T0348819

Kamahl

KAMAHL

The Triumph of Hope

An authorized biography by
KEITH CAMERON

NEW
HOLLAND

First published in 2024 by New Holland Publishers
Sydney

Level 1, 178 Fox Valley Road, Wahroonga, NSW 2076, Australia

newhollandpublishers.com

A record of this book is held at the National Library of Australia.

ISBN 9781760797669

Managing Director: Fiona Schultz
Publisher: Olga Dementiev
Project Consultant: Deborah Stellason
Designer: Andrew Davies
Production Director: Arlene Gippert
Printed in China

Keep up with New Holland Publishers:

NewHollandPublishers
@newhollandpublishers

Contents

Foreword

It was an ordinary Tuesday morning, much like any other before it, when, my wife Amy informed me that we were headed to Sydney's upper North Shore to pick up two large ceramic garden pots. She added that as they were bulky items she needed me to lift them into the car. Even though this was the first I had heard of our impending purchase, after all these years together, I realised the futility of pointing out that I did have things to do, so I thought better of it and dutifully headed to the car. En route, Amy informed me that the purchase had gone through an agent, who had told her that as she would not be present for the pickup she had arranged for her client to be there to meet us at his home. I mentally calculated travel time and concluded that I would be back behind my desk in a little over an hour and a half, leaving ample time to complete my work and make an appointment that afternoon as I had initially planned.

Around 10 am, we arrived at the rather grand gated property, Amy pressed a buzzer, and a sizeable electronic security gate slid open. After letting her out, she walked toward the equally elegant front door and I parked the car on the large courtyard driveway. In the shadows of the doorway was the outline of a figure behind a security screen. As the figure approached, a great voice boomed, "Good morning, I take it you are here for the pots." The voice was instantly recognisable, it was the deep bass-baritone of show business legend Kamahl. Amy was surprised and a little bit starstruck, the surprise led to her exclaiming. "Oh, Kamahl, wow, it's you!" in a volume and tone that was a workable impression of a twelve-year-old girl meeting her pop idol. We briefly exchanged introductions, entirely for his benefit of course, as we already knew who he was. Without much ado I set about the task of humping these two rather huge ceramic garden pots into my car, being ably assisted by an Australian entertainment icon.

Kamahl explained that he had recently sold his home as he was downsizing from this property to a more 'manageable' apartment. As a part of that process, he needed to offload decades of valuable items, which he was doing in a large online auction within the next couple of weeks. The pots we had bought had not been included in the main auction as an oversight along with a number of other pieces.

When I saw the pots it was clear that fitting these monsters into the car would need quite a bit of planning. After considering several alternative approaches most, if not all recommended by Kamahl who, possibly sensing my ineptitude with such tasks, had eagerly assumed the role of director of operations. We finally managed to find an angle to squeeze both of them into the boot. Whilst they now sat snuggly, we faced yet another vexing issue, the lid couldn't close as they were too tall. Kamahl obligingly located a sturdy looking cord in his garage and volunteered to tie an elaborate knot securing the lid. Tying knots is just another one of those things Kamahl lays claim to as a hidden talent, although I must add that as those same knots came undone whilst crossing a minor speed bump a few hundred metres from his home later, it's a talent he'd do best to keep well hidden. Whilst we had toiled away uploading my garden's soon to be feature pieces, Kamahl had entertained me with a few of his stories. It would appear that when interesting things have so richly populated your life, just about anything acts as a cue for an anecdote.

Once we were loaded up and ready to go, Kamahl assumed the role of genial host and insisted on offering us refreshment before heading home. Anticipating that we would be refreshed by a cup of what I assumed would be Dilmah, we would be able to be back on the road shortly after, so gladly we agreed. Upon setting foot in this magnificent house, the first thing that I noticed was a glowing monument to his career. It was a long wall covered almost top to bottom with Gold and Platinum albums. In addition, framed pictures featuring him along with a veritable who's who of international celebrities, stars, royalty and other highly notable people. As we had tea, which incidentally wasn't Dilmah, we chatted, and he shared some stories about his life, how he came to Australia, his career and his plans. Kamahl was far from reticent or guarded with information, he was most eager to share his experiences candidly and transparently with the self-deprecating humour for which he is known. Actually, one of the most interesting aspects of our discussion to me was the fact that he genuinely showed interest in our story, a trait not often demonstrated by people who have enjoyed his level of fame and celebrity. The more we talked, the less likely my plan to be back on the road in half an hour seemed. As the clock ticked onward without our noticing, well over three hours had managed to slip by. We had been distracted by the entertainment of Kamahl's rich tales delivered by his even richer voice. I realised that unless I was to break several speed records and just as many road laws, I needed to send off a quick text message to my appointment requesting a reschedule.

Like many people of my age, I have always known of Kamahl. As a part of the Australian TV generation, to us he was seemingly ever-present on a whole raft of Australian variety programs. Whilst familiar with his celebrity, I was by no means able to lay any claim to a deep knowledge of his life, his career or, for that matter, his achievements. The more he spoke, the more I learned, and I became engrossed in his story. Like most successful entertainers of his vintage, Kamahl has showbusiness and celebrity anecdotes to burn; beyond that, however, it was clear that there was a far more compelling story. To me, his was a tale of a triumph over the odds, it was about overcoming challenges, an inspirational migrant tale overcoming ignorance and bigotry. In many ways it was also a story of how much Australia had changed over the years. Just like many great personal tales, it even featured a great life-changing epiphany for its hero, which led to what he had always sought from his birth, to be accepted.

When we finally headed to leave that afternoon, it was clear that we had just made a great new friend whose company we thoroughly enjoyed. He seemed to concur, suggesting that we should stay in touch. We even agreed that we should try to catch up for dinner in the coming week. After a long career in the communications industry, I am well-conditioned to suggested 'must catch ups', seldom coming to fruition no matter how well-intentioned the suggestion is at the time. I was therefore surprised, to say the least, when good to his word, a couple of days later, he called me to invite us to go to dinner with him that evening. Several hours later, we were sitting in a local restaurant, continuing to share our collected lessons on life and our views on the World. We had many such catch-ups over the weeks leading up to Christmas that year. During one of our 'get-togethers', Kamahl asked me if I would be kind enough to do him a favour. He asked if I knew anyone who could write some copy for a particular item that he was auctioning, a collection of letters between he and one of his dearest old friends, Sir Donald Bradman. Without hesitation I agreed to help by writing the piece for him myself. The next day I happily tapped out a few hundred words, bringing the collection to life by explaining how it came to exist and how the histories of both men had intersected. Kamahl seemed very happy with what I had written for him and he used the copy as a highlight piece for his auction's publicity.

Several days after the conclusion of his auction, he rang me for a chat. During our discussion, he would tell me that he had a theory he referred to as "serendipitous circumstance". He explained that there had been many fortuitous chance meetings with people throughout his life that had led to alliances that would bring surprising good fortune. He claimed that almost all of his big breaks in life had all been preceded by serendipitous circumstance. He said this theory had been such a regular feature in his life, he had almost come to expect it to happen. He went on to pay me a great compliment by stating that our meeting, was serendipity in action yet again. This story hopefully proves his theory correct.

Postscript

As part of my initial research for the book, I read anything and everything that I could lay my hands on. Many hours of sourcing articles, film clips and interviews, were all readily available. I also decided it would be prudent to read Kamahl's last published biography, *An Impossible Dream* written by Christopher Day back in 1995. As the book was released so long ago, it had been out of print for quite a while so was not readily available. For days I scoured the internet to find somewhere to purchase it second-hand. I finally located a site specialising in such books, I placed my order, and it arrived three days later. Upon opening the book's cover, I found that it had been autographed way back in '95 by Kamahl himself. The hand written inscription remarkably read, *"Best Wishes Keith. From Kamahl '95!"*

1

To a brave new world

If one is different, one is bound to be lonely.

Aldous Huxley

In September 1953, a reed-thin, chronically shy, dark-skinned Tamil teenager named Kandiah Kamalesvaran arrived in Adelaide. He had travelled alone from his home in Kuala Lumpur to attend Kings College, a prestigious private school located in the leafy suburb of Kensington Park. He had limited exposure to Western culture, his English was poor and he found the food offered so unpalatable, he'd survived on milk, eggs, and cake for weeks. The eggs being consumed raw, as he had remembered that his sister when entering puberty was fed raw eggs as a supplement to her vegetarian diet as means of providing her strength.

Travelling from KL had started with a perilous train ride to Singapore, where, for safety, he had remained on the floor for the better part of the trip. Not entirely his choice, as back in the fifties, the train route from KL to Singapore ran straight through parts of Malaysia that were deeply impacted by the 'Malayan Emergency'. This was the euphemism used for what amounted to a full-blown bloody civil war, a conflict that would consume the country for around twelve years. During this stage of the War, it was pretty standard for trains to be both the intentional or incidental targets of gunfire. As many stray bullets found their way into unintentional participants in the war, most passengers opted for the safety of the floor over upholstered seating.

When he arrived in Singapore, he boarded the strangely named MV *Gorgon*. This Blue Funnel passenger-cargo vessel would take him down the Western Coast of Australia to Fremantle. He would then go on to complete the last leg of his journey by plane from Perth to his end destination, Kings College Adelaide. It was here that he would complete his education. The MV *Gorgon* was not a luxury cruise liner; far from it, it was the type of cargo vessel that took on a few dozen paying passengers to make extra money. For many, a ship named after the three hideous sirens of Greek mythology whose day job was luring sailors to run their boats aground it may have appeared to be a bad omen. Still, for a young traveller not versed in ancient history, it didn't. He was focused on the promise of a brave new world full of adventure. Weeks at sea lay ahead without the company of anyone of his generation or ethnicity, he was indeed the only person of colour on the passenger list. It was the very first time he had ventured further than short distances from his home, aside from when he was first born and was taken by his mother f or a couple of months to her homeland, Sri Lanka, or as it was still referred to the Ceylon. He was to discover much later that the purpose of the trip was recommended by her doctors after childbirth. At the time within their culture it was quite common for doctors to suggest the separation of men from their wives after childbirth to allow 4–6 weeks to allow women to heal before resuming sexual activity.

The MV *Gorgon* in which he was to travel to Australia had several stops on the way. These stops were mainly to pick up precious cargo, specifically cattle and sheep to take to markets in Fremantle. Those stopovers in Derby, Carnarvon and Broome, for a young lonely man, made the trip seem to drag on even longer.

When the MV *Gorgon* arrived in Broome there was another surprise for our young traveller. Passengers were disembarked and taken into town by some crew members for a few hours to get their land legs and be fed. Returning to the ship a few hours later he was shocked to see the vessel sitting next to the dock as they left it but one thing had changed, there was no water underneath it. It was sitting on muddy sand. He was not aware that the wharf was a 'spring tide port' meaning that trading vessels could only enter and leave on the high spring tide. He was shocked and couldn't understand the calmness of those around him who seemed to be unfazed by this incredible sight. Didn't they know that the ship had run aground? He remembers, "I was so shocked to see the ship sitting on the ground, I asked one of the crew members what was going on and he rather mischievously answered that we may be there for days waiting for the tide to come back in. Of course he was just playing a trick on me and we were away as soon as the sea returned … I must admit he had me going for a while though" he laughs.

Back at sea Kamalesvaran was initially quite pleased to see the cattle when it was loaded onto the ship in Broome. He was very familiar with cows, having grown up in a strict Hindu household where the family cow was the object of worship and revered accordingly. The Kandiah's cow was named Lakshmi, and to them, she was a sacred creature given as much respect and love as any family member. It is hard to fathom how he would've felt when his curiosity got the better of him one afternoon, leading him to sneak a peek behind a screened-off section of the deck. There to his great shock, he was to witness the slaughter of one of these sacred creatures. The cow was then butchered on the spot and subsequently served as meals for passengers and crew later on that day. One of his very first encounters with Western culture was to witness the slaughter of a religious deity. It would be fair to say that there had been more welcoming introductions to a new culture! Needless to say, young Kamalesvaran did not eat dinner that evening. He recalls the menu featured, among other things, ox tail soup and some type of beef stew. He was to skip many more, in fact, most meals on that trip.

Once he had finally arrived in Adelaide and presented himself at school, he was utterly aware of how much he stood out from his classmates. This was hardly surprising as this was the 1950s and Australia had still not shaken off its xenophobic and racist White Australia policy. A policy is also known as The Immigration Restriction Act 1901 designed for one primary purpose; to forbid people of non-European ethnic origin, especially Asians and Pacific Islanders, from immigrating to Australia. To be specific, it fundamentally blocked anyone who was black or brown. This law, combined with the after-effects of World War Two, which in itself had stoked the distrust of outsiders even further, made Adelaide in 1953 a particularly challenging place to be an 'other'. Someone who looked different, sounded different, and most of all felt different to the majority of society. As a highly self-conscious teenager, he already felt different back in his homeland. Yet, this new world took those insecurities to a whole new level. Being different is challenging for any teenager, but to stand out so dramatically bordered on being overwhelming.

One of Kamalesvaran's earliest memories at school was being instructed by his teacher, DD Harris to stand up and to share the experience of his flight from Perth with his classmates. In 1953 as very few kids had ever been on an aeroplane, so presumably, the educator, reasoned that sharing this experience would be an interesting ice breaker for the young man to share. Reluctantly he rose to his feet. Acutely conscious of his limited English, he stated that his flight had been excellent. Intending to say that that the airline hostess had been kind to him and very hospitable, he spluttered that "The trip was very good, and the hostesses were most serviceable". His unintentional gaffe was met with a gale of laughter from both the boys and teacher alike. Needless to say, he felt buoyed by the response and repeated it thinking that he had inadvertently struck comic gold. When it was pointed out to him later that it was not the 'joke' but he that was being laughed at, he was filled with embarrassment. It had turned out that the well-meaning gesture of the teacher had unintentionally left him feeling humiliated and yet even more self-conscious.

So how did young Kandiah Kamalesvaran overcome this less-than-ideal introduction to Australia? How did he eventually become one of Australia's most beloved entertainers with a career spanning well over sixty years as a performer? How did he sell more than 20 million records worldwide and receive 76 gold and 14 platinum records? How would he achieve Australian national honours in recognition of his standing within his adopted home? How did he become Kamahl?

2

Challenges presented – challenges accepted

You may not control all the events that happen to you,
but you can decide not to be reduced by them.

Maya Angelou

From a very young age, Kamahl had to develop skills and strengths to survive, in a world populated by so many people he would go on to aptly describe as "so unkind".

Throughout the early part of his life, the challenges he faced and the barriers he had to overcome paradoxically drove him to adopt a positive, optimistic approach to life. He learned that to overcome adversity, he had to be heard and remembered or face scorn or, worse yet, anonymity. The trials and tribulations he faced, far from defeating him, made him understand that getting on the front foot was imperative when no one expected you to succeed. Borne, out of the basic need to survive he focused on his interpersonal skills. He worked on reading people so diligently that it practically became a sixth sense.

By Kamahl's harsh self-assessment, he was never blessed with an abundance of natural talent. What he had been supplied with at birth was a sense that being accepted was the key to overcoming his weaknesses. It is surprising to many that he would include his trademark rich bass-baritone voice as one of his weaknesses. In describing it, he says. "I am a good but not great singer. I see myself more as a communicator than a performer. As far as my singing is concerned, I'm a bit of a hybrid, I'm neither one thing nor the other, a cross between my two greatest influences, Nat King Cole and Paul Robeson … by trying to sound like both of them, I ended up somewhere in the middle, I'm an operatic crooner if you like." Despite his dismissive assessment of this voice, whether used to sing or speak, it became a core strength, his calling card. It remains distinctive enough and good enough to be instantly recognised by most Australians. It has proven to be a highly lucrative meal ticket for well over six decades.

However, the self-doubt of his singing talent was dwarfed by a much bigger issue, the root of all of his insecurity, his chronic shyness. It is hard for people to reconcile the image of someone performing at ease in the public eye with a tremendously self-conscious person who feared rejection for many years. His easy-going, engaging manner and sense of humour, always regarded as one of his essential characteristics, were consciously crafted. He used them as a defence mechanism through a variety of tools and techniques. His spontaneous self-deprecating wit proved to be a helpful quality that allowed him to disarm critics, converting audiences of all ages into dedicated fans.

His tremendous work ethic and his stubbornness have helped him in every pursuit. Whilst his English comprehension grew exponentially since 1953, there is one word he still struggles with to this day, and no doubt will never learn, and that is the word 'NO'. His approach to his career has been guided by a single-minded philosophy to do, as the cliché goes, bite off way more than you could chew and chew like hell. He has consistently refused to accept rejection and would push to overcome whatever hurdle was placed in his way until it was behind him. His resolve was founded on his need to survive against great odds from an early age. He realised that when working without a net beneath the high wire, failure is not just a learning moment. It was simply a luxury he merely could never afford.

The spectre of failure has always been his constant companion. It was his omnipresent motivation coach; it followed him closely like a threatening stalker, pushing him faster and further in his attempt to escape from it. Much of this drive was a recognition that to have turned back from where he started was simply never an option. To turn back would affirm and validate the insecurities he had fought since the very start.

In his life, he claims that through a series of unique circumstances, a continual stream of remarkable, almost inexplicable events, he has benefited in extraordinary ways. He says, "My life has been so full of serendipitous situations that have led to great, sometimes fantastic and crazy unexpected opportunities. I have been so fortunate to have been blessed with so many of these wonderful experiences. People that I have met along the way that have opened doors for me, who have given me support and counsel are too many to count." This may be but a belief that his successes have been achieved through pure kismet alone and it wrongly gives the impression that he was passively in the right place at the right time. This, in turn, was solely responsible for his fame and success. However, any objective review of his life and career events tells us that this is far from accurate. It is, after all, confirmed that many entertainers have found themselves in similar remarkable positions. Still, the majority either overlook or ignore those opportunities by failing to understand the potential that they held. Tales of people who missed out on their 'big break' are legion. Ponder for a second that there were Beatles who quit before the band took off (with apologies to Pete Best). The notion of success through luck also discounts or overlooks the level of perception required and the ability to grasp the nettle and turn it into a flower. The ability to read fortuitous situations is a product of having faced incredible adversity, experiencing significant obstacles. This informs how to recognise the breaks for what they were and ensure that they were not passed over.

Many equally or more talented contemporaries of Kamahl's struggled or disappeared throughout his career, yet somehow he managed to flourish. He believes that this was due to his never losing sight of the need for acceptance. In essence, whilst most others tirelessly worked on building and developing an act, he managed to fashion himself into a brand way before the term became fashionable. The Kamahl brand was the amalgamation of all that he brought to the table. He had a likeable easy manner. He was handsome, had an air of old-world charm, was well-spoken, clearly intelligent, and had a great voice. To top it all off, most importantly, he was unique. He looked and sounded so different when he started in what was a very white Australia. He just couldn't help but stand out. Ironically his race and colour, the cornerstone of his insecurity, the things that could have become an albatross around his neck, became the essence of his unique selling proposition.

To illustrate his awareness of his strengths and weaknesses, he tells this story, "In the early seventies I was in New York to perform at Carnegie Hall which was a pretty big deal at the time not just for me but for any artist, let alone one from Australia. Legendary Australian TV Journalist Ray Martin contacted me requesting an interview for *60 Minutes*, and I gladly accepted. Before seeing me that week, he for some reason had interviewed fellow entertainer, Terry Kaff. He asked him what he thought of me, you know, how did he feel about a fellow Aussie performer appearing at the sacred space of Carnegie Hall, then regarded as the very pinnacle of US venues. He responded by saying that he was shocked because he didn't think that I had any talent. Ray asked what I thought of Kaff's rather blunt appraisal of me. I said immediately with a deadpan face, Ray, he is 100% right, you know I don't … but please don't advertise this fact … we don't want it getting out … Ray, for a second, did a double-take, then realising that I was joking, laughed out loud, which made the rest of the interview a very positive affair. I have always believed in not taking myself too seriously. I felt that I could always win people over by putting myself in the joke. Lucky for me, it works most of the time, so I always resort to humour to diffuse tension in conversations because I hate awkward situations. I believe that showing vulnerability makes you appear more approachable and accessible, more human if you like. There is nothing Australian audiences hate more than a celebrity who is, and I quote, 'up themselves'." The anecdote illustrates another great Kamahl brand attribute… the ability to think on his feet.

Kamahl learned a lot of his personal branding skills by keenly observing people identified as successful who came from many different walks of life. Quickly recognising that those people had valuable lessons to impart, he learned from their wins and their losses, which were equally instructive in many ways. It seems ironic for someone who, as a student, would never realise outstanding academic achievement that he would dedicate most of a lifetime to so diligently studying at the school of life. He began to fastidiously apply himself to these practices from his early youth by reading people and interpreting human behaviour. He realised the key lessons he needed to understand may not come from a book. They were in interpersonal relationships influenced by the power of presentation, language and actions.

This journey he has been on since boarding the MV *Gorgon* in 1953 was not a straightforward one. It had many significant twists and turns. He has been on many side roads, some of which turned out to be cul-de-sacs. However, throughout his career, Kamahl has always approached everything with incredible gusto despite the obstacles along the way. Before GPS was a thing, he would find his way on the long path to success by reading signs left by situations. For many people, the very fear of failure would lead to taking a safe or conservative direction through the point of least resistance. Yet, for Kamahl, he fearlessly chose to take risks and accept challenges that seemed impossible to most. Using a very Australian metaphor, Kamahl says, "I have always been prepared to swim outside the flags." Whilst this analogy is entirely apt, there is much more to it than that. Kamahl never thought that those flags were there for safety. He believed that they were placed there in celebration of his presence.

3

Beginnings

The first step towards getting somewhere is to decide that you are not going to stay where you are.

Chauncey Depew

Kamahl was born in Kuala Lumpur on November 13th, 1934, in an area called Brickfields, a Kuala Lumpur neighbourhood on the western edge of the city commonly referred to as Little India. Brickfields population, culture and observed customs supported its nomenclature perfectly. It is common for Tamils to have no family name, their name is generally their father's personal name which appears first, followed by their own name hence he was named Kandiah Kamelesvaran, literally translated as Kamelesvaran son of Kandiah.

Before Kamahl's birth, his Tamil Hindu parents decided to move to Malaysia from Sri Lanka, then known as Ceylon, to seek a better life for their family. Historically Ceylon had offered great strategic and trade opportunities and was therefore ripe to be exploited by Western colonial powers. From its initial colonisation by the Portuguese in 1517, replaced by the Dutch in 1658, and subsequently the British in 1796, Ceylon would remain a traditionally managed colony until achieving independence in 1948. Each of the colonial powers, not surprisingly, had left a cultural and political impact. As was also common, they each used a 'divide and conquer' strategy to retain control of the population. In Sri Lanka's case, the Sinhalese majority population preferred by all colonists to act as their nominated representatives of power. By providing this elevated role, religious and ethnic minorities were marginalised and oppressed. In times of economic hardship, unrest would generally rise among these minorities resulting in bitter conflict. In the 1930s, such tensions were once again brewing specifically within the Tamil population. Kamahl's parents determined that the life they wanted for themselves would be away from this fractious, unpredictable and sometimes dangerous environment. They would follow the path to Malaya that a number of their family members had done before them.

Kamahl's father Mayilvaganam and his mother, Elyathangam, were very traditional Tamils, devout of faith and fiercely proud of their highly evolved culture. Kamahl nowadays characterises his home as a "loving but very strict" environment. Although he was the second eldest of six children, significantly, he was the most senior boy. The role of the eldest boy within this culture had many implications and responsibilities that he would quickly learn to appreciate. His family was not given to any outward displays of affection. It was essentially a serious household leading a pretty serious and pious life. By Western standards, his family's living arrangements were highly unusual. He, his siblings and his parents all lived with his mother's brother in law V Arupillai and her sister, Periamah, along with his mother's younger sister and husband. All major household decisions were approved by the man known simply as 'Uncle', including those relating to the household's children. Uncle was the clan's patriarch and took an authoritarian, no-nonsense approach to run domestic affairs.

Uncle and his wife had no children of their own. In fact, Kamahl's eldest aunt had been pregnant a couple of years before Kamahl's family lived at the home. Tragically, the child had been stillborn. Due to complications arising from the labour, it would prevent her from ever having her own children. However, the couple would become very involved in overseeing the raising of the household's children, and they were respectfully and deferentially consulted with almost all decisions related to their upbringing.

The family's modest home was provided to Uncle by the General Hospital, where he held the position of Chief Medical Officer. The house had ten occupants, all under one roof. This did not include servants who also shared the home from time to time. The close-quartered living arrangements required that the strict order of the house was not only valued but treated as an imperative to avoid a descent into chaos. It was an environment where children literally only spoke when they were spoken to and whose opinions were neither sought nor valued.

Kamahl had some justifiable fear of the authority that was wielded by both his father and uncle. Their rules, if defied, would be met with swift and what seemed at the time to be significant and harsh punishment. The penalties ranged from a short slap around the ear or being made to stand on one leg. Whilst the former could be meted out by any adult member of the family, this latter was his father's speciality. He says with a broad smile, "If standing silently in a corner on one leg for an hour or so doesn't sound hard to you, please give it a try for me and let me know how you get on".

He remembers that whilst his father's administration of justice and punishment was harsh, it had a predictable and logical nature. The penalties were consistent and clearly on message; therefore, whilst unpleasant and disagreeable, the rules were clearly understandable. His mother's punishment, however, seemed to be far less predictable. Her justice was more instant and reflexive, she was prone to improvisation; hence her punishment was harder to anticipate and sometimes impossible to comprehend. He remembers returning from school one afternoon and complaining to her that he had been roughed up by some bullies on the way home. Her response was to clip him around the ears for complaining. As he puts it, "I literally got hit for bringing to her attention that I got hit."

This was a stoically religious and serious family unit. The children were expected to reflect these values completely both within the home and whilst in the close-knit community outside of it. Complaining was seen as a weakness. It demonstrated that you were a person of poor character and therefore, it was actively discouraged, barely even tolerated. The children of the household were drilled into accepting that life was a serious business and that there was little room for self-pity and even less for frivolity. He recalls "My first experiences of racism come from my childhood in KL. My own community of Sri Lankan Tamils who were themselves largely exiled from their homeland due to the perils of being a racial minority there, now in another country looked down on the Indian community they found themselves alongside in Brickfields." The racial boundaries that he experienced as a child would certainly go some way to prepare him for what lay ahead in the years to come.

He remembers vividly that whilst he always felt cared for, loved, and protected, there was very little joy or laughter in his childhood household. His father, in particular, who was a devout Hindu, spent much of his spare time practising his faith in prayer and devotion at the temple. He also embraced the various pastoral activities associated with his faith throughout the community. Kamahl recalls, "Every week, we would attend all services at the temple on a Friday, it was the most important of all of the disciplines that we had to conform to, and to my parents, my uncle and aunt, this one was totally non-negotiable." While the seemingly stern atmosphere in the home may have sometimes seemed stifling for a child, in fairness to the adults of this household, these were very serious times with plenty of things to be anxious about.

Kamahl's father worked as the Chief Clerk in the engineering department of Malaya Railway. This was an upper middle management position with a great deal of responsibility and quite a bit of social status. He was a very ambitious man consequently he held similarly high expectations for his children to do well and make something of themselves, particularly his eldest male child. Along with, and in many ways linked to his Hindu faith, his father was also a founding member of the Sangeetha Abvirthi Sabha, the Indian Tamil Music Academy in Kuala Lumpur. The Academy would become a focal point of Indian music, dance, and drama within Kuala Lumpur and throughout all Indian communities within Malaya. Kamahl became very familiar with Indian music that he had heard on his father's recordings or in the temple where it was a crucial part of worship, however in his early years, he showed very little interest in music, neither did he feel particularly inspired by it. In fact he rarely gave it much thought at all. At this time of his life, he related singing mainly to religious service rather than something that provided joy or happiness. Therefore, it was relegated in his mind to being more of a domestic ritualistic observance than a pursuit of genuine passion. This mindset made it all the more confounding to him when the household matriarch, his aunt, actively encouraged Kamahl's father to enrol him in the Academy. He agreed, and this would see Kamahl become the only boy in a group consisting of ninety female students. Little did he know it at the time, but this was possibly the first but not the last time he would feel like he didn't fit in. Sadly the experience, rather than inspiring him to take up music as a pursuit, achieved the opposite completely. After finishing only one year at the Academy, much to the disappointment of the family, especially his father and aunt, he dropped out. Kamahl's great love of music had evidently not as yet fully developed. When it did, initially at least, it would align with the popular western genres, the very type of music that his father dismissively referred to as both mechanical and soulless.

As a student, Kamahl was quite erratic in his scholastic performance. He confesses that he now wonders if he had an undiagnosed form of ADHD as a child. Little if any knowledge of the syndrome existed back then. He says, "I am sure that these days they may have pumped me full of Ritalin or something, it was particularly hard at school, I found it so difficult to concentrate, it felt like it was impossible" For those who couldn't perform back then much to Kamahl's chagrin, there was only one remedy for poor concentration, unsurprisingly it was the same answer for most problems, harsh discipline through punishment. It was a major frustration for him and his family that he struggled with studying as he was obviously intelligent. When he applied himself, he was a competent student, albeit one who spent a great deal of his time looking out the window daydreaming. Even more frustrating for them was when threatened with physical punishment or even, on some occasions, expulsion from school, he would quickly regain focus on his work. He remembers, "I would spend most of my time daydreaming. The teacher's words in class or textbooks would just wash over me, and none of it seemed to sink in. That is until I was facing exams or had been scolded or punished for not keeping up. Then as if, by some miracle, I suddenly found that I could understand the lessons and easily catch up and then I'd go on to get a passing grade." It was indeed a vicious cycle, one that would persist for his entire academic life.

Kamahl, despite his somewhat stifling surroundings, was a highly active and sociable child who was very keen to participate in games. His great love at the time was cricket, a sport he still keenly follows. To his dismay, his family, most notably his mother, forbade him from playing any sport at all. Her reasoning was that playing sports in the Malaysian sunlight would darken his already dark skin. As a Tamil, Kamahl already belonged to the darkest skinned of all Indian ethnic groups, making his family extra-sensitive about the issue. Within the broader Indian ethnic community, having lighter skin was a highly coveted physical feature. It was more than just a representation of appearance; it spoke of class and status. Colour and caste determined social standing and instantly communicated where a person stood on life's pecking order. In practical terms, this meant that a boy's dowry or financial value at marriage could be significantly and directly impacted by his skin tone. Quite literally, the lighter the boy's skin, the higher the amount that would be paid to his family by the bride's parents, the darker his skin meant the exact opposite. It was Kamahl's first but certainly not last experience with skin colour politics and the preposterous inequity it represented. Not only did this system discriminate based upon skin colour, it actually placed a financial value on a human being … even worse, a scalable price. He reflects, "My earliest and most significant experiences with racism were definitely within my own culture. I didn't have to travel far and wide to experience racism. It played a major part in our everyday lives. In addition to my own community's obsession with colour, the other racial groups around us all had their own distinct codes of discrimination. On top of all of that was our white colonial rulers."

His family's preferences aside, young Kamahl gave into an emerging rebellious streak and decided on playing sports secretly anyway. Initially sneaking off to play soccer he would then follow one of his life's great passions, cricket. His secretive sports life, however, was set to be exposed and relatively short-lived. One fateful afternoon, under the guise of offering to deliver a letter for his elder sister, he was, in fact, opening the batting for a group of local kids. On the first ball of the over, he badly mistimed a full toss. Instead of clearing a fence as he had visualised, he collected the six-stitch leather missile straight in the face. The ball clattered directly into his mouth as hard as a rock, his vision clouded, and his head swam. He collapsed to the ground in shock, and blood was sprayed everywhere. He then recalls seeing stars just as his mouth exploded in pain. His immediate fear was that he had lost his front teeth. However, his more significant concern was not of the cosmetic damage from the injury but something far greater than that. It was the fear of going home to face the music about the deception he had committed in his skin darkening secret sports activity. With the disclosure of his closet cricketing career exposed, he had pretty reasonably deduced that the punishment that would follow would be of epic proportion. It would definitely eclipse the prospect of a permanently disfigured, gap-toothed smile.

On arriving home that afternoon, his fears were somewhat validated by his mother's initial reaction. Upon seeing his condition, in a strange but somewhat expected sequence of events, she almost immediately gave him a whack around the ear and then asked him to explain what had happened. Kamahl's dread grew as he thought this was merely the opening act on what was sure to be a headline performance of pain that he faced when the male heads of the household returned for the day. However, to his great surprise, when Uncle, the adult whom he feared most of all in life, arrived home, he issued him with a stern verbal rebuke, instead of the more physical punishment he anticipated. He was then picked up gently and bundled into a waiting trishaw and taken to the hospital for treatment. After rather clumsily yanking away at Kamahl's front teeth, the attending doctor confirmed that none were lost and proclaimed that he had indeed been fortunate … Kamahl could not have agreed more with the good doctor. Not only had he kept his smile intact, but no further punishment would eventuate that day. While undoubtedly a strict disciplinarian, his uncle was a fair man and had evidently concluded that the boy had suffered enough pain for one day. He even showed the boy a little sympathy and good humour on the way home. Kamahl was so relieved sitting in the tricycle on the way home, he even managed to spare a sympathetic thought for his mother. He figured she would've been beside herself at home, painstakingly calculating the discount each lost tooth could've required on his dowry.

Whilst his life to this point had seemed somewhat harsh and strict, it was about to become so very much more severe.

When Kamahl was only seven years old, the Second World War came raining down from the sky in fierce Japanese bombing raids. This daily bombardment forced he and his family from the city with all their possessions loaded in bullock carts to a safer location until the threat had passed. When the bombing eventually stopped, the capital had fallen to the Japanese Imperial Army's military machine, which had overrun the entire country. Kuala Lumpur had been transformed under strict Japanese control and was the base for thousands of occupational personnel. During these times, the life of the family changed significantly. Whilst his environment had been stifling and strict, the world outside the front door had now become a thousand times scarier. He now looked upon home as his safe haven protecting him from harm.

Kamahl's father's life also changed dramatically under occupation, he had been forced into the service of the occupying forces, given a Japanese military uniform and made the Head of Railway Security. Acceptance of this role was non-negotiable; he had limited options. He either took the job without question, or his life would have quite literally been over. Kamahl distinctly remembers seeing his mother pray for her husband's safe return from work every day he was to leave home. These were tough times for his father as he had to navigate his way through cooperation for survival without crossing the line in becoming identified as a collaborator. He was torn between doing what he needed to ensure his safety and family, without compromising his commitment to his community and countrymen.

Following the war, Kamahl's father would in fact be jailed based upon false accusations of collaboration. Some within the community who had attempted to gain material favours from him when he was in that authority position had been his accusers. After a hearing conducted by the re-installed colonial powers, he was found not only to be innocent of all accusations but totally exonerated. Whilst he was released, he still had to spend a gruelling four months in the infamous Padu Gaol whilst he awaited his hearing. Kamahl remembers clearly visiting his father in this miserable and frightening place with his mother and siblings. His ever-stoic father never spoke of the peril he had faced during wartime or his time in Padu Gaol. Some year's later, Kamahl discovered how his father had taken many personal risks through intervening and preventing the execution of staff in Sentul wrongly accused of theft. He had also opened the rice stores during a food shortage, organised food and medical treatment for prisoners and supplied food to British POWs. His humanitarian efforts were to be recognised after the war by the Royal Netherland's Forces, who reimbursed him for his expenses of $16,000.

Kamahl's memories of these times are filled with fear and brutality, having witnessed first-hand totalitarian rule's cruelty, barbarism, and inhumanity. "Whilst the Japanese treated the Indian population reasonably well relatively speaking, the Chinese were slaughtered in their thousands after the fall of Singapore. Those identified by the new rulers as standing in the way of their regime had their lives quickly and viciously extinguished. On the Batu Road roundabout, bamboo poles were erected and crowned with the severed heads of those tragically slaughtered who had been accused of resisting authority and summarily dealt with. It was a terrifying sight for me when I was just seven years old. It is a vision that has remained with me my whole life, one that contributed significantly to my abhorrence of violence and cruelty," he says. Kamahl discovered that when absolute power sets out to make a point, it never relies on subtlety nor gentle persuasion. Fear is the main currency of authoritarianism. He reflects that "I was always afraid that I too may end up on that roundabout every single time I saw those soldiers. I had nightmares about it for years and must confess that it still sends a shudder down my spine."

Kamahl also recalls the sight of the daily morning ritual that their occupiers and overlords went through. Dozens of men would march straight past their front door each day at the same time. The Army Unit would stop at the field opposite and totally disrobe. Once wholly naked, they would perform their ablutions in plain sight. In his mind, they evidently felt no need for modesty, as to them, he and his people were less than human. There was no respect at all for the people they ruled over. Such memories of overt disdain from people in total control abusing their power burned intensely into Kamahl's mind and informed his attitudes toward justice and fairness throughout his life. These were indeed harsh times, he says, "Each day, army trucks would drive past our home filled with shirtless and clearly starving POWs packed in like cattle. These poor souls were being transported off to some hellish camp or other. It was horrifying to contemplate the fate of these men. I still can't comprehend what makes a person become so corrupted by power that they can commit such cruelty against any creature, let alone a fellow human."

In one strange incident during this time, he was on his way home with only Lakshmi, the family cow for company. He was confronted by a young Japanese officer; he could be determined to be an officer by his uniform, sword, and authority he appeared to comport himself. He approached Kamahl and attempted to communicate with him. He seemed to be quite a young man, from what Kamahl recalls. This didn't prevent him from striking fear and dread in Kamahl's heart. As the soldier approached, with his hand placed near the hilt of his sword, Kamahl's fear intensified. Fearing that this may be the last day of his short life, he heard the soldier say something Japanese to him and then make a sudden movement with his hand. He saw a flash of silver reflected in the afternoon sun. Kamahl braced himself in anticipation of his head being separated from his body, without breathing and with eyes clamped tight. He was then surprised to find a chocolate bar wrapped in tinfoil placed in his hand. What he thought would be his last moment on earth had surprisingly turned into a moment of unbridled joy. This act of totally unexpected kindness juxtaposed with his impending sense of doom taught Kamahl a valuable life lesson. Humanity and compassion exist inherently within all people. No race or group of people has ever been born evil or cruel. It is taught behaviour driven by circumstance, and indoctrination from those who have power resulting in the most awful reactions from people of all types. Kamahl rushed home that day, naturally elated by his acquisition of the much-treasured bounty. He was eager to tell his family of his experience and confident they would share his happiness. Sadly, he wasn't met with the joy he had anticipated, but instead an interrogation. There was disbelief in his story; he was subsequently accused of stealing the chocolate and punished accordingly. It appeared clear to him that happiness was an even rarer commodity than the luxury of chocolate in these awful times.

He reflects, "Whilst it all seemed so incredibly cruel to my childish mind then, having now been a parent and grandparent myself, I completely understand their concern was for my welfare. We lived with such incredible threats all around us. So I suppose it was an extreme form of stranger danger tuition."

Kamahl's formal education during the War was quite fractured. It comprised home lessons and infrequent informal groups convened by community leaders, which provided the little he was being taught. Formal education did eventually return, but what there was existed under Japanese direction. He can still perform the Japanese National Anthem, 'Kimigayo', and remembers the words to 'Theno Hikai Banzai', a Japanese marching song.

When the War finally ended, Kamahl was eleven years old. He and many others had lost around three years of formal structured schooling at a critical time of childhood development.

By the time he was 12 years old, his life experiences had been very extreme, to say the least. He had witnessed first-hand more inequity, injustice and cruelty than most of us will be exposed to in a lifetime. Whilst his life had been hard, he always had the reassurance that his family was there to protect and care for him. He said, "Ours was a strict but loving household. We were always clean, well-fed, well clothed, and provided a clear direction from the home adults. We were also afforded a good education at good schools when it once again became possible. My siblings and I all knew that our welfare and future prosperity was the major priority for the household." This was reassuring and gave strong feelings of security. However, the protection he had taken for granted could not shield him nor prepare him from being the victim of three individuals which would shatter this assumption. Before he had reached his teenage years, Kamahl was sexually assaulted by people who were trusted and respected by his family.

His first assailant was a tutor, who had been selected by his parents to help Kamahl catch up from his war years interrupted schooling. Although the man was not a teacher, he was a well-educated and a much-respected member of the Hindu community. To all outward appearances, a knowledgeable, sober person, regarded as a pillar of society by most. He was a happily married. With a conspicuously beautiful wife and had a child of his own. Kamahl recounts that it was during one of his early lessons late one afternoon when he was suddenly and violently forced to the ground by this man without any warning sign. He was held down and then assaulted. He vividly recalls, "My parents had arranged for me to have lessons at this man's home which was quite close to where we lived. I think he was supposed to be teaching me mathematics, but to be honest, I can't reliably remember. During this lesson he pushed me to the ground and got on top of me all of a sudden. He then grabbed my legs and forced them around his erect penis. It was placed between my thighs mid-way up. I had no idea what he was doing. I was in a complete state of shock. He was quite a mild-mannered and cultured person who became like a deranged animal. He was holding me down and gyrating back and forth whilst forcing my legs together until he evidently had satisfied himself." Kamahl was left horrified and confused as, unbelievably, his assailant matter-of-factly regathered his composure as if nothing had happened at all. Kamahl was totally shaken by the incident. He didn't know how to deal with what had happened or what to do about it. Like many children who are the victims of a sexual assault, he did not report the matter to his family or authorities. It is now accepted that many children suffering sexual abuse are victims of someone they know. When it happens, they are reluctant to come forward, even many years after the event. Those attacked fear that they are in some way guilty of an unspeakable act themselves rather than being the victim of one. He simply dealt with it by convincing his parents that he was gaining little from his tuition and they shouldn't waste their money with continuing. Luckily they agreed to end the man's services negating what would most probably have been ongoing abuse. Whilst this allowed the assailant to go unpunished, at least he reasoned, he would never have to face him again.

As devastating as it is for kids in society in current times to deal with a situation like this, the cultural pressure within Kamahl's world in the 1940s was overwhelming. His strict religious upbringing with an environment where children were not regarded as having anything valuable to contribute until they were of age meant a self-imposed silence. Hence, a gross injustice was all but guaranteed. He felt that speaking out was practically impossible as he believed that the consequences of doing so would be far worse than the assault he had endured. His young mind figured that as he was a mere child, he would not be believed over this much-respected individual or any adult for that matter. In a society where children are not provided with a voice, it is common for them to remain silent and to elect to deal with things in their own way. Whilst profoundly disturbed by the incident, he chose instead to compartmentalise it and assure himself that it was something that would never happen again. He believed that his assault was now over, and any punishment that would result from disclosing the incident would be borne by him and him alone.

Managing to block the first incident from his mind proved almost impossible. Still, he felt bereft of options other than to suffer silently and continue to block it out. Sadly, just as he succeeded in blocking the first assault out, through another perpetrator there was a second incident, another person of trust. The young man in question was a local handyman and gardener who plied his trade for local neighbourhood families. Regularly he used to tend the Kandiah yard and take care of the odd maintenance issue as required. He was a very outgoing, friendly and unthreatening character with whom Kamahl felt totally at ease. Whilst he was working at the home, he often talked to young Kamahl, who was yet to turn thirteen. The social interaction he engaged in with the older man was welcome. As is the case for boys entering the early stages of manhood, having an adult speak to them almost as a contemporary makes them feel more mature. This is particularly true in a culture where children are to be seen but not heard.

Kamahl can't recall most of the detail of any of their discussions, just that they were always light-hearted and friendly and that he enjoyed the man's company immensely. He distinctly remembered one frequent topic of their conversation, the obsessive lustful desire he had for a beautiful young neighbour lady in the adjacent property. Kamahl remembers that whilst the discussions were relatively light, they were sometimes ribald, which amused rather than shocked a twelve-year-old boy nearing manhood. One day the gardener summoned Kamahl over to him in the yard, a request that he complied with unquestioningly. It appeared that the neighbour lady who was the object of the gardener's unrequited lustful interest was visible from where this man was located. She was tending to laundry in the yard and was totally unaware that she was being observed. When Kamahl dutifully arrived, he had his hand grabbed and forced onto the man's member. The man then sternly commanded him to masturbate him whilst he fixated lustfully at the blissfully ignorant neighbour.

His demeanour was no longer friendly; it was threatening. Once the gardener had reached a climax, he dismissed the boy and, just like the tutor, acted as if nothing had occurred. Kamahl's trust of adults had been breached yet again. If anything, this attack was much more brutal for him to process as it involved someone with whom he had been comfortable. The experience left Kamahl wondering if this was normal behaviour for all adults. He states, "Was this how I was to be treated my whole life?

Does this happen to all children? If not, why was this happening to me? Why me?" Once again, he was confused and traumatised but, as before, simply vowed to pack up his feelings and the pain of abuse, revulsion and disgust. He decided that at this point, he would never be alone with this individual again and purposely avoided being in his company forthwith. He was also determined to not be alone with any adult, for that matter. He decided that he would bury the incident and be less trusting of adults to protect himself. However, despite his best efforts to defend himself, he was unfortunately set to be a victim again. It was to happen in the strangest and most unexpected of circumstances. This time the assault also came from the most unexpected of assailants.

When he was barely thirteen, Kamahl and his family attended a large wedding in Brickfields. Among the many guests was a relatively young couple his parents knew, who had two children both of whom were considerably younger than Kamahl. He recounts, "I was quite surprised when the lady asked my parents if they would allow me to accompany them to their house and stay a few days. They lived around sixty miles away and I believe the reason behind the request was so that I could keep the kids amused and occupied on the long trip home. They stated that as they were returning to Kuala Lumpur at the end of the week, they would then ensure my safe return home. It seemed like a most reasonable request and one that drew no objection from my parents or me for that matter. To be honest, I was always keen to get a break from the strict environment of the home. So, it was like a small holiday, sort of a little adventure."

When the family with Kamahl in tow arrived back at the family home, it had been a lengthy and tiring trip. It was very late, and sleeping arrangements were quickly organised. This wasn't by any measure a complicated process as all slept on the floor on mats in the one large room. Once settled, the young children almost immediately dozed off. Their father, who had been drinking heavily throughout the day at the wedding, was also quick to nod off and was snoring loudly. During the night, Kamahl, half asleep, sensed someone being next to him. Soon he realised that this was the mother of the children. Initially startled by her presence, he was silenced by her motherly gestures. Then he was shocked when she then fondled his genitals and then fellated him until he climaxed for the first time in his life, leaving him startled and confused.

Once this happened, she crept back to her previous spot by her husband only a few feet away to leave a thirteen-year-old wide awake, anxious and confused over what had just happened to him. He couldn't sleep and decided to leave just before the sun came up the following day, whilst the house occupants were still asleep. He picked up his few belongings and, without a word, was gone. He just knew that he couldn't face his abuser, her husband or their kids. Neither could he subject himself to the potential of several more days of abuse or the unthinkable prospect of her being caught in the act by a less sleepy husband. As he hit the road, he hadn't even worked out how to get home, much less what to say when he got there to explain his early return. He left in the pre-dawn darkness without money and without a notion of which direction to head. As he had arrived in the dark and was going in the dark, he had to rely heavily upon his wits to find his way home. He says that he was in such a confused state that to this day he can't recall precisely the details of that trip. It was just a blur. He was consumed by the more monumental issue at hand… to return to the safety of his home. He recounts, "I had no idea where I was and only a vague notion of where I was headed. Still, I knew I needed to be away from there… Every instinct I had compelled me to get out. I had not one clue what I would use as an excuse for my early return. Of course, I knew that there would be questions and recriminations for my early arrival. The risk that I had taken travelling on my own without an adult to protect me was huge. It seems ironic that I should need the protection of an adult after what had happened to me that year. I reasoned that all that I could say was that I missed being at home… I knew that they would not find this reason acceptable nor believable, but what choice did I have? How would I say that I had been sexually assaulted by a young mother and wife of two small kids?" He vaguely recalls that the return trip had involved hitchhiking but not much of how many lifts he got and from whom. It is a testament to how threatened he must've felt to prefer to set out alone, placing himself in danger rather than facing this person again. When he arrived home several days earlier than planned without explanation or at least one he felt he could divulge, he was not surprised at all that once again there was trouble and punishment. The injustice of being punished for being a victim of abuse did not elude him, but he reasoned there was nothing at all he could do.

Kamahl believes that this last incidence of abuse was the worst and most confusing for him to deal with. From a young age, he had always been aware of the brutish behaviour of men. Whether it was on the receiving end of punishment or the exertion of the total raw power he witnessed from occupation forces. To him, men were hard, seemingly heartless creatures, the frequent deliverers of excessive violence and cruelty. Whilst he had sometimes been on the receiving end of his mother and his aunt's punishment, their type of justice was swift, not as significant, and it lacked cruelty. It was always a case of punishment being forgotten and forgiven almost as quickly as it was issued. He had also witnessed maternal love and a compassion at a level he felt that men were totally incapable of delivering. In his young mind, there was a clear delineation of characteristics of the gender roles. To him, women were nurturing caregivers whilst men were tough and uncompromising figures of authority. Therefore, it was confounding that he had now gone on to be abused by a woman, herself a mother of two children. For the first time in his young life, he now felt safe from no adult, and his positive albeit stereotypical view, on women had been badly dented. This incident would impact his perception on women, for a couple of years, even affecting his relationship with his mother, aunts and his elder sister. It made him feel mistrustful, withdrawn and vulnerable. He had been victimised and could not fathom how to deal with the whole situation. He now reflects with amazement that eventually and almost inexplicably, he just managed to overcome these feelings and was able to trust again after a relatively short period.

All of these incidents had one thing in common: he had been violated, and to compound the matter, he believed he had nowhere to turn. There was no one he knew that he could talk to. In many respects, his upbringing had somehow conditioned him to be able to repress his feelings and commit them behind a blanket of secrecy in his mind. It was this ability under adversity that bred a strong survival instinct in him. Arguably, the extreme experiences of his everyday life had developed within him an ability to suppress what he believed at the time was his own shameful secret.

By the time Kamahl was fourteen, he had effectively sunk the abuse he had suffered deep within him. It was only much later in his life that he allowed himself to remember the incidents. He had successfully applied the only therapy he believed was available to him. He pretended it never happened so that it just couldn't hurt him anymore. As he now reflects, "Child abuse in all its forms is so abhorrent and inexcusable, as a survivor of such abuse myself, I am greatly heartened by the modern-day approach to addressing this sickness far more seriously. Children should always be cherished and treated with the utmost sensitivity and respect. I would not like to see any child ever have to deal with this kind of situation in the way that I felt I had no other choice. To be perfectly honest, it took me years to get over what happened. And even when I thought it was gone and forgotten, it was still there. You never really get over it."

By the time Kamahl was in his teens, his dark experiences had presented two distinct options, one that could make him strong and resilient, and the other could break him. He believed that as there was nothing to gain from the latter, he chose to suppress and compartmentalise his trauma. Of course, the approach had its limitations and would leave scars, but for him, he felt he had no choice but to push on.

4

From anchors away to g'day

Man's mind stretched by a new experience can never go back to its old dimension.

Oliver Wendell Holmes Jr.

As he turned fourteen, Kamahl, now fully reconnected with his formal education, had managed to, as he puts it, "scrape through the entrance exam of the Victoria Institution". The School considered one of the leading education centres in Kuala Lumpur. Unfortunately, Kamahl's fractured schooling had left him wrestling with an even greater inability to concentrate on his academic work. If anything, it was worse than ever. He struggled to maintain interest in any of his subjects unless being bullied or coerced into it with threats. It became a vicious ritualistic cycle of falling behind and then managing to catch up but only when required. This played out many times over the next five years. However, this absence of application was far from the case when it came to sports, as he had become an accomplished soccer, hockey and cricket player whilst at the Institution. He would in fact be recognised as the house captain of his soccer team. This sporting activity was never disclosed to his mother, who would've been far from impressed with these crazy dowry sabotaging activities.

As the end of his education approached, the family had to plan where he, the eldest boy of the house, would finish his studies. It was resolved that he would have to spend his last year overseas to complete a yet to be determined degree in an English-speaking university. A degree from overseas was highly coveted by the community. It would establish him with excellent prospects along with a substantial increase in his opportunities, including, of course, his dowry value.

Several options were discussed, initially referencing international weather reports. They convened a meeting to discuss and debate the pros and cons of the options. The sessions had collectively concluded that Britain was too cold for a boy from tropical Malaya. From the international news America, it was feared to have too much racial disharmony. Australia was put forward as an option even though the country was still operating under the infamous White Australia immigration policy. South Asian students were now being permitted study visas under the Colombo Plan. At least the place was closer and more temperate than the other options. Australia it was to be. Since 1949, British and Australian schools had been enrolling a quota of Asian students under this plan. While not yet ratified nor enacted, the previously immovable rules were relaxed to raise the prospects of people within Commonwealth Countries within the South East Asian Region. While Kamahl's parents were very much involved in the discussion, his uncle made the final decision in his capacity as the household head. It turned out that Uncle had a friend who had sent his own eldest son to Kings College in Adelaide. As his uncle's much-respected friend spoke so highly of the School, it was appropriate that his eldest nephew would be dispatched there to make a man of him.

So it was to be that within a couple of months of that decision being made, Kamahl assembled with his whole family on Kuala Lumpur Railway Station. They bid him a fond farewell as he travelled south to Singapore to make that voyage on the MV *Gorgon*. He remembers that all he had with him to take to the new world was one suitcase crammed with all his possessions. Unfortunately, that did not include an overcoat, a significant oversight considering the destination had winter far colder than any he had ever experienced in his life.

After the voyage to Australia, Kamahl finally disembarked in Fremantle. He remembers it felt like he had landed on another planet. Onboard, he had been surrounded by white people. However, it had not prepared him for what he describes as finding himself in a city that featured a "sea of white faces". Worse than that, all of those white faces seemed to be staring straight back at him. He says, "I wasn't sure if it was curiosity or fear that made them stare at me, but I had never felt as different or as self-conscious in my life as I did that day… I wanted so desperately to be invisible". He was alone in a strange land, and not for the first or last time in his life, he needed to use all of his survival skills to deal with the situation ahead.

Upon landing in Adelaide, he was met at the airport by the School Bursar, Mr Geoffrey Folliot, a former Malayan Police Force officer. Mr Folliot was an impressive character, so pukka that he could have stepped straight out of the pages of Kipling's Raj. Originally from Highgate in London, he joined the Colonial Police Force in Singapore during the 1930s, with a heartfelt commitment to serve King and Country during the last days of Empire. At the fall of Singapore, Folliot had been captured by the Japanese. He was imprisoned in the notorious Changi POW camp for the duration of the occupation. After his release and his health's eventual recovery, he took a role with the Colonial Police Force relocating to Kuala Lumpur, assisting in transforming the service into what became the Malayan Police Force.

In 1948 the Communist uprising had all but sunk the country into yet another bloody war. In 1950, a police station in Keluang was attacked, and Folliot was sent with a small group of officers to investigate. Unfortunately, he and his men were ambushed, leaving several dead and himself very seriously injured in the affray. He suffered multiple bullet wounds, one of which permanently paralysed one of his arms. Another shattered his jaw and deeply sliced his tongue. Shrapnel from a grenade explosion had also hit him in the legs and face causing significant damage. He was left severely impaired physically, which meant his recovery was a very long and excruciating affair. After several months of treatment and rehabilitation, he was released from care. He was offered and accepted an honourable discharge from the Force. In an attempt at showing their gratitude, the British Government gave him the option of resettling anywhere within the Commonwealth, and so he sensibly chose Australia.

Folliot was a formidable man who had spent many years in Malaya and, as a result, was very familiar with the people and its rich culture. It was he who convinced the School Principal, Lieutenant-Commander Cecil Shenkfield, to enrol more Asian students. Both were the type of men who were firm believers in colonial ideals. They saw it their duty to take an almost paternalistic and protective role in educating young men from what they saw as countries facing the perils of communism. They firmly believed in the ideals of the Commonwealth and all that it represented. They thought they could support this by providing education and exposure to the Western, or more precisely, British way of life, to young men. This logic dictated that this would possibly prevent these young men from radicalisation, which would lead them to a way of life more aligned with their own. As quaintly patriarchal a view as this seems now, men like this had strong beliefs that had a type of patriotism forged in conflict and required a dedication to serving King and Country. Kamahl says, "They were really very interesting characters, Folliot in particular. He was very much a man of his generation. He was tough, having been hardened by everything life had thrown at him and yet somehow very compassionate. I still feel great respect for him as even though his worldview looks strange by today's standards, he was entirely genuine in his beliefs, and his heart was definitely in the right place."

Arriving at Kings College, Kamahl realised that he may have been in a brand-new country in a brand-new school, but his old problem, a lack of application to study, had come with him. It may as well have been packed in his luggage. It was as if it took that space that had been left by the missing overcoat. In fact, he now had the extra burden of not fitting in and being very self-conscious and socially awkward to contend with. He confesses, "My study habits were abysmal. I always just did barely enough to get through exams. As hard as I tried, I struggled with studying. I was just so disinterested. Within the school, I just tried desperately to not stand out for any reason at all. I tried to fly under the radar. I was extremely self-conscious. To make matters worse, I was 19, so I was older than most of the other boys, which made me feel quite awkward even though it was only a year. At that age, it felt like I was an adult amongst kids, and that made me insecure."

Whilst he had learned a reasonable amount of English before his arrival, he was far from fluent, which also restricted his academic achievements and ease in social settings. The English he had been taught back home also did not come complete with Australian pronunciations nor colloquialisms. It took time to adjust his hearing to interpret. As a result, he was very nervous about speaking in class or in public for fear of being ridiculed. His focus continued to be on areas where speaking was limited, his sporting pursuits of Cricket and Hockey. Now unshackled from his parent's obsession with devaluation from solar exposure, he found himself totally free to use sport as a means to gain acceptance and develop friends. He had found that sport in Australia provided a means of social expression where action is far more significant than words.

He recalls that he felt that he experienced very little racism at the King's School. "At King's, I felt like I was just another student. There were a small number of other Asian students there, which helped. Some had been there before our group, and they may well have paved the way for our acceptance at the School, so we were not the novelty we seemed to be in the world outside the school gate. However, I often wondered what it would have been like to have been among the very first students of colour at King's."

Australians being notorious for abbreviating names and coining nicknames, found a two for one deal with Kamahl. The one thing that did irritate him at King's was the mispronunciation of his name by his fellow students. His real name Kandiah Kamalesvaran was evidently way too long and cumbersome for his classmates. Hence he was christened 'Camel', which he absolutely hated. Still, his desire to fit in and his self-consciousness prevented him from speaking up about it. He eventually learned that his schoolmates meant no harm. He realised that he was living in a land where they eat Brekky, celebrate Chrissy and have Barbies with Tommo, Kevvy and Stevo.

Outside of the relatively protected environment of the school, it was a different picture. Kamahl was always aware, continually reminded of not fitting in. He was an 'other' not treated as a part of the community. He was marginalised and treated as a part of a feared minority simply because of his appearance. When he, along with a small group of other Asian kids, would occasionally venture out, they were constantly stared at. He recalls seeing young kids literally run off the streets into their yards to avoid contact. He says, "I don't think that it was prejudice that motivated their behaviour but a fear of the unknown that motivated them. They hadn't seen people who looked like us and didn't know how to deal with us. The fact that their parents may have taught or encouraged this type of behaviour I didn't dare think about. I preferred to believe that it was simply fear through ignorance. Their ignorance was to be pitied."

He also vividly recalls one day before a cricket match seeing the expression on a small child's face who was watching him pad up. It was evident that he was genuinely confused not only by Kamahl's dark appearance but how his hand's colour had not stained his gleaming white pads.

Kamahl sees racism as something so pervasive that it can have influence through indirect conditioning. He cites an example of how it manifested in his own life "I recall when I was at King's and just starting to appreciate classical music. Lying on my bed, I listened to a performance on the ABC of a Chopin prelude marvelling at the playing. It was so good, quite unlike anything that I had ever heard before. When the piece was back announced, they read the performer's name, and it was Fuo T'song who was this incredible Chinese concert pianist. In my adolescent mind, and much to my great shame, I could not reconcile the artistry of the performance with his ethnicity. It was almost as if my brain was hard wired to only accept specific roles for each ethnic group. As ridiculous as it sounds now, I felt less about that wonderful performance even when faced with the evidence that this performer and his performance were peerless. Such is the insanity and irrationality of racism. It has no rational foundation. It eats at reasoning with things that are taught or passed on by our individual conditioning. That incident sticks out in my mind and always reminds me that racism, like any disease, can be caught if you are exposed to the sickness. It can even lay dormant, raising its ugly head out of nowhere, triggered by something random from past experiences or taught behaviour. Worse still, it doesn't even need to be demonstrated with an overt act. It can live in our hearts and minds without us even realising and can just surface unexpectedly. I suppose it had a lot to do with the type of society I had grown up in where race, caste, social standing was so evident in daily life they became entrenched feelings, unashamedly accepted as the norm. As I often say to those who don't believe this, racism is real. It isn't just a 'pigment' of my imagination." He laughs, adding, "Interestingly, I thought of the Fuo T'song anecdote when it was reported that he had died at the age of 86 from COVID disease in London in December 2020. He had a long and illustrious career, celebrated the world over for the genius that he was. Evidently, his outrageous talent and skills had been unencumbered by the ridiculous racial profiling of a skinny Sri Lankan kid lying on his bed in Adelaide almost seventy years before."

At this stage of his life, Kamahl had started to become acutely aware of the role race was to play. He learned that if he was to overcome the prejudices faced in this new society, he would need to find a weapon to disarm those who would prefer to marginalise him with their prejudices. He began to understand that as Kandiah Kamalesvaran, aka Camel, the sportsman and struggling student, would not gain acceptance. He would have to invent another approach. He hadn't as yet fully realised it, but that approach was right there all along. He just hadn't realised it yet. It was literally sitting right under his nose.

5

Nature boy

Your life can change in an instant, that instant can last forever.
Laura Kasischke

It was whilst he was still attending King's College that Kamahl discovered his deep love of music. However, it wasn't the music that he had been raised with, not the music that his father had encouraged him to appreciate and revere. Initially, the vocal stylings of the famous duo, tenor Jussi Bjoerling and baritone Robert Merrill sparked his interest. He would gain his first exposure to this music at the home of Gordon and Edna Boerman. They were always keen to share their knowledge with any youngster showing interest in music. Edna was herself a trained classical singer who performed as a contralto with various musical societies around Adelaide. Her husband Gordon was a highly decorated war veteran. He totally supported his wife's altruistic approach to promoting musical appreciation. Kamahl reflects, "Gordon Boerman was a very impressive man, he had served during wartime with great distinction, and yet he exuded humility, stoicism and quiet dignity. Each year on ANZAC Day, I perform 'Soul of Australia', that wonderful poem by J.H.M. Abbott. The poem beautifully honours the sacrifices of the ANZAC's. Every time the image of the estimable Gordon Boerman is always in front of my mind as he represents to me the physical embodiment of the sentiment contained within those moving words."

During the Boerman's musical evenings, a pianist would always be in attendance to accompany the singers. These were quite formal occasions that left quite an impact on Kamahl as his interest in music grew. There was a gramophone generously stacked with classical recordings that the boys were permitted to play. Kamahl, who was already a committed dreamer, absorbed like a sponge, the escapism that music delivered. The sense of grand occasion that each of those evenings provided was intoxicating for him. He confesses that initially, his attraction in attending the Boerman's soirée was less than cultural or spiritual. He remembers distinctly that a niece of the family occasionally dropped by who was very attractive. Whilst he was still so chronically shy, he would never speak with her. Just being able to get the occasional glimpse of her provided a much-needed distraction from the drudgery of school and his humble boarding house.

Nonetheless, whatever his initial motives, music proved to be a far stronger motivation after a while. He actually began to understand his father's almost obsessive devotion to music, even though it was a completely different form of music. He reasons, "My father had tried desperately to get the whole family to share his love of traditional Hindu music. I think he wanted us to feel the beauty and power. After experiencing music that I loved, I began to understand why he wanted us to have something so special in our lives too."

Whilst the classical singers he heard at the Boerman's may have baited the hook, it was at another nearby home, that of Mr and Mrs Morecombe, where he was reeled in. The Morecombes owned a local delicatessen, where Kamahl, along with a group of other Asian boys from King's, used to congregate after school. It was a place where they played games, talked and some would occasionally sing a song or two. As the family became more familiar with the group, they invited the boys into their adjacent home to relax. Some of the kids would perform little comedy skits, and others would sing. It was at the Morecombe's that he first heard Nat King

Cole. He recalls, "The first time I heard Nat King Cole singing 'Nature Boy', it was at the home of a couple of lovely people called Morecombe …I was completely sold. His voice was so unlike the classical singers. It was silky smooth. He had a restraint quite unlike that produced by the exertions of the opera singers. I actually thought that the slight rasp in his voice may have been due to his having a damaged throat and the restraint was his way of avoiding further damage. After a short time, however, I realised that I had finally heard a voice that had inspired me to sing and not just listen." Kamahl's shyness prevented him from singing initially, as he had little if any confidence in his voice. 'Nature Boy' changed everything for him. He loved the song so much he had memorised every word and would practice whilst on his own. He says, "Once I remember, I even hid under a blanket in the middle of the King's College Oval in the middle of the day so that no-one could see or hear me. Believe it or not, that is how shy I was then." On one of his secret rehearsals in the shower, he was overheard by a friend who told him that he thought that he was "pretty good". That modest praise from his friend proved to be a far more significant piece of encouragement than intended. He decided right then and there that he would attempt the first of his many thousand public performances. It may have been a long way from Carnegie Hall. Still, that night, the Morecombe Family Home living room was just as big if not more significant, a career milestone for Kamahl. He was extremely nervous. He took Gladys Morcombe aside to let her know that he would be singing, adding a request. He asked if she didn't mind turning off the lights, it would really be appreciated. "The request was in equal parts my desire to keep my anonymity and to not be able to see the reaction of the group."

He stood up. He gave his own rendition of 'Nature Boy'. The response was positive enough to persuade him that this singing thing might prove quite valuable as a means of providing him with a way of fitting into that sea of white faces. "Once I developed the confidence, I used to go with friends to cafés and clubs. As I was still too shy to speak for myself, I would have them ask the owners to allow me to sing a few songs. They seldom, if ever, refused. After all, it was free entertainment for their patrons whilst being a great experience for me."

Even though he had started performing quite regularly in his spare time, he remained incredibly shy. He recalls, "Like the other Asian boys at King's, all of my fees and expenses were paid for by our families back home. We saw very little money at all. What we did get, we had to earn by doing odd jobs. In that regard, singing provided me with a little amount, generally through tips from generous patrons."

Toward the end of his final year at King's, Kamahl went on another one of his by now, trademark crash courses in cramming. He managed to pass his exams with a good enough mark to gain acceptance into the University of Adelaide. Only one reasonably major problem emerged… what was he going to study? He had no idea, and worse still had given it practically no thought at all to that point. His family's only direction was to get a good education and make something of yourself, which hardly provided a clear pathway to career choice. Kamahl desperately wanted to stay in Australia first, foremost and last, and he saw the improbable choice of singing was going to be his meal ticket. Just how it could be, he had absolutely no idea. Still, he knew that if this dream became a reality, he had to pick something to buy him time lest he is sent packing back to Kuala Lumpur. He needed desperately to pick something, and for reasons that to this day he can't fathom, he chose Architecture.

"Whilst I was still at the Victoria Institute in KL, I entered some drawings into an art competition. My motivation for doing so perversely was that I wanted to prove that I could compete with the Chinese students. They were always regarded as the best drawers. I have always had a competitive streak and eagerly accepted a challenge, so I entered two drawings. Both were awarded a laudable second prize. As ridiculous as it sounds now, I thought at the time that drawing was all there was to architecture. Therefore my decision was made." He quickly learned to his dismay that drawing is just a part of the skill set required to be an architect. Indeed, the discipline was made up of a whole host of things, none of which he was particularly good at. As he increasingly discovered this, the study grew harder and harder. His interest grew weaker and weaker, which, when teamed with his booming interest in singing, did not bode well for his architectural prospects. "I was singing everywhere I could, skipping classes, ignoring assignment deadlines and obsessively collecting vinyl records with what little money I could scrape together. The lack of commitment to my studies hadn't missed my uncle's attention, even from afar in Malaysia. He corresponded regularly with the people who were hosting me at the time, Merle and Leslie Moeller, for updates. They were the parents of a school friend of mine. Barry was a couple of years below me at King's. The family had taken a bit of a shine to me and had me lodge with them for several months, which was great. They were a very nice family, very generous and hospitable. The only problem was that they provided no cover for me at all with Uncle as nice as they were. Uncle was regularly corresponding with them as the heads of household, asking questions and being the lovely honest people they were, felt duty-bound to provide answers. Needless to say, Uncle was far from happy and to make matters worse, my poor grades had not gone unnoticed by the Department of Immigration. They communicated through the University Registrar that if improvement wasn't forthcoming, I would be headed back to KL in no time at all. It was like some kind of hellish pincer movement." Luckily for Kamahl, both the Immigration official, Bill Schneider and the University Registrar, Harry Wesley Smith, were highly decent and reasonable men who looked for a solution rather than looking to close the door on a young life. "When it was obvious that Architecture was definitely not my thing, I switched over to an Arts degree. However, that was proving to be a massive interference to my music as well. One day I was called into Harry Wesley Smith's office, and immediately I panicked. The last thing that I wanted to hear from him was that I was to be sent home, but I feared that was precisely what I would be told. To my delight and surprise, he instead offered me an alternative which proved to be my lifeline."

Harry Wesley Smith told Kamahl that no syllabus existed at University to study music. He stated that there was a chance for him to enrol at the Conservatorium of Music and he had already made the appropriate enquiry on his behalf. Kamahl was elated, finally the opportunity to immerse himself in something that he genuinely loved. "Harry was a terrific person who had a profound impact on my life with that incredible gesture of kindness."

The previous year Kamahl had been invited by Harry and his wife to their home for dinner. He told Kamahl that he had heard from his sons that they had heard him performing at venues around town and was a great singer. Intrigued, Harry requested that this troublesome student Kamahl come and literally sing for his supper so that he could judge his talent for himself. Kamahl sang yet another Nat King Cole number. Harry commented that whilst impressed with the performance, he didn't understand why Kamahl was 'making faces' when he sang. Kamahl told him that the exaggerated facial expressions were part of singing in the 'Nat King Cole style', which Harry found amusing. Although unaware of it at the time, Kamahl had not only found a fan, but he had conscripted a very useful advocate.

Several days after being summoned to Harry's office, he was sitting in another office, that of Professor John Bishop. The Professor was the Director of the Elder Conservatorium of Music. He asked him to sing, after which he called Harry Wesley Smith to tell him that he agreed Kamahl had a 'pleasant voice'. A week later and he was enrolled, avoiding the dreaded return to KL.

Through the late fifties into the early sixties, deportation was ever-present in Kamahl's mind. He was barely keeping his head above water academically. He had now chosen a career path that was definitely not approved by those who made Student Visa decisions in the Department of Immigration. Nonetheless, he had determined that he would be a singer and was prepared to do whatever it took to achieve that goal. He went very close to taking the one-way trip back to Kuala Lumpur on numerous occasions when the Department was continually reviewing his progress. Lucky for Kamahl, he was being monitored by a very sympathetic immigration officer, the aforementioned Bill Schneider.

Bill was responsible for overseeing foreign students on study visas in South Australia. While Bill had the onerous task of deciding who would stay and who would go, he was prepared to give a sympathetic hearing to this young man with a genuine passion for his art. Kamahl had flunked out of the two-degree courses that he'd chosen, and at this point, he should've been headed home. However, Bill Schneider agreed to permit him to attend the Conservatorium of Music. This is even though, the course was not within visa guidelines.

Furthermore, Schneider told his superiors when questioned on the case's progress that he simply couldn't locate Kamahl. Therefore he could not push forward with deportation. Once again, Kamahl had benefitted from a great kindness shown him by someone he barely knew. Whilst this situation came as a great relief, it did provide Kamahl with a bit of a conundrum. How to be missing when his chosen career path was to be out there performing in public. He was now a full-time student at the Conservatorium and very grateful to those who had made that happen.

Whilst attending at the Conservatorium, Kamahl was befriended by another student named Pam Newton. Pam was a tremendously talented harpist with a bright, friendly disposition and warm personality. Shortly after their meeting, she invited him to join her at the Newton family home for their Sunday lunch. Pam's parents Stan and Gladys, just like their daughter, were extremely generous people who took an instant liking to Kamahl. He had not realised it when accepting that first invitation that it was an invitation that stood each week for almost three years. As if the generous offer of a home-cooked meal wasn't incentive enough for any young man, there was also a surprise additional bonus.

Kamahl recalls, "The Newtons were a wonderful family who treated me as if I were one of their own. Gladys Newton was an excellent cook, and the meal she would feed me would be the major highlight of my week. She was so considerate that she would try to make me feel more at home by introducing curry to some of the dishes she prepared. I would sing for her and her husband Stan, and they really seemed to like that. They were musical people and were very supportive of my singing. They always gave me great encouragement to continue with my studies and performance. As if that weren't enough, the biggest surprise for me was when I arrived back at my lodgings that very first visit and took off my coat. Either Gladys or Stan had placed a ten-pound note into my jacket breast pocket whilst it had been hanging in the hall. Ten pounds was a small fortune back then. It was much more than my rent. It would be remarkable for someone to be that generous on a single occasion, but this didn't happen once. It happened every single time, every week for around three years. They were such wonderfully warm people. I have always been so grateful to have had people like the Newtons in my life. I will never ever forget their generosity and incredible kindness. The Newton's were indeed extraordinary people."

6

The evolution of a lyrebird

*Use what talents you possess; the woods would be very silent if
no birds sang there except those that sang best.*

Henry van Dyke

In nature, a lyrebird is a creature that is capable of imitating almost
any sound with ease. They have been recorded accurately, copying
human voices and practically all the noises they hear that are
generated by humans. Sounds such as a chainsaw, a car engine, a siren, a
fire alarm, gunshots, camera shutters, dogs barking, crying babies, music,
mobile phone ring tones. The ability of the lyrebird mimicry knows no
bounds. Kamahl, when he was a young man finding his voice, like the
lyrebird, he relied upon his ability to mimic the sounds produced by the
singers that he greatly admired.

He muses that this mimicry may have resulted from learning a
language quickly when he arrived here. Whilst his English was workable
and Australia's accepted language, the Australian accent is quite unlike
the English he had been taught as a kid in Malaysia. He, therefore, had to
work extra hard to comprehend plain old everyday conversation through
an Australian accent filter. This meant that his concentration on detail
became quite acute. So he would develop an ear that could detect even
the slightest variation in delivery when he heard anything unfamiliar.

It was yet another survival technique employed to ensure that he knew what was being said and, more importantly, what was meant. He now bemoans the fact that age has impacted his hearing quite significantly and these days needs to be helped by science via state-of-the-art hearing aids. "My hearing which was always one of my greatest tools was almost stolen from me by age," he says. "Thanks to science and technology, I am still able to perform and listen to music. It would be really terrible to consider a life in total silence."

As for Kamahl's singing, he was initially influenced by the classical stylings of the operatic vocalists like tenor Jussie Boerling and baritone Robert Merrill. He then copied the velvet smooth crooning of Nat King Cole through the early to late fifties. He recognised the deep timbre he had been blessed with naturally. He then discovered and subsequently evolved his style to imitate his other great singing hero, Paul Robeson. The Robeson style remained from the late fifties and into the early sixties. When he wasn't crooning 'Unforgettable' like a cocktail lounge lizard, he was a very young 'Ol' Man River' on the Mississippi. Stylistically, these two influences had very little in common other than being united in Kamahl's equal admiration of them. Remarkably, the confluence of these massive influences would result in his own kind of hybrid style. His almost self-mocking description of his vocal style is to say he is an Operatic Crooner. It's a style that allows him to be adept at contemporary or classical ballads, gives him the ability to switch and mix styles which afforded him a unique position. He wasn't just an easy-listening balladeer. He had classical capabilities that he could apply to the operatic, gospel and thematic pieces. This proved vital to audiences alienated by the rise of youth-oriented contemporary music throughout the sixties and seventies. He provided an oasis of alternative options to pop, rock, punk, disco or reggae. He was like their musical Swiss Army knife, and scores of Gold and Platinum record awards show testament to his connection with this audience.

However, for all of the recognition he has received, it is interesting that Kamahl takes the most significant personal pleasure from his spoken word performances. He says, "Whilst my career has always been about songs, to me, the words are the most powerful thing within them. Words are where the message lives and breathes. Words can be used to elevate or decimate. If you look throughout history, a great speech has actually moved nations to both greatness and devastation, such is their power."

Upon hearing 'Nature Boy', the Nat King Cole classic completely changed Kamahl's life and unlocked the key to his future. He says, "It was the powerful and yet simple central message that the song contained, to love and to be loved in return. Personally, I believe it is all that one can really hope for in life. The song itself had a fascinating back story. The guy who wrote it was Eden Ahbez, who was practically unknown, a kind of hippie before hippies had ever existed. Back in the late forties, Ahbez wore scruffy-looking clothes with sandals, had a long scraggly beard, shoulder-length hair. When he wrote the song, he lived homeless in a tent with his wife and child directly under the Hollywood sign in Los Angeles. When he directly approached Nat King Cole's manager at the stage door one day, he was thought to be some kind of freak. Thankfully, the manager passed the song on to Cole rather than throw it in the bin, and he loved it. It became a colossal hit recorded by so many famous artists. Still, my favourite will always be Nat King Cole's original version. I have recorded many Nat King Cole songs over the years, and when I perform them live, they always get such a great reaction. He was definitely one of my heroes, and like all of my heroes, I wanted to meet him personally. I am not sure why. It is possible that I felt that meeting them may result in something rubbing off on me, their skill, talent, their celebrity or all of the above." Kamahl duly attended the Adelaide Concert at Wavell Stadium, where Cole was backed by a full orchestra. He was not disappointed. He even remembers the set, song for song, as if it were yesterday. "He started with 'I'm Shooting High', which was performed acapella for the first eight bars then joined in perfect time by the orchestra. It was superb, he even forgot the lyrics to 'Darling Je Vous Aime Beaucoup' at one point, but no one cared at all. He was just that good."

The morning after the concert Kamahl, was on a mission. He spent the whole morning doing his best detective work to track down where Cole was staying. After discovering that he was located at the Highway Inn on Anzac Parade, he decided to hang around the lobby until he sighted his hero. He loitered around that hotel lobby for what he says seemed like an age. He was there so long that he was even asked by a house guest if he were Cole himself. This was 1958 and Adelaide, so a dark face in the environs of a hotel lobby was quite the rarity. After his long wait, he finally saw Cole accompanied by his manager walking through. He approached them and introduced himself, announcing that he was a student from Malaysia who would like to be a singer. "I look back on this incident and cringe a bit. I wonder what I was thinking. To this day, I struggle with the fact that I wasn't hauled away by security or, at the very least, chased away by the two men themselves. Thankfully neither happened, and they were extremely gracious… Cole said, 'you sing?' and acting as if I had been thrown a cue, I burst into 'Nature Boy' from beginning to end." Quite a ballsy thing to do for a shy guy, performing one of your hero's standards, to said hero. The two men listened attentively through Kamahl's impromptu performance, and it was evident that they were impressed.

Cole's manager responded encouragingly by saying, "You've got something there, son, keep it up." As for Cole, he dryly said, "Do you write?" Unfortunately, he was thrown by the question. Before a confused Kamahl could muster a coherent answer, the men had already moved on with his rambling response trailing off as they left. His confusion emanated from the fact that writing music was something that hadn't even occurred to him. He hadn't moved beyond performing at this point. In his mind, however, he was more than satisfied with his endeavours that day. Whilst it is rare to meet your hero in the flesh and not be disappointed, to Kamahl, his encounter with Nat King Cole was the furthest thing from disappointment he could imagine. With a wry smile, he says, "It was simply unforgettable."

As Kamahl's studies at the Conservatorium stepped up, he became more exposed to the disciplines of vocal training. While he had naively believed that a vocal range was predestined at birth rather than developed, he quickly learned that vocal training was essential to effective performance. This was brought home significantly when after hearing the magnificent bass-baritone of Paul Robeson, he knew that he would like to emulate the great singer's vocals. After all, he reasoned, he had a bass-baritone voice, and notes were just notes. Quickly he realised that he lacked the vocal strength to do this type of material any justice and would need to step up his training if he were to go further as an artist. Like so many other occasions in his life, he found the answer was not easy; it lay in hard work and dedication. One of his early lessons at the Conservatorium came from his vocal coach, who quipped, "Kamahl, you are never going to make it as a singer unless you get a handle (Handel) on the *Messiah*." It wasn't until sometime later that Kamahl got the musical pun but thankfully understood the advice immediately and sought to address his vocal training far more seriously.

Paul Robeson's tour of Australia in 1960 provided Kamahl with an opportunity to study a master up close, as it had previously with Nat King Cole. He was determined to gain insight or a simple word or two of wisdom to guide him on his journey. He knew that he needed to do all that he could to be in his presence. While international artists of such stature would typically be held at the Town Hall, Robeson was a figure of much controversy in an Australia who was still in the thrall of Cold War politics, just like his homeland. He was an outspoken socialist who was mercilessly hounded by the media and political hacks for his radical views, particularly his support of the Civil Rights movement. Like

America at this time, Australia was very conservative and firmly believed that entertainers were purely there to entertain and not engage in politics. He was mercilessly punished financially for his social views in the States. He was considered too controversial to hire, hence work dried up, forcing him to look further afield for engagements purely to survive. When the chance to tour Australia and New Zealand emerged as a possibility, he seized upon the opportunity. Sadly, he had underestimated or was ill-informed on just how conservative Australia was in 1960.

Consequently, Robeson's trip was characterised by negative press coverage who dedicated more time to his supposedly radical left-wing views than his talent. His concert in Adelaide was even relegated to the Unley Theatre. Whilst quite a suitable venue for local talent, it was a second-tier and really not befitting an artist of such stature.

Young Kamahl had little if any interest in politics at this point in his life and was just thrilled to see yet another of his musical heroes in person. He states, "Robeson was a remarkable man with an incredible presence, he had been a great Gridiron player at University making All American, he was a Rhodes Scholar, a fantastic orator, a truly great actor, but to me, at that time, I was just mesmerised by his voice, it was truly remarkable. It was a voice that my friend Bob Ellis years later would perfectly describe when he said If the Earth itself could sing, its voice would sound like Robeson". Kamahl also learned another great lesson from Paul Robeson during that one concert. He had a fabulous stage presence. He was a giant of a man. He performed with a stillness that ensured that his audiences remained captivated by his every utterance. He didn't need to move around as it would've only served to distract.

That evening as Kamahl sat in the theatre somewhat awestruck at the performance he was witnessing, he still retained enough presence of mind to plot meeting his idol. He determined that the best approach would be to make his way to the stage steps to intercept him. When he arrived, he found him in the company of his wife, who was already helping with his hat and coat ready for departure. Kamahl nervously spluttered a greeting of sorts and remembers saying that it was a privilege to meet him. Robeson turned slowly and extended his hand to Kamahl, which he eagerly shook. His wife, who seemed anxious and a little unnerved by the encounter, promptly ushered him away. Without hearing one word from his idols mouth, he departed. Kamahl was bitterly disappointed not to have the conversation he had hoped for, but watching Robeson perform and getting to shake his hand was priceless.

Kamahl reflects on the Robeson tour as an early introduction to the sometimes poisonous nature of politics. "Many years after he toured, I became aware of the circumstances surrounding his life and the awful persecution he faced. All for having a view contrary to the prevailing regimes of the day. He was a genuine socialist who, during his short visit to Australia, had visited the Sydney Opera House, which was in the early stages of building at the time. He went there to entertain the workers on the site. He also performed for wharf workers in Melbourne and Sydney, all free of charge. He and his wife were also very interested in the plight of Aboriginal Australians. He had said that he would like to return to Australia to hold benefit concerts for the advancement of Indigenous people. Possibly due to his failing health through depression that didn't eventuate. Eventually, he moved to Russia, believing possibly that it represented everything that his homeland failed to live up to. Only a year after he left Australia when in Moscow, he attempted suicide, whilst thankfully unsuccessful he spent much of his remaining time on earth a recluse." Whilst Kamahl has never been politically affiliated, he admires people of great character who choose that path. A person like Robeson, whose efforts for peace, freedom, racial equality and social justice were immense, fits that bill entirely. He claims, "Robeson's achievements should not be dismissed purely because of his political beliefs. For me, he was indeed a great man who did so much for so many."

On one fateful evening, in December 1958, whilst performing at The Lido Club in Adelaide, Kamahl was approached by an attractive young woman during a break in his set. She asked him if he remembered her. His puzzled expression betrayed him. Sensing his confusion, she politely volunteered that her name was Pat Booker. She used to work at Myer, where he used to go to buy his school uniforms whilst attending Kings College. Pat kindly asked Kamahl if he would care to join her and meet her friends at their table. He duly agreed and followed her back to her table. On arrival, Kamahl noticed a very well-dressed man smoking a rather conspicuous cigar among the group of ten. He was joking about a 'fish in his glass', a trick constructed around a piece of foil paper floating in a drink. This was a fairly lively group who seemed like a fun crew, and the banter flowed back and forth, but there was little doubt who was holding court. Kamahl says, "They seemed like they were having a lot of fun, but to be completely honest, I was struggling to keep up with the conversation. They were chatting about topics that were not all that familiar to me". Kamahl excused himself to go and complete the next and final bracket on his program.

When he was finished, the man with the cigar came up and asked him what he was doing later on. As socialising was not big on Kamahl's agenda at this point in his life, it was not a difficult question. He was doing nothing. "He asked me if I would like to go with them to a party in The Hills. I gladly agreed. He went on to tell me that his company was having a Christmas Party at the Marino Golf Club and asked if I wouldn't mind singing a few songs there. Of course, I agreed, when we arrived, there were about seventy guests. My host, whose name I still didn't know, was obviously important, judging by the reception on arrival. It was also obvious that he was Pat's husband. I sang a short set of around two or three songs and finished with Silent Night. The crowd were very generous with their applause, and to my surprise, my host rushed toward me and thrust a ten-pound note in my hand. Ten pounds was a lot of money back then, so I was literally gobsmacked. He graciously thanked me for my efforts and went back to being important, mingling with what was obviously his employees. I remained at the party until it wound down. Around 1am Pat and her extremely generous husband offered to drive me home, stating that they just needed to stop off at their place on the way. When we arrived, I was taken aback by their enormous dog. He was a Great Dane named Webster. I had never seen anything that big without a saddle on its back before. My host went to the fridge and took out an enormous plate of minced meat, which he placed in front of the dog, who devoured it in two gulps. I was so preoccupied with the presence of this giant creature that I hadn't realised that my generous host had also been cooking food for us. He had cooked massive steaks. As I was a vegetarian at the time, it was a bit of an issue. Still, I was so overwhelmed by his hospitality. I really didn't want to offend, so I managed to chew the whole thing without even sparing an apologetic thought for the memory of Lakshmi, our family cow. In a vain attempt at maintaining my spiritual integrity, I secreted the chewed pieces in a handkerchief in my pocket."

Kamahl's host drove him home shortly before sunrise from what had been a most memorable and enjoyable evening. At this point, he hadn't realised that he had been in the company of one of the most significant business people to ever come out of Australia. Pat's husband, Kamahl, discovered some weeks later was none other than Rupert Murdoch.

After their initial meeting, Kamahl didn't cross Murdoch's path for almost another year. This was hardly surprising as he was trying to build a career in performance which kept him very busy, and they mixed in vastly different social circles. Kamahl had started to develop many regular engagements across Adelaide and was beginning to feel more confident that his act was beginning to generate a following. In October, he learned that Murdoch had purchased a television station and that it would be going live on the seventeenth of the month with its first live telecast.

"I wasn't sure if it was Rupert himself who requested it, but I was asked to perform during the station's first live broadcast. I was terrified. I hadn't even performed with a full band live at this point, a pianist maybe but never a full band, and now I was to perform live in front of an audience of many thousands. When the day arrived, I was so racked with nerves, I didn't want to embarrass myself. I didn't want to let Rupert and Pat down for the trust they had placed in me as both were going to be there on the night. When I saw Pat, she obviously sensed that I was very nervous, so she offered me some of her drink. I gulped it down and, to my shock, discovered it was some type of whiskey and I had never had alcohol in my life before. If it was meant to settle my nerves, it failed as my mouth dried up almost completely. I wasn't entirely sure how the hell I could recover to sing." He still doesn't know if it was the delayed effect of the whiskey or deep breathing that got him through. Still, he managed to perform 'Autumn Leaves' and 'Handful of Stars', the latter being a challenging piece. To this day, he can't understand what he was thinking in choosing it in the first place. His reviews the next day were overwhelmingly positive, with one kind scribe opening 'of the stars that shone last night, that guy from Malaysia called Kamahl has a voice to remember. From this breakthrough performance that evening, Kamahl became a regular on all of the TV stations in the Adelaide market. Over the next few years, he would perform on numerous shows and, as a result, grew his popularity significantly, becoming one of Adelaide's best-loved performers.

By the time the early sixties rolled around, Murdoch had moved the bulk of his News Limited operation and himself to Sydney. He did have to come back to Adelaide from time to time to attend business meetings. On one of his trips, he happened to encounter Kamahl whilst he was rehearsing at Channel 9 for an upcoming show. "After I ran through 'Rambling Rose' yet another Nat King Cole standard, he came up to me and said I should go to Sydney and stated that he believed that Adelaide was too small for me. I was flattered, but the whole idea seemed fanciful to me. Firstly, there was the issue of my lack of confidence. How could I possibly make it in a big city? Secondly was the fact that I was a migrant here on a student visa that had technically expired. My movement from city to city could prove difficult without attracting the ire of immigration officials and risk being bundled on the next plane back to KL."

Resigned to the notion that his move to Sydney was a fleeting compliment from a well-intentioned friend, Kamahl thought nothing more of it. A few weeks later, to his great surprise, "I received a letter in the mail, it contained a booking for a six-week season at the prestigious Australia Hotel in Castlereagh Street, Sydney. In a suite at the hotel for the duration of the engagement and an airline ticket. Evidently, Rupert had contacted Tom Miller, a well-established and respected agent, to arrange the gigs when he had returned from Adelaide after our meeting at Channel 9. For Rupert to have followed through on his own suggestion and taken the time from his busy schedule to personally arrange this was truly amazing. I was extremely nervous, frankly overwhelmed by the challenge that I faced. Still, when someone offers you an opportunity of that magnitude and shows that much faith in you, you have to take it with both hands."

And so it was, he headed off to Sydney and the Australia Hotel's Sapphire Room. At the time, the venue was the 'in place' for Sydney society. So the chance to perform there was a massive boost for any artist trying to build a career. Performing six days a week, Monday to Saturday, he would see the Murdoch's at the show each week on Friday and Saturday, always seated at the same table. When his season was nearing its end, he approached his friends to thank them for their hospitality and generosity. To his surprise, Rupert said to him, "where do you think you're going?" Kamahl responded "Back to Adelaide, of course". Rupert stated matter-of-factly, "No, you're not. You are staying here, and furthermore, you can stay with us."

Kamahl recalls, "I did go back to Adelaide, but it was only to collect my things. I returned to Sydney to stay with the Murdochs. They at that stage were perceived as Australia's 'Camelot' couple living a luxurious lifestyle. It seems surreal to even think about it now. For two years Rupert and Pat treated me like I was a member of the family, more than a houseguest."

Kamahl had no doubt improved his address and set his career on an upward trajectory. His migrant status had been patiently waiting to raise its ugly head. He was contacted by the Department, who reminded him in no uncertain terms that they need to be assured of his intentions to conform with their requirements or get packing. He was informed at a meeting with officials, that he would require a guarantor to vouch for his bona fides in pursuing his studies if he were to remain. The registrar of the University of Adelaide, Harry Wesley Smith, again came to his rescue by speaking to Rupert on his behalf to arrange for him to be that guarantor. This basically required a letter to be sent to the Department advising them of Kamahl's dedication to his study of music and his increasing popularity as an Australian entertainer. It stated that he was studying under the direction of Harold Williams at the Sydney Conservatorium of Music and would continue his studies overseas in a further twelve months. The letter which was each year written by Rupert's secretary Nancy Gunn, would be redated, presented for the signature and mailed off neutralising the threat of deportation for another year. Kamahl reflects, "Without that great support, I would've certainly been deported."

Kamahl regards his time spent with the Murdochs at their Yarranabee Road, Darling Point mansion as very special. It was his first insight into the lives of the rich and famous, full of glitz and glamour. Big house parties, lavish dinners, meeting influential people, celebrities, politicians, captains of industry, all were part of the environment. The only thing this luxurious abode lacked was a record player. "I thought it very strange that a man who actually owned a record company did not possess a record player. I rectified this almost immediately by persuading Pat to buy one along with a good selection of LP records. Rupert was a workaholic and evidently still is, so he was seldom there when we played music each day. When he finally made it home, he wanted to play table tennis, a game he was actually quite proficient at. Our games were actually quite tense as neither of us was a good loser. As much as I would try to throw the odd game, my instincts just wouldn't allow me to."

The home hosted a significant number of large parties and get-togethers. Anyone who was anyone in Sydney Society was to be found at the many functions and gatherings. Undoubtedly, the most influential people in Australia, from politicians to business giants, the famous and infamous. If they had a profile at all, they were there. As Kamahl was the ever-present house guest, function attendee and occasional entertainer, he pressed the flesh with most. One of the most important and beneficial meetings that happened for him during his time there was with a man named Tony Rossi, himself a performer. Tony was a classically trained singer who had started his career in various opera companies in Europe and Australia. He had soon realised that a steadier income was available from the growing club circuit. Tony was married to a lady named Peta, who, like Pat Murdoch, had been an airline hostess before marriage. The two women had worked together and were fast friends of long-standing. Pat had urged the couple to come and meet their houseguest to see what Tony could do to help Kamahl get a start in Sydney. Tony was all too happy to offer what help and advice he could as someone who knew first-hand how tough it was to get that first break. Tony was very impressed with Kamahl's voice and presence. Tony offered to arrange an introduction to Bill Sadler, a veteran agent with excellent contacts.

When he met Kamahl, Sadler just looked at him and asked him if he had his diary. Of course he didn't but quickly realised that he needed a diary in a hurry, when Bill rattled off many bookings. The first was at Petersham RSL on May 4, 1964. Bill didn't even want to listen to him sing before making the bookings for him. Tony had recommended him, and if Tony thought that he was ok, he was ok, and that was all there was to it. Just like that, Kamahl had himself an agent. To this day, Kamahl maintains, "If it were not for Pat's kind gesture in helping me, who knows what may have happened? It may have taken years for me to get where her intervention had placed me in days."

At Yarranabee Road, many people were coming and going, many with their own exciting stories to share.

One larger than life character was Curley Brydon, General Manager of News Limited at the time. Curley's life was made from the stuff of 'boys own adventure' literature. Born in the New South Wales town of Armidale in 1921, Curley enlisted in the Royal Australian Airforce as an eighteen-year-old the day after the war was declared in 1939.

By 1943 he became Australia's youngest ever Squadron Leader at 22 years of age. In the RAAF, he developed a considerable reputation on the back of his fearlessness and bravery when flying bombers in high-risk operations. He was awarded the Distinguished Flying Cross for his courage. His urge for high risk in civilian life would continue and needed an outlet. He would become a high profile racing car driver for many years whilst still carving out a successful career in business. He was a passionate yachtsman and regularly sailed with Murdoch on his ketch, the I*lina*.

Curley's wife Leslie was also a keen sailor, being part of the first all-female crew to compete in the Sydney to Hobart race on *Barbarian* in 1975. Kamahl recalls, "Curley was a real-life hero. Amazingly, no one has ever made an adventure movie about his life. He even looked the part of the swashbuckling 1940's movie hero with his slicked hair and moustache. Paradoxically he was quite reserved and economical with his talking. One of his risky hobbies had left him with a metal plate in his head, as I recall correctly. It was little wonder that Rupert had hired him to run part of his growing empire. He was just so impressive and a proven natural leader under extreme pressure. I would have loved to have heard more about his interesting life but was robbed of much of that due to my fear of sailing. Well, to be specific, my fear was drowning. I have never been a swimmer and when I was young I experienced the prospect of a watery grave on two occasions, so generally speaking, I avoided water sports entirely. As a result of that fear, I was denied many afternoons aboard the *Ilina*."

A young Harry M Miller was a regular visitor to the home when he was just starting out in Australia. He relocated from his native New Zealand in 1963. He set up Pan Pacific Productions with fellow migrants Keith and Dennis Wong, the entertainment entrepreneurs who owned the fabled Sydney nightclub Chequers. Harry through the sixties promoted a glittering run of concert and theatrical tours in Australia and New Zealand, including Louis Armstrong, The Rolling Stones and The Beach Boys, to name a few. He would also go on to great success as both a personal manager of stars like Graham Kennedy and the promoter of groundbreaking musicals such as *Jesus Christ Superstar* and *Hair*.

In 1973 Harry would book Kamahl to appear at the Capitol Theatre feature show, which he used to warm up to Kamahl's last Sydney Opera House concert.

Kamahl also vividly recalls meeting a brilliant young journalist named Zell Rabin being at the home. Rupert Murdoch had headhunted Zell into the Newsgroup from arch-rival Fairfax in somewhat of a coup.

Zell was a fascinating guy who had been born Jewish in Lithuania in 1932. His parents, sensing the oncoming insanity of the Holocaust sweeping through Eastern Europe, fled to Sydney in 1939. They would join his mother's relatives, who had settled there some years earlier. His father was a chemist prevented from practising until accredited in Australia. Until this could happen, they decided to farm a small parcel of land in the Western Suburbs. When accredited, he was free to purchase a small chemical plant which he turned into a successful enterprise.

Young Zell was extremely bright. In fact, he spoke four languages fluently by the time he was six. Unfortunately, English was not one of them. Very early on, he had learned the language and became so proficient that he became a high academic achiever who would choose writing as his livelihood. Quickly moving up the ranks of journalism with John Fairfax Ltd, he was to be installed as their bureau chief whilst still in his early twenties. In New York, he recorded many high-profile interviews with people like Marilyn Monroe, Henry Miller and US President Harry Truman.

After a short spell back in Sydney, Murdoch persuaded Zell to jump ship and become the New York bureau chief for the *Daily Mirror*, which he had bought in 1960. Among other things, Rabin achieved in his time running the desk in New York was that he arranged and interviewed John F. Kennedy at the White House. Murdoch recognised the incredible talent in Rabin. He saw him as the man to head his battle against his rival Sydney publishers.

He, therefore, installed him as the editor of the *Sunday Mirror*. In 1963 Rabin also became editor of the *Daily Mirror*. By recognising the success he brought to the *Daily Mirror*, Murdoch would grant him almost complete editorial control of the newspaper. A power which he has rarely given to previous or subsequent editors. Zell had a natural flair for big, bold headlines that would capture mass attention. Under his stewardship, The *Mirror* grew to be highly successful. His editorial instinct was also fearless when offering a viewpoint. Under his direction, the *Daily Mirror* became the only metropolitan newspaper in Australia to oppose the involvement in the Vietnam War.

Sadly whilst still very young, Rabin died of cancer on November 13th 1966, he was only 34 years of age. Kamahl says, "From early in his career, Rupert always had a great perception when it came to talent. Zell was the best example of that. He was definitely his golden child. His intelligence was obvious to anyone who spoke with him, and his ability matched it.

Having achieved so much so early in his life, it makes you wonder just how far he could've gone if it were not for his tragic early death. Many people in his field had not achieved as much with careers older than he was when he died. He was a remarkable character."

Famed interior designer to the rich and powerful, celebrated socialite Leslie Walford was another frequent guest at Yarranabee Road. Walford had been responsible for the aesthetic of Murdoch's property. Kamahl recalls him as a colourful and flamboyant individual who was not only highly talented within his chosen field but could also work a room with the greatest of ease. Kamahl recalls, "Leslie definitely had a great sense of style. Born in Australia, his parents had sent him to be educated at exclusive private schools in Britain or public schools as they ironically refer to them. From there, he had gone to Oxford University to study politics. I believe he had, however, two shared passions, art and design, so he obviously decided to pursue that path. He always spoke so eloquently and had perfect diction. It was his sense of style that always impressed me."

Exposure to such prominent characters went a long way to inform Kamahl on many things, namely, how to stand out from the crowd. Many of these people were successful because they were bold, determined and driven. They all shared one key characteristic; in that they were all unapologetic for their ambition. He observed that they all had in some way been moulded by the challenges they had to face. His schooling in Australian society and culture may have started in Adelaide, but it was at Yarranabee Road Darling Point, where he would complete a master's degree in how the 'other half' lived.

Sometimes, he wasn't even aware of who some of these people actually were at the time of meeting them. "One of the more interesting people that I met at one of these gatherings was Arthur Calwell, who I was informed was the leader of the Australian Labor Party. As I had no interest in politics at all, that meant absolutely nothing to me at the time. When I met him, Calwell was still recovering from being shot in a failed assassination attempt at Mosman Town Hall. It had only happened a short while earlier that year. Calwell had been shot at close range by an anti-war activist named Kocan through a closed car window. Evidently, if the car window had been down, it would have killed him instantly. The incident affected his appearance quite considerably, with his jaw being shattered by the shooting, leaving his face with a strange appearance.

:When I learned of this during our conversation, I immediately felt sympathy for the poor man. In my opinion I felt that Calwell had been one of the major advocates of maintaining the White Australia policy. This policy took a very segregationist view on the composition of Australia."

Arthur Calwell was indeed quoted when interviewed by the press on the topic some years earlier:

'I am proud of my white skin, just as a Chinese is proud of his yellow skin, a Japanese of his brown skin, and the Indians of their various hues from black to coffee-coloured. Anybody who is not proud of his race is not a man at all. And any man who tries to stigmatise the Australian community as racist because they want to preserve this country for the white race is doing our nation great harm… I reject, in conscience, the idea that Australia should or ever can become a multi-racial society and survive.'

When we hear a politician quoted like this in more enlightened times, Australians awkwardly shake their heads, but this was the prevailing and accepted view for a significant number of Australians at that time. His ideas were not the exception but the rule. Even more incredible, this is a man who contested three Prime Ministerial elections. Kamahl says, "I have to say as a person described as belonging to the group described by Calwell as coming in various hues from black to coffee-coloured.

Well, this dark coffee coloured man is delighted that he was never given a chance to further promote his prejudice. I am even happier he was never given a chance to run the country. I would say that his views were jaundiced, but that would probably set him spinning in his grave, as I am sure he thought his thoughts could only be whiter than white."

Yarranabee Road indeed held fond memories for Kamahl. Still, as is often said, all things must pass. After well over two years of being generously hosted by the Murdochs, he felt more confident and comfortable in himself he decided that it was time to move on. Toward the end of his time there, strains were starting to show in the couple's marriage.

In 1967 they eventually moved ahead with that divorce which saddened Kamahl. He had such great affection for them both as a couple and as individuals. Kamahl says, "They were such dear friends and had been such an enormously positive influence on my life".

Sadly, Pat passed away in 1998. He remembers vividly that he was touring Europe at the time, and it was November 12th, the day before his birthday.

Pat re-established her life. After a relatively short period, she met and subsequently married a man named Freddie Maeder, who was, at the time, a celebrated hairstylist. Both Freddie and Pat were highly social people. They enjoyed the high life, which was often referred to euphemistically as part of the jet-set. This was a reasonably hedonistic environment where more was trumped by much more, and much more was far more than was healthy.

Over the years, the travel and parties eventually took a toll. When they finally settled in Spain, they were surrounded by like-minded people with a similarly high-rolling view on life. It was whilst living in Spain that Pat's health began to dramatically decline. So she returned to Australia without Freddie. She was physically and financially damaged from the years abroad. The excesses she had put herself through. About a month before her passing, Kamahl recalls that he received a call from the Hotel reception where he was staying. They informed him that he had a visitor named Pat in the foyer. He duly went down to meet his guest and claims he was excited to catch up with a dear old friend he hadn't seen for quite some time. He was genuinely shocked by her appearance. "It was terrible. She was thin as a pencil and looked very unwell, a far cry from the vibrant, beautiful woman we all knew and loved. It broke my heart to see her in such a condition. We had a pleasant afternoon chatting that day. It turned out to be the last time I would ever see her as one month later, whilst I was touring in Holland, Sahodra rang to inform me that Pat had died. It was really awful as she was still quite young. It is always sad when a dear friend dies and I understand that it was Rupert who, upon hearing of her awful decline in health, fully paid for her return to Australia and supported her treatment."

Kamahl still occasionally communicates with Rupert, who, to his credit, still takes the time to respond to each email or letter or even to catch up when their respective location permits. "Life takes people in different directions. Even though I always knew that Rupert was destined for big things, never would I have believed how powerful he actually became. It is truly remarkable to witness. To me, he has never changed. He has always been the same person. I will always think of him as that impeccably dressed, charming young businessman, who I met in The Lido nightclub in Adelaide one night close to Christmas in 1958."

On the subject of politics, Kamahl concedes that he and Rupert have significantly different views on very many issues. In fact, there would be very little that they would agree on politically. They have managed to largely avoid the topic. Kamahl says, "I have never allowed the poison of politics to pollute our friendship. He has his views, and I have mine and that is all there is to it.

"His conservative views are well known, and mine are significantly more progressive. To be honest, I don't really believe that Rupert's political persuasions are as clear cut as people believe they are. Over the years, he has famously supported both the Tories and Labour in the UK. In Australia, he has supported both the ALP and Liberal parties. His position in the US seems to have been less flexible as it has mainly rested with the Republicans. I think that is because they seem to be more aligned to his business objectives rather than any particular ideology he holds."

With some incongruity, he observes his lifelong friend, providing such a powerful propaganda platform to a person like Trump through his Fox News network. He says, "I cannot reconcile his support of Trump with the person that I have always thought that I knew so well. I simply don't understand how someone with an almost genius-level intellect can relate to the unintelligible words coming out of Trump's mouth. To employ people like Hannity, Carlson, Ingraham, Dobbs, or Pirro is in such great contrast with the magnificent Zell Rabin. It saddens me. In my mind, there is absolutely no way that the insanity that is spouted on the opinion side of the Fox Network could possibly align with his own true beliefs. People ask me whether his motivation is about profit or power. I doubt if it is either. Let's be honest; it isn't about wealth anymore for him. He has genuine wealth and all the power anyone could possibly have. I suspect it is something else that drives him so much. In my view, I think that he still has a deep-seated desire to prove himself to be as successful as his father, who died when Rupert was yet to realise his business talents. Sir Keith's death robbed him of the opportunity to prove his worth to his dad whilst he was alive.

"So maybe he has to prove it to the rest of the world instead. People are indeed very complex creatures. Actually, when I hear people berating him, it hurts me very personally. When I hear the criticism and people demonising him for his direct support of far-right politics. Still, the hurt is not because that criticism is unfair, it is the fact that the criticism is at times correct. I almost feel that he has left me powerless to defend him on specific issues.

"Even though we may never agree on politics, I know that he has a character beyond that. Therefore, I am still eternally grateful to him for all he did for me. After all, is said and done, we always have remained friends as I have the utmost respect for him. He has directly demonstrated great kindness to me over the years. When it mattered most to me, he ignited my confidence by providing me with such tremendous opportunities. I genuinely mean it when I say who knows where I would have been without Rupert. My best guess would be driving a tour bus back in KL."

After Yarranabee Road, Kamahl's following address was nowhere near as salubrious. It was a small one-bedroom attic apartment in Liverpool Street, Paddington. He paid the princely sum of three guineas a week, around $100 in today's money. The apartment's location meant that it provided easy central access to most of Sydney's entertainment venues, so it was quite the bargain, even for the time.

Whilst a considerable step down in prestige from harbourside Darling Point, it was his own, which meant a lot to him. He was no longer a houseguest. He was the lord of his own manor, even if the manor was tiny. It gave him a feeling of permanency and belonging, almost enough to distract him from the 'Sword of Damocles' hanging over his head by the Department of Immigration.

The new place was not without its own unique challenges; the on-site landlords, Cathy and Jim Lockerie were quite a charming couple. Unfortunately, they had a far less than charming Doberman Pinscher named Rex. Rex was 10% pet and 90% psychopathic terrorist with a specific disliking for Tamil bass-baritone singers, so it seemed to Kamahl. Rex's domain was the rear yard of the house which unfortunately was also the location of the flat's only accessible toilet. He mused, "That bloody dog played havoc with my ablutions. I would have to run the gauntlet whenever I needed to spend a penny, each and every time it felt like a near-death experience. I used to joke that the damned toilet was closer to neighbouring St Vincent's Hospital than the House. If Rex ever did get hold of me, I may as well keep running straight over the back fence and into the Emergency Ward rather than risk trying to get back in the House."

He does still have fond memories of the home despite the perilous canine capers. He recalls, "It was very tiny but quite comfortable. I remember we had to dispense with the handrail on the stairs to fit my piano in. I don't think I ever replaced it when I left … sorry, Cathy and Jim".

7

The wind beneath my wings

She walks in beauty, like the night
Of cloudless climes and starry skies.
And all that's best of dark and bright
Meet in her aspect and her eyes.
Thus, mellowed to that tender light
Which heaven to gaudy day denies.

One shade the more, one ray the less,
Had half impaired the nameless grace
Which waves in every raven tress,
Or softly lightens o'er her face.
Where thoughts serenely sweet express,
How pure, how dear their dwelling-place.

And on that cheek, and o'er that brow,
So soft, so calm, yet eloquent,
The smiles that win, the tints that glow,
But tell of days in goodness spent,
A mind at peace with all below,
A heart whose love is innocent!

(Lord) George Gordon Byron

Sydney's Mandarin Club was opened in 1964 by businessman Dennis Wong and his brother Keith. The Wongs were among the many great immigrant success stories in Australia, having fled the revolution in China in the late forties to build a new life in a new country. Initially landing in Brisbane, they opened and ran a very successful restaurant named Paradise. From there, they found their way to Sydney, also initially getting involved in the restaurant business. However, they did take a meaningful detour by branching out into the city's rapidly growing live entertainment scene. They went on to establish two legendary venues, Whisky a Go Go at King's Cross and Chequers in Goulburn Street Sydney. Chequers being Sydney's number one international cabaret venue featuring a heady list of headliners like Sammy Davis Junior, Liza Minelli, Matt Monro, Shirley Bassey and Dionne Warwick to name but a few. A little walk down the street was the site that became the Mandarin Club. It was quite a unique venue, not only because of its location so close to the heart of Sydney's CBD, it was the only fully licensed legal club to trade 24 hours a day. The venue featured an excellent Chinese restaurant credited with being the first to offer Yum Cha in Australia. For this, it was popular with the many performers who, after night plying their trade, were looking to wind down from the adrenalin high of their own shows to drink, eat and be seen. Given its celebrity patronage, it was literally a place you never knew who you may bump into. Therefore, it was a great spot for late-night networking. Kamahl recalls, "One night I was in there after some show or other, and I was spotted from quite a distance by Norm Erskine, who was a mainstay of the club and cabaret scene at the time. He was a big loud character and had quite a following. When he spotted me, he howled quite loudly, 'Ladies and Gentlemen, it's Kamahl, the Mahatma Gandhi of Australian entertainment!' Whilst I was being stereotyped, I wasn't in the least bit insulted. Far from it, I was actually quite flattered that he even knew who I was, and even better, he announced it to everyone within earshot…if you knew how loud Norm's voice was, you'd realise that was quite a coverage area."

It was fitting that in such a unique setting, one night in 1965 that Kamahl would meet someone who would change his life forever.

Kamahl reflects, "I had been performing at Granville RSL Club that night and after the performance decided to go to the Mandarin Club along with my support act. People are often surprised that entertainers after work don't just simply head off home for peace and quiet to hit the sack to get some rest and unwind. The reality is that performing energises you, and it takes you some time for the mind and body to reset. After dinner alone, I was still wide awake and decided to waste some money in a poker machine. I have never been lucky as a gambler from early in my life, so this was purely an exercise in mindless time-wasting until I felt that I could head back home. As I sat there, I noticed in a mirror above the machine that I could see people moving back and forth. I wasn't really paying too much attention until I noticed what I thought at the time was a magnificent vision. Among a group of Asian ladies was the most beautiful young Indian woman I had ever seen. She was wearing a traditional green sari which made her stand out like a beacon of light. Even though I by then was an established performer and making a living from being in front of strangers, I was still painfully shy when it came to approaching girls. However, I was compelled to say something in this case, so I blurted out 'excuse me' without thinking of what I would say next. She turned to acknowledge me, and then I said, 'Are you a model or an airline hostess?'. She responded by just saying 'no' in a matter-of-fact way and then moved straight on. I can hardly say that my nervous opening line would ever rank as a great moment in seduction. Still, I reasoned it was a start, and as they often say, every great journey starts with one step. I suppose mine started with one single stumble. Still, at least I hadn't tripped up and fallen flat on my face." Showing all the dogged determination that was now emerging as one of his significant characteristics, Kamahl was not in the least deterred. He took advantage of the next time she walked past to step in front of her and further his earlier line of enquiry. He said, "If you are not a model or an air hostess, what are you?" She encouragingly replied with a smile this time, saying, "We are nurses celebrating our graduation." This time buoyed by the friendlier response, Kamahl plucked up the courage to ask her if she would like to meet up sometime soon. To his surprise, she agreed, and so he asked for her name and a phone number where he could contact her. She informed him that her name was Sahodra Tikaram, and she was living at the Crown Street Women's Hospital. In what he describes as an attempt to 'play it cool', he said he would give her a call in the next couple of weeks. He recalls, "I wanted so badly to call her straight away. I was besotted, all I could think of was her, but I had to put myself through the agony of waiting just so that I could appear relaxed and in control." So it was that two weeks to the day, hour and minute, he picked up the phone and called Crown St Women's Hospital Nurse's Quarters and after a brief exchange of pleasantries, they arranged their first date.

Kamahl remembers that their first date didn't start all that well. They went to see a movie, *A Shot in the Dark*, a comedy feature starring Peter Sellers. This film, as it turned out, was a movie that neither of them enjoyed all that much. Seller's bumbling Clouseau hardly provided the inspired romantic backdrop he had wished for on their first date. Luckily his fortunes changed at the dinner that followed immediately afterwards. They talked for hours about their respective lives and life experiences. They found so much in common that they actually felt like they had known each other for years. During their conversation, Kamahl discovered that Sahodra had been sent to Tasmania for a couple of years to study and then to Sydney to finish her studies for the last twelve months. Upon completion of her studies, she was to return home to start her career.

One aspect of their lives they definitely shared was their respective families' expectations and plans for them. Sahodra was born in Fiji to a respected Indian family. Like Kamahl, she had been sent overseas to complete her studies.

After her return it was expected or to be more accurate, ordained, that she would be married. Unlike Kamahl, however, Sahodra's plans were quite a bit more advanced. The family had already gone to the next step in planning her life by actually finding her a husband. Like her, he was an Indian Fijian whose family was well known to her family. The selected husband to be, like both of them, had been packed off overseas to complete studies, his being a law degree in New Zealand. Whilst this did add a degree of complexity to the early part of their relationship, it may have made the relationship more intense than it otherwise may have. "I didn't really feel like the third wheel in the relationship because Sahodra hadn't even met the man" he says.

Kamahl did his best to explain his own career path and plans in a bid to impress her. A life in show business must've sounded quite a radical notion for a very traditional Indian girl.

After they had been going out for a few weeks, he decided to bite the bullet and take her to one of his shows so that she could see for herself what he was working with. He was performing at Sutherland RSL Club. It was the first time she ever saw him perform, and thankfully for him, she was suitably impressed.

They continued to date, and their affection blossomed. Yet both were almost resigned to the relationship to be doomed for failure in the long term. Both knew it would almost certainly be considered and confirmed by respective families as untenable. The cards were stacked against them by the conventions they were raised with and the culture that fostered them. They were of different castes. Their respective cultures, while sharing many similarities were different enough to matter. Their common language was English, as neither spoke the others native tongue. In each of those languages, they were no doubt about to hear a thousand familial objections, none of which made any sense to either of them. Still, they understood how things worked within their cultures. Sadly this made them resigned to their unlikely potential future together. There was also the not too minor issue of Sahodra's selected beau being already picked. He was a lawyer no less, almost at the zenith of preferred son in law occupations. Kamahl, on the other hand, was an entertainer, the nadir of Indian parent in-laws vocational selections. It mattered little that Sahodra had never even spoken to the man in question. The closest contact they'd had, was when her mother had pointed him out to her at a party from the other side of the room.

Nonetheless, he had been chosen, and a dowry had been discussed, so it was practically game over. While Kamahl was getting by quite well as a singer, the profession was never reliable nor steady enough to be taken seriously as a suitor. This overriding issue was one that Kamahl nor Sahodra could do anything about and one he had faced so many times in his life already … His skin was deemed to be too dark.

With all of these things going against the couple, even with their prediction of a bad ending, their love continued to strengthen.

When Sahodra's family became aware of Kamahl, their reaction was not at all unexpected. "We were from totally different cultures, both of whom held deep-seated prejudices against each other. At least our relationship was no longer a secret with Sahodra's family. I hadn't even dared broach the subject with mine, particularly my uncle. I really wasn't looking forward to that discussion. I knew for a fact that it was going to be almost exactly the same, if not worse. Here I was pursuing a career that they were not happy with, and now in a relationship that was not officially sanctioned nor approved of by them."

Growing concerned about the welfare of their daughter, Sahodra's family despatched their eldest son to Sydney to check out this nightclub lothario that their cherished daughter was consorting with. Much to Kamahl's relief, he got on very well with him, and he was given a big fraternal thumbs up by the man who would become his brother-in-law.

"Sahodra's brother Moti is a really great guy, and we hit it off very well almost immediately. He was very well educated and highly articulate. He was a lawyer who actually became Sir Moti Tikaram, Fiji's first-ever Indian magistrate. He would later become Fiji's Chief Justice. I pride myself on surviving a cross-examination from one of the great judicial minds of the Pacific," he laughs. Her family still had severe misgivings about the man they would later accept as their son-in-law. They arrived at the pragmatic view that at least they could save the money set aside for Sahodra's dowry. This would be used for one of their other four daughters. Being the parents of daughters is a costly business in traditional Indian families.

Since meeting Sahodra, Kamahl knew that she was the person he wanted to share his life with. His life was still full of so much uncertainty. Not only was the predictable adverse reaction from his family a hazardous bridge yet to be crossed, but there was also the little matter of his potential deportation…Not to mention his relatively insecure career choice. Whilst the Department of Immigration had been unseen and unheard of for a short while, he had started touring the country quite a lot. He feared that this would inevitably result in him finding himself in their crosshairs yet again. He didn't dare share any of these concerns with Sahodra for fear of losing the woman he was now convinced he would be with him for the rest of his life. The more he toured, the more he dealt with the fact that the couple were often apart for days, sometimes weeks, and he started to find this separation harsh. They would console themselves by writing to one another during these times and sometimes call to remain in touch. It was a poor substitute, however, for the time they spent together. In the sixties, this was before Facetime, Skype or even instant messaging to fall back on, all of which may have eased the long-distance communication gap. All there was were pens, paper envelopes and stamps or ridiculously priced 'trunk calls'. Whilst he always had an affection for elephants, he was far from keen to go broke using a service that named itself after the creature's most visible feature. Hence calls were kept to a minimum.

In the Autumn of 1966, he was booked for a season at Lennons Hotel in Brisbane. Lennons was regarded as one of the premier venues in Queensland in its day. Therefore an engagement an entertainer with ambition was one that could not be refused. At the end of a successful season at Lennons, he noticed a family in the audience at several of his shows. After the final performance, he introduced himself to the mother, father, and daughter group to thank them for their kind support. Word had evidently gotten out that there was a 'wrap party' for the band, crew, and a handful of invited guests in Kamahl's suite that evening. The teenage daughter approached him to say that she would love to come to a show-business party asking if she could attend. He knew that this would be an extremely tame affair with little alcohol consumed and a reasonably early ending by show-business standards. He agreed, telling her to inform her parents. After a most uneventful party shortly before midnight, Kamahl ensured that the girl returned safely to the floor where her parents were staying. As the lift doors opened, he was confronted by a furious father who immediately slapped the girl in the mouth, dragging her out of the lift. He snarled at Kamahl, "We don't need the likes of you in this country!" Kamahl returned to his suite shaken by the incident. He had done absolutely nothing wrong, and yet he was in the mind of the overly aggressive parent guilty of God alone knows what. With his tenuous immigration status, he was fearful that the man may lodge some kind of confected allegation that could jeopardise his residency.

This incident further darkened the cloud he felt over him during the previous few weeks. He had found the time away very difficult as he had been missing Sahodra immensely. "I found the separation during that season at Lennons excruciating. I loved this woman deeply and wanted to be with her every available minute. I could not wait to get back home to Sydney and have that incident added on top. It made for a tough time indeed," he said.

Whilst overjoyed to be back in Sydney after his Brisbane stay, he was brought down to earth with a massive thud. When he entered his apartment, he discovered an urgent telegram waiting there to greet him. It was from the Department of Immigration. The telegram was extremely brief. It asked him to urgently contact their offices to arrange an appointment. His spirits plummeted to a subterranean level. Surely this was it, and his time had come to face the music, and he was to be headed back to Kuala Lumpur on the next available flight. Kamahl recalls, "I sat there with my head in my hands wondering if it was even worth unpacking my suitcase. I was so certain that the guy in Brisbane had followed through with his veiled threat and lodged some type of complaint. No matter how baseless, I was not going to get a fair hearing. I was going back to Malaysia. That was all there was to it. When I caught the bus to their drab-looking offices that awful rainy day, I could not have felt lower. When I arrived, I presented myself at reception and was made to wait a short while, after which I was ushered into an office. There a rather officious stern-looking woman sat behind a big desk. On the desk, she had a large pile of papers upon which sat one file with my name on it. She looked at me and asked if I had anything to say for myself about my status. I muttered something about being a student and studying in Australia since 1953. She curtly replied, 'I can see that. Then she talked, and I tuned out, it was like I was back in the classroom daydreaming again whilst the teacher spoke. Although this was more of a day nightmare, I honestly thought she was delivering the Immigration Department equivalent to the proclamation of a death sentence. I simply tuned right out. I wasn't listening at all, already resigned to my fate. All I could do was feign attentiveness by nodding and saying yes where the appropriate gaps appeared in her diatribe. Meantime my mind raced through the problems with each potential scenario that I was about to encounter. When the woman finally stopped talking, I realised that she was staring at me to react to what she had told me. I blurted out, 'Pardon?' and she repeated the words that I must have heard but couldn't process. 'You have been here for thirteen years and are now entitled to permanent residency should you wish to take it up. Do you wish to take it up, Mr Kandiah?' I initially thought that she must be joking, but I quickly realised that she had never told a joke or even laughed in her entire life." Kamahl felt like the weight of the world had been lifted from his shoulders. It wasn't until later that in avoiding contact with the Department of Immigration that they had, in fact, changed the rules three years prior. Asian students who had been in Australia for ten years or more could proceed with application with residency which would be granted automatically. No longer did he have to worry about being returned to somewhere he no longer regarded as his home. He was home already.

"I ran down the street as high as a kite. I was so happy. There was only one person that I needed to speak to at this time, so I got into the nearest payphone and furiously dialled the number for the Crown Street Women's Hospital. When someone finally located Sahodra, they put her on the phone, and I asked her, 'What are you doing for the rest of your life?' She was taken aback but humoured me enough to ask what I meant. I said, 'Do you want to get married' I was certain that she thought I was joking as she just said 'when?' My response was 'How about next week?' I was so overjoyed that I possibly sounded a bit mad. I had to gather my thoughts and explain everything to her and stress that I was very serious about marriage. I wanted it more than anything in the world. My only concern now was that she may think I was a madman and just say no. After all, she hadn't until that moment known that I had been an immigration fugitive. I am eternally grateful that she didn't think I was mad and agreed to be my wife. The following weekend the two of us were accompanied by Marie and Bryan Spurrs, an English couple that I had met whilst performing at Drummoyne Rowers Club several months prior. They acted as witnesses, and best man and maid of honour, respectively. The celebrant was supplied by the Sydney Registry Office. The setting was the harbourside venue of Lady Macquarie's Chair with the Sydney Opera House in a very unfinished form in the background. Little did I know at the time that I would perform in that wonderful building that it finally became only a few years later. I wore a plain black suit, and she wore a yellow sari that I had specifically chosen for her. It was a straightforward affair indeed. It is somewhat ironic that two people deeply in love really only needed such a simple setting for their vows. When massively opulent ceremonies would have been lavished upon us in our respective home countries if we were to be married to complete strangers."

8

Home sweet home

*A house is made with walls and beams; a home is built with
love and dreams.*

Ralph Waldo Emerson

Kamahl and Sahodra's honeymoon was brief, very brief in fact. A
single night in a hotel in George Street. He says, "I remember
breakfast the next morning feeling a little worse for wear from
the celebrations of the day prior. We had gone to the nearest open
restaurant for breakfast. As we sat there I noticed the great violinist Isaac
Stern sitting at a table quite close by. I took his presence as an omen that
music had really chosen me, not that I believe in such things like that at
all." He laughs, "That evening they went to Chequers nightclub to see
the cabaret performance of the legendary Matt Munro. With that, the
honeymoon was over, and it was back to work."

Kamahl was now a married man and, within a year, a very proud
Australian citizen. To celebrate his being chosen by music courtesy of the
Isaac Stern omen, he could now stop the pretence of studying and quit
the Conservatorium of Music for good.

Now married, they could no longer continue being crammed into
the tiny Liverpool Street attic that he previously regarded as his manor.
So he immediately searched for a new place to call home. To say that

they didn't look too far would be understating it. They found themselves a one-bedroom 'apartment' in Glenmore Road, Paddington a mere 150-metre eastward stroll up Oxford Street. "It was an improvement on Liverpool Street, but not by very much. It was, we assured ourselves, a temporary residence. One that we had taken hurriedly through necessity and would quickly move on when we had the time to properly find somewhere that we would then call home. Somehow, we managed to live there for two and a half years. I had been so busy building my career at the time and working all hours under the Sun that my availability to look for a new home just slipped by. I remember the place in Glenmore Road being quite cramped and uncomfortable. I remember that there were problems with the electricity supply which we never managed to get to the bottom of. It was very noisy, the neighbours were this Eastern European couple who evidently didn't like each other much. They seemed to argue very loudly, almost constantly about everything. They were always irate and never smiled or spoke to us. I never took it personally. I just felt that if they couldn't get along with each other, it was doubtful they wanted to connect with anyone else."

The search for new premises took on greater significance in 1969 and rapidly accelerated in importance with the arrival of the couple's first child, son Rajan, in May of that year. Soon after this joyous arrival, the family purchased their first real home in the heart of Sydney's northern suburbia in St Ives. Kamahl, now charged with all of his new responsibilities, worked like a man possessed to provide for them and secure that new roof over their heads. This is not to say that he became careful with money, indeed far from it. Still, a mortgage brings with it a focus and becomes a number one priority. He was now an Australian, and he firmly believed that he needed his own piece of Australia for that fact to be taken seriously by anyone. The sooner that there was no debt on that property, he would achieve that goal totally. As for 'saving for a rainy day', it remained a pretty foreign concept. He never had in his life thought too far into the future and it was a struggle for him to do so even when responsibility grew. Luckily this was not the case for Sahodra. "If it were not for me having a wonderful, intelligent wife, we would have quite likely ended up destitute." He jokes, "She has always been aware that whilst I was a great provider, I totally lacked the skills needed in money management. On the other hand, she is astute and practical with those things and masterfully took on the role of the financial manager. She wisely invested our money, researching and buying shares, putting money aside for unseen contingencies. She always knew that I looked at myself as a business, and my focus was on my strengths of branding, marketing and performing, which is very much a right-brain thing. She always understood that I needed massive left-brain support to make us successful, so she thankfully took on that role and did it superbly. I was truly blessed that we have the balance of right and left brain aligned, making us such a great team," he states.

Of all of the high spots Kamahl has experienced in his life, he believes that he has achieved nothing more incredible than being a father and husband. Whilst he concedes at times, his obsession with his career has translated into his being overly self-absorbed, his genuine love of his family was always impossible for him to ignore. He states that he has eternal gratitude to Sahodra for her love, strength and wisdom. It ensured that the sometimes crazy things he put their family through, like so many entertainers, were neutralised by her tireless efforts. "She has been a remarkable wife and mother; above all things, she always knew when to rein in my sometimes erratic impulses. No man has ever had a greater partner. I could never repay her for what she has done for me.

"My children are wonderful people who despite having grown up in sometimes extraordinary circumstances and even having their own careers have been thrust into the limelight. But they have all done so well without it affecting who they are as people nor impacting their values" he says.

For his young family, there was always the occupation supplied challenge of continual absence. For Kamahl working hard meant working away from home, and so he toured constantly. Even when at home, his engagements were both time consuming and demanding. In 1971, when the couple's second child, daughter Rani, arrived, this became even tougher. "I seriously don't know how Sahodra being home alone, with two little kids, for so much time, put up with it.

"I could be away for anything up to six months at a time back in those days. I can't begin to imagine how tough it was on her. I know that the kids both found it really hard, even though they seemed to deal with it. I was always sad that there was so much that my not being there would make me miss in their growing up. Quite a lot of landmark events were missed, and I still regret that a lot. It is a great credit to Sahodra's strength of character. She treated the situation and me with such calmness and superhuman patience.

"I have been astoundingly fortunate in my life materially, but far more important than any of these things, I was gifted with such a wonderful family. A beautiful, brilliant, and very patient wife, two beautiful, gifted children, and a gorgeous granddaughter are all my greatest sources of joy. The older I grow, the more I regret not having been there for each of them, more than my career would allow. It is truly my only regret in life."

In the early eighties, the family would move to Turramurra to a rather grand home. So elegant in fact that Rajan rather cheekily but appropriately dubbed the house The Taj Kamahl. Regular travel for his music meant being away constantly. Still, Kamahl always had the comfort of knowing he had created for himself and his family, a home to return to. They would live at the Taj Kamahl for over twenty years. Whilst there, he became an active member of the community and always took a great interest in his neighbours, including the then Coca Cola CEO Dean Wills and a very young Chris Lilley, before he went on to the heights of comic fame with *Summer Heights High*. Radio celebrity Mike Carlton was also close enough to have had the odd dinner or two at the Taj.

He confesses that winning 'Father of the Year' in 1998 came as quite a surprise. The Australian Father of the Year Award is organised by The Shepherd Centre. This group raises funds for deaf children. It is presented annually to "a distinguished father who has demonstrated support, guidance and love to his children or other children through his working role or family life."

In 1998, much of the years of early career climbing had been scaled back, and I was becoming more settled in my life. Anyway, I must have fitted the bill somehow at the time, but I do confess that I was a bit sheepish as a recipient. For so much of my children's growing years, because of my career, I was not there enough at home. And you can't help but carry some guilt for that being the case.

Rajan and Rani now have their own career stories to reflect upon, both having been bitten by the music bug from a relatively early age.

Rajan took to music like a duck to water with piano lessons, taking on violin and then saxophone, ultimately leading to a deep connection with the computer-based music technology of synthesisers. He formed various bands in high school and would spend his school holidays doing work experience at Fairlight, the Australian company rightly credited as world pioneers of digital sampling. His prodigious talent was quickly recognised by many Australian acts. This led him to session work and touring with artists such as Dragon, Jenny Morris, Ross Wilson, Kevin Borich, Margaret Urlich, Tommy Emmanuel, and Kylie Minogue. In more recent years, he has been a composer, producer and arranger. He always looked to improve his art and gain experience. He took a scholarship position in Los Angeles with legendary composer Mike Post. After earning a deal of great experience in the US, he eventually resettled in Sydney, where his work has led to many notable credits.

Rani also managed to forge out her own singing career in the late nineties.

She achieved success with a hit song, 'Always On My Mind', a sophisticated house dance track, reaching 33 on the ARIA Single Charts that year and receiving a nomination for 'Best New Talent' and 'Best Pop Release' at the ARIA Awards that year. She had first come to the industry's attention providing the stunning soulful vocals on Hatman's house hit 'I Had A Dream' in 1997. She was rewarded with a recording contract at Virgin. The hit single was followed by another single, 'Trust In Me,' leading to an album later that year, *The Infinite Blue*. Rani's musical style was vastly different from her father's. Whilst Kamahl had long been a high-profile artist on music stations with an older middle of the road playlist, Rani featured mainly on alternative youth music station Triple J. Despite the critical acclaim and early success, she was evidently not as severely bitten by the show business bug as her Dad. She made the decision to leave the industry quite a while back and has lived for the past five years in Singapore with her husband Michael and their teenage daughter Izzy.

On reflecting on his life with Sahodra, Kamahl believes that there is one anecdote that provides a sobering insight to the world of fame and how it has the ability to impact relationships significantly. It is a little-known fact that Kamahl was one of the first artists to record the Hollywood classic 'Wind Beneath My Wings'. He says, "I was recording a Country and Western album in Nashville in 1982 with the legendary sound engineer Ernie Winfrey. He was one of the all-time greats in the industry when a song recently been written by Jeff Sibar and Larry Henley was offered to me. Whilst I liked the music, as it had a nice enough melody, the lyrics truly blew me away. I absolutely loved those words as they spoke to me deeply and personally about my true feelings for Sahodra. Like the subject in the song, she has provided me with such great strength from her love and support… Whilst I was out there in the spotlight, she was always there, inspiring me with her love, providing me with assurance when I felt insecure and vulnerable at times. Throughout our life, she has never sought celebrity, in fact, far from it. If anything, she studiously avoided it. With the patience of a saint, she supported me in my pursuit of it. I am the first to acknowledge how hard it must have been sometimes to be forever in the background. I know how it takes an incredible person to be able to do that. There have been hundreds of instances over the years when we have been somewhere together, on our own or with friends, and people would just decide that they needed to have a chat, get an autograph or a picture. I have never been able to say no to fans. This meant I was being engaged for reasonably lengthy periods whilst she would have to wait until it was all over. Whilst fame provides you with a great life. It is a very seductive thing. Of course, I can completely understand how it can lead to resentment and pressure within any relationship. Nonetheless, it does place an enormous burden on those you love who may feel that they are being ignored and are playing second fiddle to it. Added to this, I know that I can become wrapped up in my own priorities, which has made me quite challenging to live with. Throughout it all, she has never given me anything but her unflinching support.

"If I were to live a dozen lifetimes, I doubt that I could ever repay her for the love and inspiration she has given me over the years. Recording 'The Wind Beneath My Wings' may not have given me a chart hit, but much more importantly, I had to capture it as it has been a theme to our life together. I just had to record it, if for no other reason than to dedicate it to her."

It must have been cold there in my shadow
To never have sunlight on your face
You were content to let me shine, that's your way …

He reflects on this line of the song as he finds an irony in the fact that in his mind, it was she who provided the sunshine.

As for the recording of the song in 1982, he says, "Sadly we didn't release the song commercially at that time with the album. According to the producers, it wasn't 'country enough for a country album', whatever the hell that was supposed to mean. Many very high-profile artists did the song during the eighties, and it was met with some modest success. In fact, a brilliant version, my very favourite, which I attempted to emulate when recording it, was released earlier by the wonderful Gladys Knight. It was, in fact, performed by so many great artists and was met with only mediocre acclaim. Then along came the movie *Beaches* with Bette Midler singing it as its theme song, and it took off like a rocket. There is no denying that she did a wonderful job with the song, and it got all of the accolades that it deserved. Whilst I had personal reasons to record 'Wind Beneath My Wings', the competitor in me often wonders what may have happened if I had pushed the record company to support a bigger release. I know that a hit record is made up of many things, not just the song itself, so who knows what may have been? It has become a bit of a running gag for me that when I am asked what I think of the Bette Midler version, I often reply that I absolutely hate it," he laughs.

He reflects, "Whilst I would have loved to have had a hit with the song, what mattered to me the most was capturing those wonderful words as a testament to my beautiful wife."

After fifty-four years of marriage late in 2020, in what to almost anyone who knows them would come as a bombshell, Kamahl and Sahodra would begin a trial separation. Kamahl says, "We've had a long and wonderful life together. We have raised two fantastic people and have shared so much. We have had so many good times together that it saddens me more than anyone could ever understand that this separation has happened. I hold myself totally responsible. I understand how Sahodra has felt overshadowed in our relationship by me being so often caught up in things that I considered important. I have never intended to make her feel like that, far from it, but I completely recognise how she does. She tirelessly dedicated almost her whole life to both me and the kids.

Well over fifty years, in fact, so I can completely understand why she feels like she needs some time to herself for almost the first time in her life. We are truly still the greatest of friends. We speak almost every day and still eat together a couple of times a week. I genuinely hope that this trial separation will end and lead us back together one day soon. She is and always has been the one great love of my life."

9

A dark journey

*Acting is really about having the courage to fail in
front of people.*

Adam Driver

In 1967 with his star now in the ascendant, 33 year-old Kamahl was offered an opportunity to further cement his celebrity credentials. This came from the offer to play a starring role in a feature film entitled *Journey Out of Darkness*.

Although he had limited acting experience, he was chosen to take on the very challenging role of an indigenous man responsible for a ritual killing. His character was to be transported by a racist outback cop to face the white man's justice. Kamahl says to this day, he has no real idea why he was chosen to play the role. "As far as I know, I was picked from a headshot. They seemingly had no understanding of my ethnic background. I also found out much later that it got down to a choice between myself and Jimmy Little, the late great indigenous country singer. Jimmy was not only authentically Aboriginal, he was an experienced actor. It is quite peculiar why they'd settle on me, a Malaysian born Sri Lankan Tamil who had never seen the Bush and lacked acting experience. I suppose one black face was the same as another to the makers of the film."

In the movie, the Trooper is dispatched from Melbourne to Central

Australia to arrest the character played by Kamahl, referred to in the film only as 'Prisoner'. The Trooper and Prisoner are initially accompanied by an Aboriginal officer who dies early on in the journey. Following the death, the Trooper becomes increasingly reliant upon the Prisoner for his survival and protection not the least of which was his security from the prisoner's own Tribe, who had followed the two men throughout their entire journey. The Tribe provides an ever-present threat and menace in the harsh terrain, threatening survival each step of the way. As the journey unfolds, the Trooper becomes increasing enlightened and begins to question his own prejudices, developing a respect for a man that he initially thought to be less than human. Whilst the casting of a Malaysian born Sri Lankan Tamil as an indigenous man would have certainly raised more than a few eyebrows in modern-day Australia, Kamahl's hire, although strange, was not the most bizarre casting choice by a long shot. Neither was the casting of the Trooper Peterson played by American Konrad Matthaei, who himself had never set foot in Australia before being cast in the role. The biggest misstep in casting was reserved for the role of Jubbal, the Aboriginal officer. Jubbal was played by Ed Deveraux, a legendary Australian actor famed for his decades of prominent roles performances in both film and TV, including the Ranger/Dad in *Skippy*. Ed was as white as the driven snow, and producers had to resort to blacking him up each day to manufacture his Aboriginality.

The film itself may have had quite noble intentions by further educating a wilfully ignorant society about indigenous culture, but its ham fisted approach was regrettable. Ironically the film was entirely conceived in the United States, a country with even less knowledge on tribal matters than Australia and a very dim history of civil rights issues.

The film's American producer was named Frank Brittain. According to Kamahl, "I only remember him only for one thing. His insistence on the pronunciation of his surname. He stressed that it was pronounced Brit Tain, like it was two words. Apparently, he was a theatre manager who had aspirations to produce and decided this was the vehicle to launch that career."

After reading Howard Koch's script, the man who co-wrote the classic movie *Casablanca*, Brittain, decided to package the project and bring it to Australia to produce and launch. In 2010 he recalled, "Koch wrote the script in upstate New York where he lived. I don't think he ever had anything to do with the Aborigines." Brittain claims that Koch agreed to let him have the script. Still, there was a proviso. He insisted that Australian born James Trainor had to direct the film, or it was no deal. Being unburdened to find a suitable director, all that was left for Brittain was to source the finance to make the film and cast the key roles. Brittain had a friend who was a lawyer who himself had read the script and liked it. Evidently he in turn took it to his friend Konrad Matthaei a TV actor most known for his roles in daytime TV soap operas. Matthaei agreed to put up the entire budget, conditional upon him playing the leading role. Brittain decided to accept, although he must have wondered if all films were driven by such narrow self-interest.

When completed, the film enjoyed some critical acclaim. It was even being suggested as a possible Cannes winner by some. Still, it could hardly ever be regarded as either a box office or a creative success. As a work of social commentary, it has not aged well at all, particularly for the somewhat heavy-handed way it dealt with the topic, not to mention the casting. This was, after all 1967, a highly significant year in indigenous history in modern Australia. It was the year of the landmark referendum. After decades of activism, over 90% of all Australians voted in favour of amending the two sections of the Australian Constitution that had excluded Aboriginal people from being recognised as part of Australian Society.

Filmink magazine later wrote, "Its heart is in the right place, albeit in a nineteen fifties Hollywood liberal way…but it's fatally compromised by the casting of Sri Lankan Kamahl and a white Ed Devereaux in blackface

as Aboriginals, not to mention Konrad Matthaei being simply dull in
the lead. The film's main problem is structural – there is no urgency in
the trip, and nothing interesting happens on the way. Once you stop
laughing at Devereaux, it's just boring."

Kamahl's own experience with the film was eye-opening, to say the
least. When filming in Central Australia, a large homestead was used as the
film and crew's base. "On the first day of shooting in the outback, we had
a very long day in sweltering conditions. We repaired to the homestead
to rest and eat. When we all arrived, Julie Williams, the indigenous
actress playing my wife and me, were told to stay out on the balcony, and
refreshments would be brought out to us. Everyone else retired to the
comfort of the house, and we were left out on the deck with a few bloody
sandwiches. I was incensed but chose to say nothing, more the pity. I just
didn't want to be seen as difficult, particularly as this was my first acting
role. It was a rather interesting treatment for two of their film stars, which
was about prejudice, societal inequity and racial insensitivity."

Sadly for Kamahl, it was his first and last role in a feature film, which
was a shame as he showed reasonable ability for a novice actor in a
challenging nonspeaking part. Unfortunately, he had boarded the wrong
vehicle for movie stardom as subjects handled so insensitively seldom
stand the test of time, and this movie was a textbook testament to that
fact. The best evidence of how badly the film has aged is that despite our
living in a time when practically everything on film or tape can be found
somewhere on the internet, other than a few small clips, *Journey Out
of Darkness* went back into the darkness from whence it came. One of
the movie's only legacies for Kamahl did however have an impact several
years later when performing at his first nightclub in Britain, where he was
billed as "Kamahl: The Australian Aboriginal."

On the subject of the indigenous people of Australia, he says, "Being
black in Adelaide in Australia in 1953, was a very different experience to
how it is now. It was glaringly obvious that I was in a part of a minority.

As a brown person, I felt of little or no consequence. I identified with Aboriginal Australians in so many ways, but that is not to say that I could have ever totally understood the struggle they have faced. In many ways, the white society has been even slower to accept the Aboriginal people who were here thousands of years before they arrived than it has for migrants. In so many ways, that is wrong. For them, it would be like being treated as a stranger in your own home." Kamahl has a hope that the current focus on reconciliation is genuine and progress is made. "I do sometimes fear that well-meaning people come to strange and ill-guided positions on how to provide meaningful reconciliation. I would like to see more support going into outback communities that face so many issues like education, nutrition, health, and addiction. These things are almost as bad today as when I spent time among those communities back in the sixties. To me, it seems many feel more inclined to assuage their guilt of white privilege by participating in more symbolic and ceremonial gestures. Whilst it is terrific that we finally recognise the traditional owners ceremonially, I would hate to think that this is all we are capable of as a country."

An interesting side story to Kamahl's brief movie career was his co-star, the rather wooden Konrad Matthaei. Evidently following his career as a thespian who couldn't do an Australian accent, he became a Broadway producer of note and the President of the American Shakespeare Company. He also had several kids. One of his sons even ended up in a serious relationship with Rupert Murdoch's daughter Elisabeth. Kamahl recalls meeting up with them when they were still together in New York in the mid-nineties, leaving Kamahl to yet again marvel at how small the world is.

10

Of risk and reward

*'Sometimes when fortune scowls most spitefully, she is preparing
her most dazzling gifts.'*
Winston Churchill

In 1968 the year had started very well. Kamahl was now a married
man and an Australian citizen. He landed a stage production starring
Reg Livermore named *Follow the Sun* at the Doncaster Theatre
Restaurant in Kensington. Livermore was a rising star of the stage.
Somewhat of a prodigy he had already found considerable fame in a host
of TV acting roles and critically acclaimed stage productions. The cast
also featured Lola Nixon, a great veteran of the boards from starting her
career way back in 1949 at the legendary Tivoli Theatre. To be involved
in this ensemble production was a tremendous opportunity and one that
Kamahl seized with both hands. The show was a great success running for
around six months and warmly received by critics, and the public.

Kamahl also got to perform 'The Impossible Dream', a big crowd
favourite lifted from *Man of La Mancha*, a massive hit movie of the
day, along with several other popular numbers. Needless to say, he was
delighted with his involvement in the show. It was a slick and professional
affair and an excellent showcase for his profile. The warm reception that
he was getting week after week, he confesses, did go to his head a little.

"I was releasing an EP whilst I was performing there and thought that I would seize a bit of initiative for some self-promotion. I had some flyers printed advertising the record and placed them on all tables throughout the venue. Later I was sitting in my dressing room preparing for my performance when I heard a heavy knock on the door. Before I could get up, it swung open, and Reg Livermore was standing with a flyer in one of his hands, pointing to it with the other. He had a face like thunder... he said rather loudly, and I quote, 'Who the f**k do you think you are? ... I am the star of this show!!' I would have loved to have come up with a witty retort, but with my best sheepish smile, I said, OK, I won't do it again." he laughs. "Let's just say he got his point across. He was probably right, but you can't blame a guy for trying to make the best out of a situation."

It was also in the late sixties that Kamahl had engaged a management representative, the NLT Agency. The business was an off-shoot of the NLT Production company, founded by principals Jack Neary, Bobby Limb and Les Tinker. Each of them were giants in the Australian entertainment industry at the time. Kamahl had been assigned Bill Marshall by the Agency as his personal representative. Before joining the Agency, Bill had been a journalist and hence had a very well-developed sense of promotion and publicity. It was almost written in the stars that such a perfect union of promoter and self-promoter was to happen. Bill was so confident of the potential success of their collaboration; he told Kamahl mid-flight, en route to London in 1971, that he was leaving NLT to represent Kamahl exclusively. Kamahl was not entirely enthusiastic at the prospect of having a dedicated personal manager. NLT had served him well and were somewhat of an institution in the Australian entertainment industry. "I couldn't fault Bill for his energy and ability. The question for me was whether it was due to his being with a company whose name and reputation opened so many doors, or was it his power of persuasion? He did continue with me for a while, but we never formally committed to any formal agreement."

One of Bill's early successes on behalf of his client was to get him entry to the International Song Festival in Rio de Janeiro in 1972. The Festival Internacional da Canção, is the American continent's equivalent of the Eurovision Song Contest. Kamahl would win through to the Grand Final, where he'd perform a Tony Hatch and Jackie Trent song 'Nothing More. 'He was pipped at the post by David Clayton Thomas of Blood Sweat & Tears fame with his song 'Nobody Calls Me Prophet'. The trip was not without its fair share of issues, not the least of which, narrowly avoiding serious injury in a head-on collision in Copacabana when sight-seeing.

Bill Marshall would represent Kamahl for only a short while longer as by 1973 Kamahl, who always struggled with the concept of personal managers, a role he dispensed with entirely by the end of the decade. Kamahl says of Bill, "To this day, I don't know whether or not my expectations of what a manager was meant to do was unrealistic. I always maintain that Bill did do a great job for the time he was with me. I just felt that the relationship wasn't working anymore. He was spending an increasing amount of time overseas, and I felt underserviced. I am sure he didn't agree at the time, but I honestly felt parting ways was the best option for both of us."

Back in 1969, yet another unexpected set of circumstances arose for Kamahl that would have a big impact on his career. It came though the actions of a fading British comedian.

Jimmy Edwards was a British comic and actor with a colossal trademark moustache, big burly frame and a bellowing voice. At his peak during the post-war years, he was one of Britain's best-loved comic characters on TV, radio, stage and film… and had maintained a sufficiently high profile to still pull an audience. In Australia in the early seventies, where international acts were far scarcer than now, he was a big-name performer. This thinking persuaded Melbourne's Chevron Hotel's Celebrity Room to book his one-man show for a season in 1969. Edwards, they hadn't realised, was definitely on the decline as a performer at this stage of his career. He had become quite an ill-disciplined performer causing managers and promoters alike to live on their nerves whilst he took to the stage. Generally much the worse for wear after consuming a few drinks. One evening, poor old Jimmy took a little too much to settle his pre-performance nerves which resulted in Jimmy Edwards being on the next flight back to Heathrow, leaving a substantial hole in the Chevron's schedule they had to fill pronto.

Dennis Smith, who had been a successful TV producer of entertainment programs in the early sixties, had by this time started his own independent production and promotion business. Seizing upon the Edwards vacancy, he was quick to offer Kamahl a deal to take over the shows. It was to be a massive opportunity for Kamahl to be the headline act in such a significant venue. The arrangement was not without its challenges. Dennis's business was rapidly growing on the back of his reputation as the go-to guy for live entertainment, which met with the relaxation of licensing laws in Victoria. This new paradigm saw a massive lift in the number of live entertainment venues available across Melbourne. Suddenly, around six hundred new venues were open to the market, all hungry to get acts, and there was only so much talent to go around. Kamahl's deal for the Chevron came with an attachment, another performance a one-hour drive away at the Dorset Gardens in suburban Croydon on the same day every day. It made for a hectic schedule, but in show business, the key is always to make hay whilst the sun shines, and it was indeed a sunny Melbourne that greeted Kamahl in 1969. There was only one further minor problem: the Chevron's owner … Eddie Kornhauser, who was totally unaware that Kamahl was booked to do both venues each night, something that he may have never agreed to if he had been told at the time of doing the deal. Smith was a very canny manager who knew that if he got his logistics right, no one would be any the wiser, and all would be fine. Dennis was definitely a risk-taker, but they were calculated risks. He knew his way around the industry like very few others and, he proved it. Denis was an excellent ally for Kamahl to have in the corner at that stage of his development. It was he who convinced Kamahl that he was more than capable of headlining his own show. Smith had also not come to his conclusion that Kamahl was his answer lightly. He had actually conducted research with the patrons of the Dorset Gardens to ask who they would like to see at the venue. Kamahl featured very highly on the list of usual suspects, which unsurprisingly included high profile acts at the time like Johnny O'Keefe and Col Joye. It began a great relationship that would last well into the eighties.

Dennis recalls, "Kamahl was great. I really enjoyed the many years we worked together. He was not only a real professional, but he was a performer who was really good to promote. He was unique in the business at the time. No one looked like him nor sounded like him. Being talented is always a great asset but being talented and different as well is much better. It makes you stand out, and it makes you memorable. Whilst we always had a good relationship, I remember that we almost became unstuck in that first week at the Chevron, over one important thing … Money! I was swamped during those days, handling multiple acts at many different venues. I was run off my feet. I had arranged with Kamahl to pay him for his shows. I would meet him in his suite at the Chevron and fix him up at the end of the last one. Back then, payment meant payment in cash. There were no electronic transfers those days. It was all about cash. I went to the venue before the concert and met him in his room and, not wanting to be carrying around a wad of notes, decided to put it somewhere secure. There weren't personal items safes in rooms back in those days either. I looked around the room for a safe hiding place, and the only thing I could see was the old phone book on the bedside table. In haste, I opened the thick book and placed the wedge of notes inside the pages. After the show, we headed back to the room, and I totally drew a blank. I forgot where I had left the money. Whilst he would never say out loud, his expression said it all. I am sure he thought that I was doing a number on him. Thankfully through a lengthy process of elimination, we found the money in the phone book, and trust was again restored. A good thing because it may have prevented a couple of decades of a great working relationship from ever happening. I suppose the Chevron's housekeeping staff would have been delighted the next day, though," he laughs.

Indeed Dennis and Kamahl forged a very productive working relationship well into the nineties and have maintained a friendship far longer.

"Dennis is a tremendous manager; he has a terrific instinct. His confidence in me pushed me to accept chances that I may have otherwise neglected or felt I wasn't ready for. Sadly, he and I stopped working as regularly in the eighties only because he got a tremendous opportunity to work with the great Barry Humphries, which took up most of his time… I guess the Dame Edna's gladioli proved to be more alluring than Kamahl's kaftans," he laughs.

The partnership realised the transition of Kamahl from cabaret to concert artist. Mainly driven by Smith, who had quite reasonably concluded that if Kamahl was capable of headlining two shows a day over several weeks to highly appreciative audiences. Doing two forty-five-minute slots, a one and a half-hour show with an intermission, shouldn't be that big a stretch. As it turns out, he was proven right … it wasn't at all. He chose a venue, the Dendy Cinema in Brighton, which had been staging live shows on Sundays for a while, and they booked it. They promoted the show, and it sold out. Kamahl recalls, "I was so nervous at just the thought of occupying a stage for that length of time… but I did it. What's more, I loved the experience. From there, it was almost all that I wanted to do, it had been a big risk, but it had paid off". Having been introduced to the benefits of calculated risk, it quickly became a constant companion, one that Kamahl would never fear again.

It was through Dennis that another great opportunity presented itself. Dennis was one of few promoters who saw great potential for regional tours to supplement the metropolitan markets. Country people were avid and very loyal music fans and yet had been ignored mainly by tours of top-line acts. By the time they got to see big names in their hometowns, it was generally when the stars were past their prime and were no longer commanding a big following in the city. It made little sense as these major centres had sizeable populations. Most had town halls with decent seating capacity located in markets with eager audiences, desperately keen for entertainment. Dennis had made many regional tours and had realised the potential from the success he had experienced. He knew Kamahl would do exceptionally well in these markets and convinced him to tour, firstly in Regional Victoria. As the mechanics of such tours required local support via promotion, ticket sales and logistics support. Dennis had developed a network of highly competent local operators throughout regional areas. They would pull all aspects of the show together to the point that all the act had to do was turn up a few days ahead. They would rehearse, do promotional appearances, perform and then move on.

In the major regional hub of Horsham, that go-to person was Helene Davidson. Her organisational skills extended her capabilities well beyond the town itself. She would deliver excellent local support for the entire Victorian north west. Helene had previously been in a highly successful real estate business that the family had built, but being a show business tragic, she had decided to branch into the industry, leaving it in the very capable hands of her husband. It was a relationship for Kamahl that would span for years. He recounts, "Helene was a gem, complete efficiency, she never left a stone unturned in making sure that my tours went off without a hitch. I would tour around January and arrive in each town I was performing in, and everything was ready. Helene's son Bill became involved later too, having decided like his mother that he preferred the crazy world of show business over the real estate game. In my view, a very

TOP: Family members in Malaysia includes top right, father Mayilvaganam Kandiah, eldest sister Vijayalakshy, mother Elyathangam, middle his Uncle Arupillai and younger siblings in the front.

BOTTOM: Kamahl aged 4 with his eldest sister, Vijayalakshy.

TOP LEFT: In his first ABC TV series, the eponymous *Kamahl*.

TOP RIGHT: A 1970s ABC publicity shot.

ABOVE: In 1961 in front of Hotel Australia, Adelaide.

LEFT: Having a pearler of an evening in 2008 at an Australia Day function G'Day USA at the Waldorf Astoria New York.

ABOVE: Kamahl with Mick Jagger in the 1970 film *Ned Kelly*. Kamahl claims he didn't know who he was until he appeared in the film.

BELOW: Kamahl presenting a cheque in 1975 to World Wildlife Fund Patron, Prince Bernhard of the Netherlands from the proceeds of the massive hit 'Elephant Song'.

LEFT: At the *Round the World* album release with the family in 1978.

RIGHT: Kamahl and Sahodra's wedding day in 1966.

BELOW: Kamahl and Sahodra at the premiere of *Evita* at Adelaide Festival Centre, 1980.

ABOVE: Being presented the keys to the city by Lord Mayor Doug Sutherland, accompanied by Sahodra, Rani, Rajan and Rupert Murdoch.

BELOW: Pictured with the Royal Coach used in Prince William and Kate's wedding, 2011, made in Manly by Jim Frecklington.

ABOVE: Meeting Queen Elizabeth II after Royal Command Performance Brisbane, 1982.

BELOW: Kamahl and family catching up with Prince of Wales, now King Charles III, whilst still during a break from Polo at Warwick Farm in 1981.

Kamahl has met with a number of US presidents: by far his most memorable, Barack Obama; George HW Bush; and Bill Clinton seen pictured here along with actor Lawrence Fishburne.

LEFT: Kamahl with Australian Cricket Captain Michael Clark in 2018.

RIGHT: With Prince Harry after his stirring performance of the poem 'Invictus' at the launch of the Invictus Games in Sydney, 2018.

BELOW: With Sahodra and Harold Williams in 1973, his former vocal teacher at the Sydney Conservatorium of Music where Kamahl studied.

sound choice, he is still a major player in the business."

Throughout the years, these tours provided great memories for Kamahl and his audiences alike. Dennis Smith recalls, "The first thing we would do upon arriving in town was to drop our things off at the hotel and head to the local golf course. It was like a ritual." On one of these afternoons, Dennis recounts, "Kamahl has an insatiable appetite for crude jokes. At the time, there were a lot of gags that came in almost a series featuring characters based upon clumsy and possibly offensive racial stereotypes. One such joke featured two characters called Rastus and Lulabelle. Neither of us can actually remember the joke, but we still call each other Rastus to this day. So whoever he may have been, he must have been one hell of a decent bloke."

Bill Davidson has excellent memories of those tours too. He says, "Kamahl was always so meticulous in his approach to the tours, he was always punctual, always committed one hundred percent to his audience. He would stay around after the show for hours to sign things. The thing that always struck me was his inability to take no for an answer. On more than one occasion, when I had to tell him that the local radio station had passed on an interview, he would give me a gentle rebuke. He would leave it at that. In an hour or so, I would be contacted by whichever station had delivered the knockback to me to confirm the time. Kamahl would be interviewed the following day. He would just call them himself and convince them to do it. His dedication to fans was something else, though. We toured Bendigo on many occasion and there was a lady who was a major fan by the name of Mollie Driscoll. Mollie was a widow quite young in life and had been left to run the family farm and raise thirteen children. Her eldest daughter Jacinta made sure that she and her mum had front row seats at each show. One year they weren't there, and Kamahl asked me where they were. I found out that poor Jacinta had suffered a massive stroke and had been in hospital for well over a year.

We were shocked because she was only in her thirties and had always seemed quite healthy. Without hesitation, Kamahl decided to visit her in hospital. I remember that it was a Catholic Hospital as it appeared to be totally staffed by nuns. When we got there, we were taken in to see her, and she was in a terrible way. She was totally immobile and couldn't speak. Kamahl spoke with her for about an hour, managed to get a few smiles out of her. As we went to leave the room, one of the nuns told us to look back, and she was waving. According to the nun, that was the only sign of life in all the time she had been there. Tragically we discovered that Jacinta Driscoll passed away only a few weeks later."

In the late sixties, Kamahl's recording career began in earnest. He was far from being an overnight success. He had released several singles and two albums, *A Voice To Remember* and *Dreams of Love*, both received a lukewarm response selling only a couple of thousand records. While enthused by his potential, Polygram was like practically every other label in the late sixties, very focused on finding the next breakthrough pop chart act. For an artist like Kamahl, other financial implications had to be addressed in terms of production costs. Entirely unlike groups who were cheap to record as they arrived with their instruments to literally plug and play, Kamahl's genre required lush accompaniment and that cost money. Also, the active part of the market was definitely youth-oriented. Middle the road fans were well serviced by the recordings of international artists.

Getting sales for a domestically produced balladeer by tapping into that well-serviced market was, therefore, a challenge, one that many may have overlooked. When recording his third album, *Sounds of Kamahl*, he insisted upon including a little-known country music song named 'Sounds of Goodbye'. Unlike the other tracks, mainly show tunes, the song did not feature orchestration but a simple instrumental backing. The number was written by Eddie Rabbitt and Dick Heard in the US and had been a country charts hit for Nashville based singer George

Morgan in 1968. After considerable debate in Polygram, the song became the album's single release and became a big hit. Not only did the single sell well, but it also opened his back catalogue up to a market that had previously overlooked his earlier work. Suddenly, the media were interested. Kamahl became a staple on shows like Brian Henderson's Bandstand, which had a substantial weekly audience. Being a visual act helped sales enormously. As Kamahl puts it, "People sometimes listen with their eyes and by adding the other elements of performance has always helped me." *Sounds of Kamahl* went on to great chart success, and he as an artist went on to become an essential part of Polygram's business plans in Australia. Dermot Hoy, who was Polygram's A&R Manager for the early part of his career, moved into the Producer role around this time and sat behind the desk for a significant proportion of Kamahl's career. Dermot says, "Kamahl was a really unique artist. For us, his albums may have cost more to produce than some of the groups at the time, which caused a little bit of angst in upper management, but his sales were great. CEO Ross Barlow understood that and was prepared to back him by pushing back on the naysayers. He and I both knew that, despite the production cost, putting out a Kamahl album was a very low risk as he had a growing dedicated following. They bought pretty much everything he released. Having an artist like Kamahl on board allowed us to take those risks on other artists as we knew we could always rely on the income Kamahl was generating. He was never difficult to work with, although he could be stubborn when he had his mindset on something. He was a really terrific self-promoter which was helped by the fact that he had a totally different look and presentation style."

Dermot clearly remembers his introduction to Kamahl, the recording artist "He rolled up to the studio and asked us to screen off the control room window. I was surprised that someone with that huge booming voice and outgoing personality was so self-conscious when it came to having people at the desk looking on. Nonetheless, we complied, and all went well. He quickly got over the nerves." Dermot also recalls getting the call to get to New York to produce the live album at Kamahl's first concert at Carnegie Hall some years later. "It was a really challenging venue for live recording. That is surprising when you consider the place that Carnegie Hall has in show business folklore. You would imagine that it would have been a state-of-the-art venue with the latest and greatest in recording facilities. No such thing, surprisingly. We had to use local contacts in an outside broadcast van in the back of the theatre. So whilst I was definitely there for that momentous occasion, I saw the performance on a twelve-inch monitor sitting in a van in the dark."

In his career, perhaps no story exemplifies Kamahl's drive and ambition better than how the 'Peace on Earth' album came into being. Straight after a decade where he seemingly posted winner after winner at every turn, he had become so used to that success that he had almost forgotten what failure looked like. After the giddying rise, he had experienced in the previous decade, when 1970 came around, it must have seemed like he had hit a career brick wall. Things were headed in the opposite direction. His release of Charley Pride's 'All I have to Offer You 'following his successful 'Sounds of Goodbye' was met with a lukewarm response in terms of radio airplay, which led to sluggish sales. Frustrated, he found himself seeking advice from all and sundry. Their standard answer was that singles were the best route to album sales and that he would need to get himself a Top 40 release backed by heavy promotion to get himself back on track.

As this had been precisely the route he had been taking, the advice proved less than helpful. He continued to tour and tirelessly perform live whilst stewing on what he could do to once again reset his career and push it to its previous ascendency. After one performance at the Chevron in Melbourne, he was met backstage by a couple of friends, Dorothy Durham and Lillian Tobin, who came to offer their congratulations on the show. Kamahl was deeply distracted by his career predicament. He was not really in the mood for the company but, ever polite, he greeted his friends warmly. The subject of his career funk came up in conversation as his friends had noticed that he seemed a bit 'down'. He explained his predicament to them, and they asked him if he had ever thought of marketing his records on TV. They said that in the business they both worked, *Encyclopedia Britannica*, they had enjoyed great success by being featured on a popular TV show. *BP Pick a Box*, the quiz show, had been around for well over a decade at that point and was one of the most viewed shows in Australia. Sponsored since its inception by the BP company, it was somewhat of an institution in the media landscape. Kamahl politely thanked them for their suggestion and agreed that massive exposure on TV would increase awareness for his product. He thought the advice, whilst well-intentioned, was rather silly as he simply didn't have the resources to buy a massive TV ad schedule. This idea planted a seed in his head, a seed that was about to sprout into a big shoot only a short while later. Whilst he was sitting alone gazing out of his window at a miserable Melbourne rainy afternoon, the thought came to him. He found his eye caught by a gaudy green BP service station's signage, which inspired a thought that made him sit bolt upright. He recalls, "If BP could sponsor a quiz show, then why couldn't they sponsor a record?"

Never one for letting the grass grow under his feet, Kamahl didn't care to research the thought or see what the appropriate channels were to investigate his idea. There was no time for that. He looked up the phone number for BP Head Office and dialled it. He had no name to contact. He did have one name that he could use… his own. When the receptionist took the call that afternoon, it is fair to say that she would not have anticipated speaking to that voice. "Hello, this is Kamahl", he announced, "Could you please put me through to the person responsible for your company's advertising and marketing?" After a short on hold wait, Kamahl was directed to a bemused Rod Taylor, BP Marketing

Manager. Rod was not all that familiar with who Kamahl was, let alone why he was meant to be speaking with him. Egged on by his assistant to take the call, he reluctantly complied. Kamahl remembers, "Rod Taylor was taken aback somewhat. After all, there I was, suggesting to him that I had a concept for a new record that I wanted his company to give their customers, and I was prepared to do so for free. That is quite a lot to take in a cold call from a stranger. Taylor politely listened and thanked me for my idea. Then he told me that they had whole buildings of people along St Kilda Road, with millions of great ideas. St Kilda Road being then the Madison Avenue of Melbourne. He politely took my number and suggested that if he had a change of heart, he would be in touch." He wished Kamahl the very best of luck with his record and bade him a fond farewell in what seemed like a gentle brush off. Less than one hour later, Kamahl received a call from Taylor asking him to explain his idea again. Kamahl says, "I explained again that I would give my single to BP as a gift to their customers, and if they decided to sell it, then the proceeds could go to a charity of their choice. He responded more thoughtfully this time with a request that we meet up to discuss the matter further."

Taylor thought that maybe he was missing something about Kamahl's big idea and went to have his Managing Director validate or affirm his decision. As it turned out, the MD had even less enthusiasm than Taylor had for the idea. Little did Kamahl realise that his proposal had something far more potent than the management at BP, and that was fan power. As Kamahl recalls, "Evidently, the two men when discussing the proposal did so whilst the MD's assistant was in the office. I'm not sure if she was a fan or not, to be honest. She voiced that it could be a great idea because 'Kamahl is a hot item right now. I'm not too certain what she meant by that, but whatever it was, I was eternally grateful."

After the second phone call, Kamahl headed straight to BP headquarters to formally meet with Taylor. BP Australia had got their thinking caps on and had abandoned all talk of a single record. They had talked it up to a Christmas Album. The idea, which had almost literally popped into Kamahl's head only hours before, had grown into an album to be released in a peak sales period. Also, it was guaranteed a non-traditional distribution network comprised of over a thousand outlets right across the country. To add to that, if it weren't enough already, the album was to be heavily advertised nationally on TV as part of BP's Christmas campaign. For Kamahl, this was the career equivalent of winning the lottery, buying another ticket with the winnings and then winning the significant prize all over again, only to repeat the same the day after. It didn't end there. BP agreed to underwrite the production as long as Kamahl's label would estimate costs and estimate anticipated sales. This was not a problem at all. After all, it isn't every day that such a deal was encountered in the music business. This was a classic win-win situation. BP was also generous enough to allow Kamahl to creatively contribute to the production of the advertisement, a contribution that he would've needed physically restraining from making.

With these words, 'Peace on Earth' was launched to the Australian market. As promised in his pitch, Kamahl donated all of his royalties to BP's chosen charity, Freedom from Hunger. He presented a cheque for $41,457 to Dame Phyllis Frost, the chair of Freedom from Hunger, at a media function held at the Carlton Social Club in March 1971. He vividly remembers staring down the barrel of the camera and announcing, "We all wish we could have the world the way we want it… but we can't, but we can help".

The album had sold 138,190 copies, far exceeding the benchmark for a gold album of 10,000. Later, the record company told Kamahl that the only thing preventing the album from a quarter of a million sales was the shortage of presses restricting the number produced. It was a meteoric success that provided a massive career springboard making 1970, which started so poorly into the start of a brilliant decade. Kamahl reflects, "Even though I had come up with the idea, the people at BP, particularly

Rod Taylor, deserve enormous credit. Despite BP not being keen on the idea initially, they had the humility to believe that although they had 'buildings of people with ideas', it never hurts to listen. To then research and make an objective assessment leading to having a judgement call showed a hell of a lot of professionalism. They took a commercial risk, no doubt, but their judgement ensured that it paid off handsomely for all concerned. It also managed to do a lot of good for needy people, something more companies should do. They were really tremendous people to work with, particularly Rod Taylor."

For possibly the first time in his career, Kamahl had a newfound confidence in his instincts and judgement. He had taken a considerable long shot risk, and it had paid off handsomely. The satisfaction he gained from going it alone and trusting his gut had paid off in spades. He believed that he was now entitled to approach his career even more boldly. The risk factor, he had concluded, was not to be feared but embraced and used as a personal motivational challenge. He realised that the size of the reward directly corresponded to the risks taken.

In the early seventies, Kamahl's career was very much on an upward trajectory in Australia. He was a household name and was in high demand. He had chart success, an eponymous TV series that ran for two seasons and recognition by the bucket load. He was increasingly financially secure from his efforts. However, he was still feeling like there were more castles to conquer.

On November 21, 1973, Kamahl performed at the Sydney Opera House. It would be the first of 29 concerts he would perform there throughout his career. *Kamahl at the Opera House* was recorded and released as a live album. Its sales went on to exceed 300,000 copies.

His self-confidence now ascending, Kamahl started to question some of the advice he got from managers. He recalls in 1974 engaging his third manager in twelve months, Ron. His appointment came off the back of Kamahl's growing frustration with the absence of management

vision for his career. He felt that demand for him was when having a
manager who would simply take bookings without a thought about how
that booking was part of a career strategy was pointless. After all, he could
take a phone call himself, and why would he pay for someone else to
perform that task? The best example of these failings was a Sydney Opera
House show sponsored by Sydney's 'Good Music' Radio station 2CH.
Ron excitedly contacted him to advise that he had been approached with
a "great opportunity". He was offered a twenty-minute bracket amongst
other artists, including Tommy Tycho and his Orchestra. The bill also
featured the Clair Poole Singers. Kamahl hated the idea. He was coming
off the back of enormously successful record releases, his own TV show,
which ran for two series, so why would he be a part of such a line-up.
He should and could headline his own show, and he was confident that
the sponsor would be more than happy to accept this proposal. He fired
Ron on the spot and decided to speak with 2CH himself. He recalls "I
said Ron if you don't know what is wrong with this deal and you think
I should be happy with a twenty minute slot then it is you that is the
problem and I don't need you. He wasn't at all happy but I didn't care, he
wasn't doing the job he was hired to do" After a little bit of negotiation,
his 2CH headline show came to be and was a sell-out. His only regret
from the show was that Ron incorrectly appeared in the program listed
as his manager. The concert was recorded and subsequently released to
great commercial success. He adds, "I knew it would work and knew the
album would sell too…and for the record, Ron had bugger all to do with
the record either."

As often happened to Kamahl throughout his career, an opportunity
came knocking in the form of Welsh entertainment legend Sir Harry
Secombe. Harry and his manager, Jimmy Grafton, had met Kamahl in the
late sixties when they were touring Australia. He had kept in contact with
both men for a few years at this point. Still, when Jimmy made contact in
1972, Kamahl was genuinely surprised. He wanted international success

and was convinced that Britain would be the perfect place to find it but had little idea how to get a foot in the door. Jimmy said both he and Harry would like him to come to London to appear at an engagement arranged at the prestigious Savoy Hotel. Whilst there, Kamahl also would appear on television, most notably on a program called *Stars on Sunday*. The program was hosted by Yates. The show was quite strange in format in that it allowed viewers to request songs or Bible readings. Kamahl thought this was a strange combination, still, he was there to advance his career and not make waves and gladly participated when Jimmy Grafton offered to take him to meet with the show's host.

Yates had a reputation for securing international acts for minimal fees. Like Kamahl, many were looking to get a break in Britain during this time. It appears that Yates wasn't so filled with holy virtue to take full advantage of ambitious singers. Kamahl recounts that their first meeting had not gone well, "It was all very awkward from the outset. I had quite a bit of TV experience by now, and whilst admittedly, I had been spoiled by the ABC. They gave me the fantastic musical accompaniment of Brian May and his 25-piece orchestra, nothing prepared for the musical backing offered at *Stars on Sunday*. Yates had noticed that I had a bag with me and asked what was in it. I replied it was my music for the orchestra. He replied rather curtly, 'I am the orchestra. It's just me and the organ!' He must've seen the look of disappointment that was written all over my face. He turned to Jimmy and asked, 'Where did you get this arrogant colonial?' Evidently, Yates hadn't noticed that the pink sections on the world map had been changing colour significantly in the past few decades and still thought fondly of the days of the Empire." Kamahl says he was a complicated character to deal with, saying, "It was a horrible start to the relationship, and it really didn't get much better. We argued over the songs that I would perform and how they were arranged." Following *Stars on Sunday,* he did get quite a lot of small shows but nothing like the breakthrough success that he was there to achieve.

Beaten but far from bowed, he returned to Australia. He was a little wiser for the experience and even more determined to push on. In fact, he would go back to London the following three years absolutely committed to making it. There was no shortage of TV show appearances being offered. Many of these were very high profile shows like *The Harry Secombe Show, The Dame Vera Lynn Show* and *The Golden Shot.* They were all tremendous rating programmes that happily featured Kamahl. Whilst in one sense gratifying that his talent was appreciated by TV executives, it had not translated into success in record sales or concert appearances. In essence, he was making a name for himself, but it was awfully slow. He, therefore, resolved that 1975 would be his last tour to Britain if things didn't turn around. One afternoon with time to kill, he was reading the entertainers bible, *Variety,* and happened to come across an article about Dorothy Squires, the former wife of Roger Moore. She had been quite a big star who had put her career on hold when she married. In a bid to reignite her singing and dancing career, she had taken the bold step of booking the London Palladium for her own show. She was going to 'four-wall' the event, a practice of hiring a venue and selling the seats exclusively to friends and industry peers. Her performance had great success setting her back on her dancing feet and into the limelight once again. Kamahl was inspired. This is precisely what he would do. He had performed at the Palladium before as support for American singer Vicki Carr. He loved the venue and everything it represented in British show business. Performing at the Palladium was the big time in Britain.

This was a huge risk as the upfront costs associated with the show were massive by the day's standards. He had to pay $30,000 upfront for the hiring fee, and of course, there were all of the attendant costs that go hand in hand with any production. There was staging, an orchestra to book and pay for and the high price of promoting the show. He says, "it was going to take a lot of money. I knew in my heart that I could fill that place, and if that was what it took, it was going to be well worth it. I had to do it right so there could be no skimping," he adds with a laugh. "I didn't bother to check if Yates and his organ were available. I went for the full orchestra instead."

Kamahl's agent at the time, Roger Henning, was charged with making sure that the right people knew about the show and were followed up to ensure the crowd. He accomplished this task well as it was indeed a packed house that Kamahl faced that evening. He reflects, "I had always had an excellent relationship with the media in the UK, they were really supportive, and they certainly got behind my show."

The show was a triumph, met with generous ovations by an enthusiastic crowd. After his struggles to gain traction in Britain over those few years Kamahl must've thought he heard Julius Caesar's words "*Veni Vidi Vici*" ringing in his head as he walked off stage that night. Unfortunately this euphoric state was to be short-lived. When he arrived backstage he was met by Roger and Sahodra and they weren't jumping up and down in victorious glee but looking like they had just lost a winning lottery ticket. The pair had the awful task of telling Kamahl that they had been advised that back home he owed $1 million. He remembers, "The debt was a combination of a bad commercial real estate deal I had invested in which had collapsed. The Bank were chasing $350,000 that the project owed. To top that off the Australian Tax Office claimed that I owed them $650,000 in back taxes. This was for an unpaid amount with compound interest which had accumulated for good measure. I was taken from the highest of heights to the lowest of depths within seconds". In true Kamahl style, he assessed his position and determined that he could work this out if he could make best use of his time left in the UK. He would take advantage of the opportunities that were now presented to him on the back of his triumph. After all, he was literally on the other side of the world and the mountain of debt would still be there to sort out when he and Sahodra went back to Australia in five months. Right now he needed to capitalise on the success he had just had and take care of tomorrow's problems tomorrow. Kamahl remembers that he nonetheless felt terrible about the predicament that they were in. He was most concerned about the impact it had on poor Sahodra who he knew was going to make herself sick with anxiety over the debt. "I had always had a philosophy that as long as you had your health and sense of humour then nothing is too big a problem to overcome, Sahdora on the other hand was raised to be extremely practical. Within her culture there was an expectation of the husband providing safety and financial security and I was failing to deliver on either. She was consumed with worry about the debt and it affected her health significantly. I had no choice but to sort this mess out and I was convinced that I could. Right then, all that I could do was reassure her and try to work out myself how the hell I could sort the mess out when I returned." With this unexpected calamity on board, Kamahl nervously awaited the expected deluge of offers to roll in. He now had a great Palladium performance under his belt and the reviews of the show were outstanding across all media. It was then that the prestigious Talk of The Town nightclub reached out with a booking four weeks after the Palladium show. The Talk of the Town was a night club and cabaret that had been opened by Bernard Delfont who was the brother of other show business giants Lew and Leslie Grade. He had adopted the Delfont name when treading the boards as a dancer early in his career in order to differentiate himself from elder brother Lew who had preceded him onto the stage. The club he had started on the site of the old Hippodrome Theatre in London's West End shortly after World War Two. The Talk of The Town since opening had hosted shows by a veritable who's who of international stars. Lena Horne, Shirley Bassey, Frank Sinatra, Eartha Kitt, Judy Garland, Barbara Streisand, Sammy Davis Jr to name a few, had all performed at the Club.

For Kamahl to be given headline billing for a two-week season at the end of July in the coveted 11pm slot was a very big deal indeed. This initial booking proved to be the start of a great relationship with the venue as he was booked for a month every single year until the venue eventually closed in 1982. Bernard Delfont, said at the time that he had no choice as the long-term lease was up for renewal and the Cranbourn Estate who owned the site, wanted to increase the rent from £15,000 a year to around £200,000. There is no doubt however if the Talk of The Town had remained, Kamahl's one month per year engagement would have gone on for years to come.

Shortly after his first engagement with the Talk of The Town he finally returned to Australia face the financial music in September 1976. When he arrived, he sought out professional advice on his predicament and it would appear that his advisors earned their keep. His tax debt was reduced significantly and the bank debt whilst unavoidable and inevitable was negotiated to make it manageable. The crisis was not as devastating as it had first appeared, no impending doom but it did guarantee that Kamahl was going to need to continue to be one of the hardest working entertainers in the country for some time to come. Hard work had never been a problem for him so and if that was the answer then he would just keep on doing what he had always done. After all he had fully intended to be doing just that anyway.

The significance of the Talk of The Town ongoing booking was far more than just providing work or providing him a base in Britain. The venue was a place that always attracted a sell-out audience irrespective of who was performing as it was a place full of A-listers and cashed up day trippers. It was the place to be seen, a venue that added a certain cache to the artists appearing there. He recalls: "It was the one venue that I could be guaranteed to be met with a throng of autograph hunters following a performance. I sometimes think that many of them didn't even know who I was, prior to coming to the club that night." London was definitely a mixed bag for Kamahl. He had enjoyed a modest (by his standards) level of success whilst providing the frustration of being just short of really achieving stardom. Realising that it was unfair and disruptive to keep Sahodra and the children following him back and forth, he was forced to leave them for several months of the year and this was a difficult reality he had to deal with. He had set himself up in a small apartment in Belgravia Mews adjacent to the stables where the Royal Horses were kept. He recalls: "The laneway behind my apartment was so small that when the horse's handlers would take them past, the horses arses rang our doorbell as they turned around." On one of the rare occasions that he had decided to have the whole family with him, he and Sahodra took the kids out for the day and were sightseeing in Trafalgar Square when they realised that Rani, who was only four years old at the time had wandered off and they couldn't find her. Trafalgar Square is such a busy location filled with crowds of people and losing a small child there must have been terrifying. They frantically searched, calling out her name and after what seemed like an eternity an Australian lady appeared, holding Rani's hand and asked Sahodra if Rani was their child. Whilst most parents have experienced losing a child in a department store or a park, they will always recall it happening for years and never lose that overwhelming relief they experience when the child is returned. For this to happen in such a busy location amongst a throng of people heightened the anxiety considerably. Sightseeing was definitely finished for the day and they bundled up Rani in their arms and headed back to Belgravia Mews. The family had been back to the apartment for only five minutes when the phone rang. Still shaken from the experience of Rani's adventure he picked up the phone. He remembers "I was still shaking from the shock of almost losing my child and the voice at the other end of the call said that she was from Leslie Grade's office. Leslie Grade was the younger brother of British TV heavyweight Sir Lew Grade. He was an agent who represented many international performers in the UK. She went on to say that Bob Hope would like to reach me, I replied that I was not in the mood for jokes. She insisted that this was not a joke and gave me with a phone number to call at his hotel. I jotted it down and then made the call."

To Kamahl's great surprise the phone was answered by a voice that was unmistakably Bob Hope's. He said, "Is that you Kaymarl?" so badly mispronouncing his name it made him feel that this may yet prove to be a prank. What he said next did little to change his apprehension: "He said to me 'say is it true you've got three balls?'" A long, stunned silence ensued. Thankfully for Kamahl he didn't hang up and Hope went on to tell him how he had seen his act at Talk of The Town and that he, his wife and daughters had really enjoyed the show.

What happened next piled surprise on surprise. Hope went on to explain that they were leaving the next day and would like Kamahl and Sahodra to join them at their hotel for supper that night if they were free. At that time there were very few if any stars bigger than Bob Hope. Of course they were free. When they arrived at the Hope's suite, he found a gracious and accommodating host. He was not intimidating at all; he was obviously at ease with his fame and didn't feel the need to laud it over others. His wife Dolores was equally warm and friendly. "Bob and Dolores were just great people. He was keen to impart his wisdom and advice which I eagerly absorbed. At one point he said that he really liked my relaxed conversation between songs and wanted to know who I had writing my material, I replied no-one. I explained that I did it all myself. He said 'great... don't change'." The supper lasted until the wee hours of the next morning. When it was over Kamahl and Sahodra returned to the reality of Belgravia Mews but not before Kamahl had received an invitation to appear in a Bob Hope TV special. It was being filmed in Dallas later that year from the man himself.

Kamahl often wonders whether the allure of Britain as a potential launchpad to international success wasn't somehow a part of the conditioning he had received from the earliest days of his youth. Having been raised in colonial Malaya and then moving to Australia, which itself at that time was still very much struggling with its own feelings of cultural legitimacy. It may have in part influenced his emphasis on making it in the 'motherland'. After a number of years of almost cracking the market he decided that even though he had a loyal following, a supportive media, great industry contacts, it had led to steady but not spectacular achievements. It just wasn't enough, so Kamahl came to the conclusion that he had tried his best and would be better to focus his attention on growing his brand domestically and relegate the international fame to a 'nice if it happens' category. This was however far from the last hurrah at launching an international career, he had just realised that he may have been starting from the wrong base. He still has many fond memories of his time in the UK and still admits to it being quite a frustration that all the great performing highlights and goodwill and affection he managed to generate in the market never realised the commercial success that he craved. He recalls "Some of my fondest memories of performing came from Britain but for some reason I always fell short of breaking through. I still remember being invited by BBC Scotland to perform on radio with their resident orchestra in Edinburgh. I sang the old standard, 'Danny Boy,' which I must have performed a thousand times before. This time around however, it was really special as I was working with a musical genius by the name of Peter Knight, who had a who's who list of superstars with whom he had worked. He was somewhat of an institution in the industry and his arrangement was spectacular and would be broadly acknowledged as the best many had ever heard. It was such a privilege and honour to work with someone of that calibre."

One more lasting and certainly positive legacy related to his connection with Britain, was his collaboration and eventual thirty-year professional partnership with musical director Kenny Powell.

Kenny was undoubtedly a musical genius almost a savant. Born in Surrey, England in 1925, he took up accordion and piano very early in life, evidently skills that he had inherited from his mother who herself was a gifted pianist. At the age of 12 Kenny became the accordion champion of southern England. After leaving school at 15 he had a brief stint in an architect's office but by 16 he was compelled to follow his life's calling and become a professional musician. Music was the most important thing in his life, save for the real love of his life Maggie McConaghy, a young lady from Newcastle NSW he had metand dated for three years in London and would later marry. As a mere kid he had toured England with the renown Harry Parry Sextet. When he was drafted into the war effort, he switched to saxophone and joined an army band unit stationed in Germany. After being demobbed, Kenny was never out of work for a day. His jazz and nightclub playing combined with his writing, arranging and playing for television, mainly with the fabled Jack Parnell Orchestra kept him well and truly occupied. During his jazz exploits he also worked with the jazz violinist impresario, Stephane Grappelli of Hot Club fame. When TV launched, his services were also in high demand. He would work on high rating programmes such as *The Benny Hill Show, The Avengers* and *Morecambe and Wise*. In one episode of that show in 1963, a little-known band growing in popularity named the Beatles appeared, joining their hosts for 'Moonlight Bay' at the end of the programme with Kenny Powell on piano.

During a stellar career he also worked with Sammy Davis Jnr, Cyd Charisse, Nancy Wilson, Peggy Lee, Juliet Prowse, Shirley Bassey, Dionne Warwick, Vera Lynn, Liza Minnelli, Harry Secombe and Frankie Howerd. In 1969, when Frank Sinatra performed in London for the first time in nine years, Kenny was at the piano. Kenny's resume would no doubt have landed him a job anywhere in the industry, anywhere in the world. So why and how he decided to throw his lot in with an Australian operatic crooner for as long as he did, still remains a bit of a mystery to Kamahl, who says: "It was truly unbelievable that as balladeer of popular or middle of the road music, I had the opportunity presented to have a musical genius agree to and remain as my music director. Even more unbelievable that we would go on to work together for decades. To be honest he was so gifted that I could never possibly make full use of his talents. It was almost like having a Ferrari to drive to the shops. Fortunately for Kenny his jazz provided his outlet to satisfy his appetite and so he kept his sanity that way … Over all those years there were occasions when things were not as rosy as they could have been between us. Sometimes it was my stubbornness and sometimes because he really enjoyed a good wine, but at all times we managed our relationship both personally and professionally with a great affection for one another. He was very idiosyncratic but that goes hand in hand with genius. It also didn't hurt that he had the most brilliant, and sometimes wicked, sense of humour." Kamahl never ceased to be amazed by not only Kenny's musical prowess but his ability to show 'grace under fire'. He recounts how at a performance in Whyalla, South Australia in the middle of a show, the piano he was playing had the bottom fall out and land in his lap. Kenny without batting an eyelid wedged it back in with his knees without missing one single note. "When you consider that this man had played in the best venues around the world and provided with the very best of equipment, here he was in a country venue with dodgy equipment and he just got on with it superbly and still managed to laugh the whole thing off. No diva outburst, no tantrums, he was too much of a professional for any of that."

Their relationship was somewhat fortuitous insofar as it was Kenny's heart that brought him to Australia not the dubious lure of playing a bad piano in Whyalla. He had met his wife Maggie, a Newcastle NSW girl, in London when she was working over there. They had been together for around three years when she succumbed to the pull of home. Realising that things would never be the same without her it was natural to him that he would follow her, to the other side of the world. Abandoning a highly successful career in the process and taking his chances by relying on his talent to pull him through. On leaving London, Kenny had a few contacts tucked away in his suitcase, one of which was a business card given to him by Bill Marshall, Kamahl's manager. Upon arrival a call was made and a meeting convened, predictably in a pub. He had briefly connected with Bill and Kamahl in London on one of Kamahl's tours. At this pub meeting in Crows Nest, Bill convinced Kenny to meet with Kamahl.

Kenny, it has to be said, was initially wary as their musical tastes were significantly different. In an interview some years ago for Kamahl's 1995 biography written by Christopher Day, Kenny claimed, "I thought he was either very square or very lacking. He didn't seem to grasp what I was talking about until we got to know each other a bit. I saw two or three gold records on the wall and noticed that one of them was for *Sounds of Goodbye.* I thought, well, obviously, he's not merely a nightclub singer. I thought maybe he is the Val Doonican of Australia [auth: the cardigan-wearing, easy listening popular Irish crooner popular in the UK in the sixties]. Then he said he loved Nat King Cole, and I thought he couldn't be such a square in that case. So I gave him points over that", thus a thirty-year relationship began one afternoon in St Ives.

Sadly Kenny Powell died in July 2011. Kamahl says, "It is such a great shame to lose any long-time friend, but more than that, the world lost a musical genius. Sadly he left us without truly being recognised for his gift by as many people as he deserved to be. I fondly remember my time with him, not just for what he musically added value to my shows. It was much more than that. It was the friendship and camaraderie, the humour and the times we spent on the road. These are the things that will always put a smile on my face whenever I think about Kenny. I can't think of him without remembering his quirkiness. Two things really stand out. One was centred on his observation about the connection between Australian country towns and cannons. He used to insist upon going for a walk through the town centre of any regional centre, where we had not been before, almost upon arrival. When we strolled down the high street, there was always a small park, where he would point out the ubiquitous war memorial cannon in the middle of it. He would howl with laughter. He mused that to be a legitimate small town in Australia, you had to have a cannon, or you just weren't allowed to be a town at all. The other thing I remember from those trips packed far more punch than a cannon when fully armed. It would be fair to say that Kenny didn't mind a drink or three, and on the road, that was no different. Early on, he introduced me to one of his favourite tipples, a drink he had concocted called a B&B, Brandy and Benedictine. To this day I shudder when I hear those two words in the same sentence as the after-effects of an evening drinking this evil brew in any quantity, could result in serious recovery time. In fact, the first time I tried to, I have no memory of the walk back to my hotel room."

In 1976, Sahodra received an extraordinary phone call from a person that we knew pretty well by the name of Ivanka Lau. A little like her American namesake, Ivanka was wealthy and had a penchant for right-wing causes. It transpired that she and an American friend of hers were trying to set up a religious anti-communist group in Singapore. She explained that they were selling a 10-carat diamond they owned to provide funding for the cause as part of their fundraising. They were wondering if we were interested in purchasing it. Kamahl and Sahodra found it amusing that Ivanka and her friend would simply assume that due to Kamahl's fame, they had 10-carat diamond money readily available. They did not, far from it. The very fact that Kamahl's strategy of projecting the image of success was obviously working and working very well, which he found very pleasing. Kamahl and Sahodra had no intention of spending a small fortune on the precious rock being offered. Still, they did agree to have lunch at some time with Ivanka and her friend. At that lunch, Kamahl was introduced to the friend, George, a very wealthy individual from the USA. George had made his fortune in timber and real estate.

The tall, soft-spoken American, explained that he had evidently discovered God after surviving a plane crash a few years before. Like many who go through life-altering significant events, he clung to the theory that God had personally intervened. As God had saved his life, he would do the Lord's work from here on in. Most specifically, he decided he would dedicate his efforts to defeating communism. Kamahl having both a developed and instinctive reservation for those who claim to have such lofty connections, he politely listened and resolved to restrain his real views for much of the conversation. When it became abundantly clear to George that the diamond was not finding a new home, he turned his attention to Kamahl's career. He said he had heard him sing and believed that he could make it big in the States. "He told me that if Helen Reddy could make it, then surely I could. He said that I could easily sell concerts in his hometown. Whilst flattering in one sense, selling out a concert in his hometown, would not rate as any kind of career highlight for any performer. It is a place that is considerably smaller than many of our own regional towns. I thanked him for the compliment and said that what I really wanted to do in the US was sing at Carnegie Hall. My comment was, to be honest, just a half-joking off the cuff comment. To my surprise, he said, 'When do you want to do it?' Again thinking that this was the continuance of a bit of light-hearted banter, I said, on the first day of Summer. To my surprise, well shock actually, he got up and, finding a phone, started making calls to the States'. Upon his return to the table, he informed me that he had been informally told that Carnegie Hall was available early for dates in Summer."

Peake would further tell Kamahl that he was highly interested in entering into a partnership with him. He was interested in the 'four-wall arrangement' that Kamahl had suggested had been so successful for him at the Palladium. For a four-wall booking to work, it is fundamental that costs are contained to a minimum to maximise income. The method ensures that the audience is guaranteed in both number and familiarity with the artist. The prime benefit is that high costs of promotion and ticket sales pressures are mitigated.

It was agreed on that day that the profits from the show would be split 50:50 between Kamahl and George. Naturally, this was after all expenses relating to the show were met. A few days after that first discussion at lunch, George called Kamahl to tell him that Carnegie Hall had been booked for Monday, June 26th. He says, "It was just like a dream. I was going to be performing at Carnegie Hall. It had all come from the misconception of a strange wealthy fellow that I was successful enough to afford a costly diamond. It is really no wonder that I have always maintained that perception and image are king."

Unfortunately, most things in life, when it involves people are rarely straightforward. In March that year, Kamahl embarked upon a three-month, heavy schedule tour of Asia and Europe. The plan was to complete this tour in New York with his appearance at Carnegie Hall. Before taking off in March, Kamahl started to become concerned that there had been a lot of back and forth about arrangements between him and George. Of most significant concern was that he would have to rely heavily upon George to drive things along as he was on tour. Hence, the potential for things to go off the rails was significant. Unlike these days, no matter where you are in the world, you remain connected with technology almost constantly. Back then, people were restricted to faxes, telexes and international calls that had to be made when both parties time zones were aligned. That is not easy when one of those parties is likely to be performing just when you need to speak with them. Even worse, stuck incommunicado on a flight for a lengthy inter-continental section of the tour. Trust was going to be essential in this partnership. Yet, even before Kamahl embarked upon the tour, cracks had started to appear.

George was indeed a successful mega-rich businessman but not a concert promoter savvy to the many nuances of the world of entertainment.

There were billboards in Times Square and Sunset Strip, posters around New York and a proposed promotional schedule of appearances on TV shows coast to coast.

Concerned that his show was on its way to being a loss-maker due to unnecessary expenses, he contacted Polygram, his record company. He had a thought that recording the concert live would generate income to offset the loss. Thankfully they agreed and organised a production team from Polydor US to record and produce that album. He reflects on that decision "I knew it was the smart thing to do, but it didn't come without its own problems. In setting up the equipment so soon before the concert, the crew were really pushed for time. Before I took to the stage, there was a glitch that needed to be sorted before I took to the concert starting. I was nervously standing backstage listening to a restless crowd for around half an hour. After what seemed like an eternity, the glitch was fixed. The musical accompaniment struck up the opening to 'Love is a Mountain'. My heart rate went down. I strolled out." He was so sensitive to having made the audience wait. He asked the conductor to stop, and he went to the front of the stage, apologised for making them wait so long, and thanked them for their patience. Predictably this was met with applause. After all, it isn't every day that audiences encounter an artist with humility.

Kamahl's Carnegie Hall concert had been a great success from a performance perspective but far from financially. Ultimately this led to the souring of his relationship with George.

The only good thing that came from all of this was meeting Mae Boren Axton to help promote the show. Mae was an incredible character. She was from the deep South and was known as the 'Queen Mother of Nashville'. Mae had been responsible for introducing a skinny white truck driver named Elvis Aaron Presley to a gentleman named Colonel Tom Parker in the fifties. She had also co-authored a breakthrough hit for him named Heartbreak Hotel. Mae managed to persuade her good friends Judi and Sid Friedman to attend the show. That took some doing as neither had any wish to attend a concert by some unknown Australian performer. Mae's persuasive powers, it would appear, were quite strong. They not only attended the show but genuinely loved what they had witnessed. At a function at the Russian Tea Rooms following the concert,

Sid and Judi invited Kamahl and Sahodra to a barbecue at their home in Wayne, New Jersey. At that lunch, Kamahl developed such a strong bond with the couple they took it upon themselves to champion his cause in the United States. This culminated in a second Carnegie Hall concert in 1978, with the Friedmans sponsoring the show as 50:50 equal partners.

When Kamahl met the couple, Sid was a TV producer of some note. He was a pioneer in the daytime news/talk, bringing legendary Radio DJ Bruce Morrow to NBC. Mae Boren Axton combining her friendship with the Friedmans with her role as Kamahl's publicist, had managed to get Kamahl a performance slot on the popular show where he would perform 'Daisy a Day'. Judi had been in many business roles throughout her life, including real estate sales. Therefore, it was surprising that the main push for the collaboration came from Judi rather than the person that Kamahl reasoned would be the more logical of the two, Sid. Kamahl says, "In life, I believe it is vitally important to continue to learn. It is more important to unlearn some of the prejudices you may have picked up over the years. I liked Judi and Sid very much and was happy to consider them business partners in the States. Still, I had always incorrectly assumed that Sid, the show business part of the couple, would manage the partnership. I now confess to being quite chauvinistic in that belief. Judi took months to persuade me that she could manage the relationship in America. I shamefully confess that I was initially reluctant to give her that chance. Still, I am more than happy to admit just how manifestly wrong I was. Within days she was opening doors for me that had previously been shut tight. She was a spark plug, full of energy and, most importantly, absolutely refused to take no for an answer from anyone attempting to put up any roadblock to my career. She and I shared our hate of the word 'no', so she was an absolutely perfect fit for me."

In the lead up to the second concert, Kamahl was back in Sydney. He was generally pleased with how things were coming together. Judi was a great communicator and went to pains to keep Kamahl appraised and agreed to every decision. However, a thought had occurred to him, who could he get to introduce him that could add a wow factor for a New York audience? That was quite a big ask. He was walking through Sydney's Martin Place several weeks before the show with this thought in mind. He noticed a demonstration for new generation fax machines taking place. While the salesman was promoting the wonders of the then incredible new technology, he asked Kamahl if there was anyone he would like to send a fax to demonstrate the machine's efficiencies. As it happened, he actually did. He had Bob Hope's fax details in the address book he kept in his pocket. He quickly jotted down a note asking Bob, who he knew was attending a fundraising concert for New York Zoo the day before the show. He wondered if he wouldn't mind staying on an extra night and doing the introduction in his message. He remembers, "I cringe when I think about the lame pun I used in the note. I was sending it to one of the world's most iconic comedians, but nonetheless, it got his attention. I said I hoped he could stay for an extra night, not for a whole zoo, but for a camel (sic). Within a day or so, he had not only responded, he agreed to do a ten-minute opening slot for me. If I could just arrange for him to be transported in a limo to and from the event. As his going rate for a ten-minute appearance in those days would have cost about $40,000, I had the deal of the century." Kamahl, Sahodra and the Hopes always remained great friends from their first meeting to Bob and Dolores' passing some years later.

The second Carnegie concert was a critical triumph. Once again, whilst live performances were keenly attended by cities where live shows were supported, this did not translate into music sales success. It was almost a replica of the UK experience only on a larger scale. Despite the tirelessly energetic Judi Friedman, who managed to move mountains to get him airplay and even a recording contract in Canada. The deal with Attic Records would see the release of an album *Somebody Loves You* featuring a compilation of Australian recordings. The record would sell well in Canada and lead to sold-out concerts at Ontario Palace and Thompson Hall. She tirelessly pestered Radio stations to get airplay and record store chains for shelf space. Sadly the latter was proving difficult as the investment for release on a grand scale and the promotion required to be put behind it to get that breakthrough hit was not forthcoming. He reflects, "I was getting airplay and great feedback from the radio stations. They told us that their listeners would want to know where to buy the records, but it was effectively a chicken and egg conundrum. It is just so different these days. The record companies and radio stations now have far less control over the product. Today's artists have much greater say over their own destiny." He had been advised by Mae Boren Axton that if he really wanted to make it in the States, he was going to need to spend a far more significant amount of time there. He was torn as he loved his home, the country that had given him so much, to risk all on relocating was just a gamble he wasn't prepared to take. It was a watershed moment, a chance to count his blessings and make a decision. He concluded that he would have to settle for America, being a garnish to his successes rather than the meal itself.

In speaking of Judi's tenacity, Kamahl recounts, "I had been trying to appear on the Variety Club LA Telethon for years. Although the show was a voluntary appearance, all funds went to a fantastic cause. Due to the stellar line-up, it was viewed by millions. Appearing on the show was almost an acknowledgement of having arrived on the US show business scene. Judi drove the assistant producer, Jeanne Brown, crazy with phone calls. When I spoke to Jeanne, she said that Judi had just worn her down with twenty-eight calls and God knows how many messages. Granted, the spot I was given, which was three AM, was not the greatest, but at least Judi had got me through that door. It was up to me to make the best of that opportunity. As luck had it, when I finished my spot, I made my way to the stage door where I ran into the producer Bob Wyn who I knew from his being involved with several Bob Hope specials. He told me that the switchboard had been busy with people requesting to see more of me. He asked if I wouldn't mind sticking around for a few more numbers. I performed eleven times that day. Each time, I was requested to do more, much to the annoyance of many local artists who had to be rescheduled or dropped altogether".

Kamahl says that the highlight of the appearance for him and those watching was his spoken word performance of *Sleeping Beauty,* a touching ode to a young girl by her father. The poem was a highly sentimental piece, made all the more compelling with a young handicapped girl accompanying him and host Kathy Lee Gifford on the stage during the performance. Kamahl recalls, "I was so overwhelmed by the words and the setting that I found myself choked up halfway through and had to collect myself. For a moment, I just couldn't continue. This was the only time that this ever happened to me in my career." The genuinely touching scene resulted in the Telethon switchboard almost melting down as teary callers sang praises for the segment. The organisers were delighted. Kamahl was made Variety Club Entertainer of the event, and offers for subsequent events flooded in. One such event was the Sammy Davis Jnr Variety Club St Louis Telethon. He was now a regular on that circuit, all due to the persistence of Judi, his doorbuster.

Philosophically Kamahl reflects, "Whilst the US was not as receptive to me as I would have liked, it was not without its positives. I've got some wonderful memories of performing to television audiences that were bigger than I could have ever imagined possible. Being on stage as the headline act at Carnegie Hall, performing in Vegas, Hawaii and countless other places. Recording in New York, Los Angeles and Nashville with unbelievably talented people were incredible experiences but of all these things meeting Judi and Sid was by far the most significant. It was a blessing too hard to put a value on because the Friedmans became such wonderful dear friends, and you just can't put a price on that. I could never have expected anyone to do more than Judi did in trying to get a breakthrough in the US. This was completely above and beyond the call of duty. She genuinely wanted me to succeed, she took it personally, and her work made it all the more special. If not for the Friedman's support and belief in me, that second Carnegie Hall concert would never have happened. For that alone, I would always be eternally grateful to them, but far more importantly, I am grateful for their friendship". Both Sid and Judi have unfortunately now passed. They were survived by three adult children, two boys and a girl Kamahl stayed in touch with via correspondence and social media for some years. Their daughter, Laurie became a chiropractor, the eldest son became an educator and the youngest son, Glenn, chose a career in security. He became a secret service agent in Washington. Glenn's career choice, he admits, came as quite a surprise. Interestingly, Glenn was by far the most proactive in maintaining contact, possibly due to his daughter choosing a career as a performing artist in musical theatre. However, the relationship dynamic appeared to change somewhat in 2016 when it became clear to Kamahl that Glenn was far from impressed with his outspokenly negative views on the incoming president. The younger man had aligned a Trumpian worldview. "It is sad how politics divides people like that. For my part, I can always accommodate someone's differing viewpoint. A testament to that fact is that I have managed to continue a relationship with Rupert all these years despite our obvious ideological differences. I suppose, unfortunately, some people can't see beyond these things. It just gives me one more reason to despise Donald Trump."

Kamahl has never had to risk wondering what may have happened if only he had done something. Once he was liberated from the shyness of his youth, his philosophy became 'those who don't ask never find out.' In 1978, he was yet again on a flight back from the UK. He had to face twenty hours where he could do very little but read, check out the in-flight entertainment and avail himself of the hospitality of first-class travel. To Kamahl, this was dead time, twenty-four hours where nothing in his career could be advanced, promoted or improved. As luck would have it, this flight was to be a different experience. Unbeknownst to him, he was seated right next to a man whose face looked somewhat familiar. Kamahl being the gregarious person, could not help but engage the stranger seated to his right. Quickly, they became engaged in a lengthy light-hearted conversation. Kamahl's genial fellow traveller handed him a card as the two men parted after disembarking in Sydney. It turned out that the traveller in question was a very senior representative of Qantas, General Manager Keith Hamilton.

After allowing himself the time to unpack, Kamahl had yet another eureka moment. He picked up the phone and made a call that would lead to Qantas being a co-producer of a hit album, *Around the World*. By introducing his new travel pal to the appropriate people, Kamahl could pitch the airline his services and a split earning model on sales plus a percentage of income donated to *Save the Children Fund*. For their part, Qantas would be required to underwrite production costs with Philips and provide Kamahl international airfares for a year to be used at his discretion. The latter was a significant offset to his operating cost at a time when his travel was almost six figures each year. It was a great deal for all parties, and shortly after the meeting, it was decided that the project be brought to life. The album was promptly released, featuring songs from around the world. The artwork used for the double album cover featured sixteen kids from different countries wearing national costume, two of whom were Rajan and Rani resplendent in Tamil costume. The inside spread featured the kids posed descending the staircase of a Qantas plane in a not so subtle example of product placement. Several other shots were arranged like scattered postcards featuring Kamahl in front of landmarks from various locations, one of which was Auckland. The underlying concept of the album was to promote better understanding between nations through the love of music. In the liner notes, Kamahl wrote:

Music turns a world of tears into a world of laughter and a world of fears into a world of hope. I hope you share the joy I experienced while recording this collection of best-loved and requested songs from around the world – tomorrow's world belongs to children so please spare a thought for those children less fortunate than our own

The album was a big hit. All was good until an anonymous eagle-eyed executive from Qantas noted that the Auckland image had one of those signposts with multiple international locations and their distances in the background. In principle, there were no issues with the shot except that atop the sign was a reasonably prominent Air New Zealand logo. It was evidently a piece of their advertising. Air New Zealand at that time was Qantas' major rival. The airline was not in the slightest bit amused and were quick to point the matter out to Kamahl, even quicker to devalue his contra deal by 20,000. No doubt he was embarrassed and out of pocket but had no choice to accept the reduced agreement. All he had done was to follow instructions to stand in the shots as directed. He was also paranoid about the goof being leaked through the industry.

11

Sound and vision

The eyes shout what the lips fear to say.

William Henry

Television was to play a significant role in the rise of Kamahl's profile. While he had featured on the first broadcast on Adelaide TV courtesy of Rupert Murdoch, his national TV break came in 1961 in the BP Super Show filmed at GTV 9. The show had a significant audience and featured the popular host Horrie Dargie. The show was a welcome break indeed. He appeared with a star-studded cast, including American crooner Jerry Vale and Australian star Lorrae Desmond, then one of the country's most prominent female singers. Kamahl was to perform a song he was really familiar with, 'An Affair to Remember.' He was also asked, as evidently was custom for the show, to participate in a medley of numbers with the show's other stars, the idea being the three singers would each carry one song, each of which would cue the other. The song chosen for him was 'I'll Get By'. The only problem was he had never heard the number, had never performed it, and worse, had little time to rehearse it and to top it off, the show was going out live. He approached the musical director Arthur Young to suggest cutting him out of the number. He was clearly struggling with the song. "I suppose you could refer to the performance as a car crash, but I have been in at least one of those, and they felt much better. I froze and just hoped that Lorrae would somehow bail me out. She didn't, although I have no idea what I expected her to do. I have remained amused for years that the title of the song was totally undermined by my performance. No way did I get by. I stank," he laughs. Sadly with the show going out live, it didn't facilitate a makeover, so once it was done, it was done. Kamahl must have forgiven Lorrae Desmond for not throwing herself on the musical grenade. They would work together many times in his career and were great friends for many years. He would never let her forget about that night on live TV, however.

"Lorrae was a great performer, a terrific friend and a real trooper, a true Aussie icon. She went on to be Shirley Dean Gilroy for over ten years in *A Country Practice*, one of Australia's most successful soap operas of all time. Sadly my old and dear friend passed away early in 2021 at the age of 91." Kamahl's less than ideal introduction to a national television audience may have been a sobering setback, if only to his confidence. Thankfully it didn't diminish his desire to get back in the saddle again as soon as possible. Luckily for him, it also didn't reduce his appeal to TV executives. More appearances would follow with fairly decent regularity.

Following Kamahl's remarkable success in 1970 with the BP *Peace on Earth* album, he had become, as someone had once referred to him, "a hot property". The ABC sought to capitalise on the hype. They approached him to be the host of his very own weekly music TV show entitled *Kamahl*. He was surprised and somewhat overwhelmed by the very notion that this was really going to happen. Of course, he had been a featured artist and had performed on quite a lot of television at this point in his career, but being the host of his own show was in a different league altogether. He recalls, "I was quite intimidated by the whole suggestion, but there was absolutely no way that I would refuse such a fantastic opportunity. To this day I am not entirely sure how the show came about. I have for many years believed that a great old friend of mine from ABC Adelaide,

Jeff Duigan had put the idea forward to his management. He never confirmed this, but I have long suspected it was."

The ABC was evidently better-funded back in the seventies. The show was a pretty lavish affair with fabulous sets and a stellar line-up of guests including Jell Perryman, noted harpist Alice Giles and Julie Felix, the singer girlfriend of famed TV journalist David Frost. There were twelve backup singers, twelve dancers. They even had the highly respected Brian May, leading his twenty-five-piece orchestra. Practically no expense had been spared, well except for one, a most important one... there was no writer allocated to the show. When he asked why they told him. "We thought you were so eloquent you didn't need one". Whilst flattered, Kamahl knew he needed help to pull the words together, so he hired one himself after fighting long and hard with the ABC about their oversight. He rightly reasoned that the linking segments he was responsible for delivering, if not polished, could fall extremely flat and awkward. He was more than capable of audience banter in shows and concerts, but TV dynamics were far less forgiving. As he says, "There is no room for umming and ahhing on national television. TV audiences are not as invested in you as a concert crowd and are nowhere near as forgiving. This was my show and my reputation at stake, so I fought hard to make sure that it was a good representation of me. If that meant that I had to pay for a writer from my own pocket then I would."

The show would run over twelve episodes in the first series, directed by Leigh Spence, who Kamahl claims he loved working with. In his view, Leigh was a complete professional and a great collaborator, fun to work with and had excellent ideas. He was always keen to listen and always looking to improve things. Leigh would later go on to great success with *Home and Away* and *A Country Practice*, two of Australia's biggest-ever TV shows.

Although sometimes questioning some of the production priorities, Kamahl really enjoyed this first series. A case in point, failing to engage a writer but insisting upon as many as four costume changes per episode. Each being custom-made for just that show and discarded afterwards. He was also disappointed in the insistence that he mime all of his songs on the show to accommodate the technical inadequacies the ABC had at the time. He reasonably concluded the lack of sound engineering capabilities may have been addressed if a little less had been spent on the rather extravagantly glitzy staging and costuming parts of the show. However, for some reason, these embellishments for the producers appeared to be non-negotiable. At the end of the day, he was pleased with the outcome. His reputation and profile had been boosted and further cemented him as an Australian artist.

When the second series came around the following year, Leigh Spence had left the show to work on other opportunities, which disappointed Kamahl greatly. On the other hand, producer Jim Davern had taken his leave too. This piece of news didn't disappoint Kamahl whatsoever as theirs had been quite a strained relationship. New producer Jon Ewing took a much different approach to the show, far more collaborative and thankfully far less combative. "I missed working with Leigh immensely because he really got it, and we had a lot of fun working together. Having said that, I had a great deal more creative input in the second series." The show's format had changed with Kamahl no longer required to meet musical guests on stage, allowing more flexibility in filming and more creative editing, providing the production with a more theatrical feel. The series was shorter than series one, running for nine episodes and had been well-received by audiences. It had provided an excellent continuance of exposure for two years from the high point of 1970. The increased exposure was also a significant contributor to the decision to re-release *Peace on Earth* after the first series, which translated into 80,000 additional record sales in just six weeks.

Following the show, it also occurred to Kamahl that he had recorded about eighty songs during production. This meant more than enough material to produce and release at least another album from those recordings. He contacted his record company, Polygram, who agreed that this was a great idea. They purchased the rights to the songs, obtained the masters, to then release the eponymous *Kamahl,* which would sell well over 100,000 units.

Kamahl's love affair with television was now confirmed and he was determined to actively seek out every possible opportunity that made sense. He now had excellent practical experience and an advanced understanding of the medium's power relative to his career. Now established on the TV landscape as one of its stars, opportunities would keep coming up. He was a regular guest on the high-profile weekend TV staple *Young Talent Time* hosted by Johnny Young. The show was well-established and ran from 1971 until 1988, with 44 episodes being produced per year.

The show had a very wholesome approach to showcasing young up and coming stars in an ensemble format. Many of Australia's most prominent artists were a part of the *YTT* line-up when they were kids and would go on to great fame. Tina Arena, Dannii Minogue, Debra Byrne, Jamie Redfern, Jane Scali, Sally Boyden are just a handful of those who went on to significant careers. In amongst the young talent performances, guest artists would also feature to be interviewed and perform. Kamahl recounts, "John was an absolute delight to work with. There is little wonder why he has been so successful in discovering and nurturing so many great performers. John genuinely cared and was so supportive to those kids on the show, and all of his guest artists were treated with great respect. He would even encourage audiences to get behind whatever it was we were doing at the time and egg them on to give a standing ovation after performances. He is a gentleman of the highest order in not only my opinion but anyone I know who worked with him."

Kamahl's career had seen him work with most of the big names in television when the medium was king. He reflects on the industry during those times as a relatively tight group of familiar names, most of whom were supportive of one another. No one exemplified this attitude to fellow artists more than Bert Newton, who sadly passed away in October 2021. "Bert was the complete professional. I don't think that I have ever worked with anyone who so perfectly understood his obligation to his audience. He was a fantastic entertainer who would do anything to please his audience. The lovable guy you saw on screen was exactly the same person he was in real life. He was funny, genial, quick-witted with incredible timing, but above all, he was extremely generous. We worked together so many times, and I enjoyed every single occasion. Bert was always taking the micky out of me. Whether it was the way I spoke or the way I dressed, nothing was ever off-limits. You always knew his jokes were never ever mean spirited. He could make me a part of a gag without making me the victim of it. If anything, he would go to pains to make sure that every time I appeared with him, I was made to feel at ease. I remember on one occasion, both he and Don Lane greeted me on to their show, both dressed in kaftans. They hadn't told me they were going to do it, so when I came to the stage wearing a tuxedo, the audience cracked up at my surprise. I have often said that Bert could make you feel like you were ten feet tall, even when you felt quite small. When he was doing the *Good Morning Australia* show in the nineties, I was a very regular guest. While all of the appearances were great, one occasion really stood out to me. I sang a song called 'Remember', a very sentimental and touching song. When I returned to the set for our interview after singing, I noticed he was a little teary. There is no greater compliment for a singer to see that you have managed to touch someone, but for it to be a man like Bert, who was all about laughter, meant a lot to me. Actually, not many people may remember it, but it was Bert, not *Hey Hey It's Saturday*, who actually started to use the line 'Why are people so unkind?' which was lifted from a song of mine, 'What Would I Be Without My Music?' I was so sad to hear of his passing. Australian show business has produced many legends over the years, but I can't think of one so respected as

Bert. He was a wonderful man who will be missed." Kamahl underscored his testament to his old friend when tweeting that he believed that Bert should be afforded the honour of a state funeral. He was delighted to see that the suggestion was quickly endorsed by many others and granted by the Victorian Government.

It has to be said that some of Kamahl's experiences during the halcyon days of television were not as positive. His frequent appearances on the *Midday Show*, where the interview portions of the appearances were invariably fun, upbeat, warm and friendly, his dealings with Geoff for reasons he could never fathom, were difficult. "I never really understood it, but Geoff was never easy for me to work with for reasons I will never know. Evidently, there was something about me that provided reasons for his icy attitude and his deliberate attempts to make me fail. Whatever they were, I decided to ignore them and found a workaround, much to his distaste. Whenever I was scheduled to appear, I would bring in Larry Muhoberac, an American recording legend who, among other things, started his career as Elvis Presley's keyboardist. Larry and I had met many years before in the US. He had emigrated to settle and retire on the Central Coast of NSW. He still did the odd show. So it gave me the assurance of getting through the performance without the stress of some meaningless shenanigans. Harvey was livid. Still, there was little he could do."

Despite his overwhelmingly positive experiences on most TV appearances and performances the world over, his Geoff experience had been a portent of things to come. When Kamahl was approached by Gavin Disney, producer of *Hey Hey It's Saturday*, to appear on the show, he applied the principle that any publicity is good publicity. The guaranteed exposure the show would undoubtedly deliver could only be a good thing for his career.

Hey Hey It's Saturday had started as a kid's show on Saturday mornings a few years prior. It had become a pioneer viral hit before viral hits even existed. This was primarily because of not-so-subtle double entendre and off-beat humour. Research had established that the format that the audiences attracted was considerably older than competitive content in the same time slot. Channel Nine realised that they had the makings of a cult following and seized upon its following to repurpose the show into an early evening prime time variety program on Saturday nights. They would throw a big budget behind it to attract higher-profile guests, slicker production values and promotion. The show was no longer bracketing cartoons but international and local artists, comic performers and bespoke skits. The gamble paid off handsomely for Nine as ratings were sensational in what was previously regarded as a graveyard timeslot. Kamahl reflects on his association with the show saying, "I was still riding high on the exposure that I had received from TV and thought *Hey Hey* was an opportunity too good to refuse. Maybe this was a little naïve, but I actually thought that my appearing on the program would work out well. After all, it was a massive show at the time. My thought was that it was an ideal way to reach a new and previously untapped audience. In some respects, that actually turned out to be true in a way."

It is fair to say that a new audience was reached, but it was pretty clear from early on that Kamahl was not there to be an entertainer or promote himself but to be on the receiving end of sometimes mean-spirited jokes. "On the rare occasion that I was asked to sing, I would be interrupted by a stunt, a joke or some voiceover wisecrack delivered by the cast. I quickly understood that my role there was not to help set up jokes, but I felt maybe in my opinion was to be the punchline in them. I have never ever taken myself all that seriously, so I thought, what the hell? At least it will show that audience that I could take a joke and wasn't just another stiff entertainer that couldn't laugh at themselves. So, I went along with it, returning time after time as a guest judge on their silly Red Faces segment. Once, I was set up by host Daryl Somers for one of their gags by being asked if I could sing a medley of Christmas songs for, as he put it, 'all the mums at home.' I was surprised, but as per usual, I complied. I was ushered over to a stool and sat whilst a recorded music track started up. I was meant to mime to the songs during the medley, but they sped up the track, cut from one part to another and generally made a farce of the whole thing. That was annoying but tolerable, and it did fit in with the generally crass humour that the show was known for. One crew appeared from the left side and hit me in the face with an oversized powder puff. I suppose the big joke was that they had turned a black man white. It was hilarious. I suppose if the bar you set for humour is the same as a five-year-old. I just went along with the 'gag' and chased the assailant with the powder puff to do the same to him and subsequently did the same to Somers. I was humiliated but wanted to look like I was part of the joke and not the joke itself."

The most galling thing about the stunt for Kamahl was not the humiliating gag. He was leaving for the US that week, where he was to be introduced by Bob Hope in his second sell-out appearance at Carnegie Hall. This was a massive achievement for any Australian entertainer.

I suppose, in a way, it exposed the elephant in the room. The silly gags aside, the thing that really hurt was that my Carnegie appearance with no less than Bob Hope as my opening for me was ignored. I was there to promote my concert totally, yet barely a word was made in reference to it. After all these years, I question why they chose to ignore it. Here I was, an Australian artist flying the flag by performing at one of the most iconic venues in the biggest city in the world, and yet they preferred to humiliate and mock me. To this day I would really like to know the answer. Even if it were an oversight, and obviously it wasn't, then it was that they thought so little of me as an artist that in their minds I was just a prop for bad jokes, and that was all there was to it. The contrast between how I was treated on this show to the good-natured ribbing that I used to get from Bert Newton could not have been starker. You see, there is a massive difference between being a part of a joke and being made the butt of one. Sadly, some of the people on *Hey Hey It's Saturday* could never or would never make that distinction. I know in recent times, some of the cast have distanced themselves from what happened on the show back then, but I struggle with that notion. I will never forget the disrespect and humiliation on that particular occasion. It was more important to them to get a cheap laugh at my expense rather than acknowledging one of my biggest career highlights.

When the show finally ran out of steam in 1999, it was cancelled. It had enjoyed a good run for a program that had started life as an accompaniment for breakfast cereal and cartoons on a Saturday morning. There was an attempt to resurrect the show in 2009 and Kamahl was contacted by Daryl Somers' personal assistant enquiring if I would be interested in making a personal appearance on the 'new' show. He had already been asked by the program producers and had said no to the first two shows in the series. However, as this approach was coming through Somers himself, he thought he should take it seriously. He says, "I said that I would consider appearing but really didn't feel good about it. I then asked about the practical details like flights, accommodation etc, to which she replied, 'oh, you would need to take care of that yourself. I was shocked but thought it might still be worth my while to perform, so I asked what my role would be, to which she replied, 'you will be sitting in the Green Room'. So, they not only expected me to buy my own tickets, pay for my own accommodation, with no appearance fee, I must add. For God's sake, they weren't even prepared to stump up for a taxi to get me to the bloody Studio.

"All that they wanted me for was to have me sit in the bloody green Room for the whole show. I had to ask myself if I wanted to be involved in yet another 'hilarious' surprise? Not bloody likely!! I told them thanks but no thanks. It was one decision I took no time over at all."

However, the association with *Hey Hey It's Saturday* was unfortunately not over. In the reunion special, the Red Faces talent quest segment featured a group of five young doctors who represented themselves as the Jackson Five. The group appeared in blackface, except for the lead singer. He had his face painted white, supposedly a far from subtle 'joke' playing off the king of pop Michael Jackson cosmetically whitened skin. They performed 'Can You Feel It'.

A crude caricature of Kamahl was placed on the screen through the song with a caption saying, "Where's Kamahl?" and another with his trademark phrase "Why are people so unkind?" played several times. It was not a great joke.

He reflected, "Had I been there all these years just as a vehicle for cheap racist jokes? I hadn't even been there for well over a decade, and yet here it was."

Times had indeed changed, and there was quite a strong adverse reaction from the piece. Harry Connick Jr was appearing on the show to perform and be a guest judge on the segment. He seemed to be appalled with the performance because they had arranged him to be a part of it in the show. He was very forthright in his comments and decided to make them live to air. Connick said, "I know it was done humorously. We've spent so much time trying to not make black people look like buffoons that when we see something like that, we take it really to heart." He added that if he'd been aware that this performance was to be on the segment he'd never have agreed to appear on it, or for that matter, to be on the show at all. The news of this incident spread like wildfire. Connick Jr was a huge international star. His voice carried so much weight that coverage of the incident spread like wildfire, particularly in the United States. The media coverage made coast-to-coast news segments and many talk shows.

Kamahl recalls, "The first I knew of this controversy was the next day when it was all over the mid-morning news. Channel Seven called and asked if they could send a crew to my house for an interview. On reflection, I should have said no. I knew that refusing would only allow them to insert their own opinion of what that refusal meant. So, I agreed, and they arrived on my doorstep asking me almost immediately if I thought the show was racist, specifically relating to my own treatment. I said not really, I thought the performance was tasteless, but that is what that show was best known for. If anything, it was just stupid toilet humour, and it was time that it should be flushed. Disappointed with that response, as it clearly was not the controversial response he was after, the journalist with crew packed up their stuff and headed to their car. Just as they were pulling out, he did ask me one parting question from the car window. He said, 'Are you going to sue Channel Nine, Kamahl?' Of course, I wouldn't have done that in a million years, but at this stage, I was growing annoyed with the questioning and sarcastically quipped, sure, why not? That's a great idea. The very next morning on the front of the *Daily Telegraph*, it read 'Kamahl to sue Channel Nine'. I should have known better, than using my own silly joke against me but to be honest, I felt like I was becoming dragged into something that I really didn't want any part of."

Harry Connick Jr ignited this whole thing because a ridiculous skit had offended his principles, and of course, he had every right to voice his opinion. He felt that his presence on the show validated behaviour that he found repugnant. That had led to it being an important story. Still, as Kamahl had been dealing with the show's gags as the punchline for years whilst suffering in silence, he became the story within the story. The Media wanted to explore how he had felt going along with the jokes, had he been scarred emotionally, how did he deal with it etc. They had failed to grasp that he had gone along with the show's jokes even when he was the butt of them because he saw them as just jokes. He never believed there was serious intent behind them. He never thought it was malicious and did not consider that he was working with overt racists. He says, "It wasn't even the jokes. It was their ignoring my Carnegie Hall performance and then adding insult to injury by expecting me in 2009 to pay my own way to appear on their show to no doubt again be the butt of their tasteless gags. I don't know of anyone prepared to get insulted for free, let alone pay for it. In all honesty, whilst the show provided me with a high profile for a few years, that was useful. I would almost guarantee that not one person in their audience ever bought a Kamahl record, but that was the trade-off for the exposure."

Kamahl did actually receive negative publicity in some quarters over the Connick Jr uproar. He was cited by some media types for being overly sensitive and thin-skinned. The irony of this criticism does not escape him "I took quite a lot of ribbing on that show for years and always did it with good grace. I had never taken myself that seriously and have always been able to laugh at myself. It was one of the many ways that I overcame my chronic shyness when I was young. It is therefore quite amusing for this to be said about me of all people."

The revival lasted only a short while before being cut. It would however appear that the memory of the show was in fact unflushable.

In 2021 Daryl Somers, when promoting Channel Seven series *Dancing with the Stars* where he was to be the host, was asked by a *Sunday Telegraph* reporter if he thought a show like *Hey Hey It's Saturday* would be able to make it on television today. His response was, "You probably could not get away with half the stuff you could on *Hey Hey* now because of political correctness and cancel culture." His little joke with the Channel Seven reporter suggested that *Hey Hey It's Saturday* dealt in toilet humour and should be flushed was prophetic.

What followed was another storm of controversy that swirled around for several weeks. Old footage of Kamahl being used as the human prop for racist gags was dug up and aired along with the Harry Connick Jr saga from well over a decade prior. Kamahl was again in high demand for interviews to get his take on the Political Correctness comment.

In an interview with *The Guardian* in March 2021, Kamahl candidly acknowledged that he had benefitted from the publicity generated by his appearances. "My basic philosophy as far as television is concerned is, when you're an entertainer and the public don't see you on television, they think you're dead. I had little control over how I would be portrayed on that program, and when I agreed to appear, I never realised it would be such a minefield. In many instances, I felt humiliated but didn't want to raise any objections or protest about it. I just kept smiling and pretending all was OK." On the show's host, he said he did not blame Somers personally. "I always got along reasonably well with Daryl. I've never had any quarrel with him at all. I don't think he had any ill-feeling toward me. I don't think he encouraged the behaviour, although he might have been able to stop it. Following his press interview, the story was followed up by every TV Network unsurprisingly, except for Channel Nine, the long-time broadcaster of *Hey Hey It's Saturday*.

John Blackman, on his Facebook page in March 2021, said, "Kamahl, if you felt so aggrieved by my 'quip' you should have had marched up and had a quiet word in my ear, and I would have desisted from making any further 'racist' remarks forever."

He added: "Keep in mind, we were all performing in less-enlightened (unintended pun) times back in the day and, when I look back over my career on HHIS (via YouTube), I sometimes cringe at what we got away with – but none of it with any intended malice." Kamahl responded on his Twitter account, stating, "John Blackman wants to know why I did not make any complaints then! Mr Blackman, you of all people know that it's all about TIMING! There's a time for everything." Blackman, after his post, was roundly lambasted all over social media for his seemingly unapologetic and tone-deaf stance with some people. It appeared clear that he had may have misread the realities of speaking out in these 'more enlightened times.

Kamahl insists that he has no regrets at all about being a part of *Hey Hey It's Saturday's* history. He feels that whilst he was very uncomfortable with some of the humour, as evidenced by the volume of support he has received from the community, that he lost no fans. He also holds no hard feelings whatsoever to Blackman. He says he had a good working relationship with him during his long association with the show. He says, "I know John really meant no ill will to me, as he says we were not as enlightened at the time and *Hey Hey* was very much a product of its time, I also understand that he has had a fair share of health-related issues in more recent years before his passing. On the jokes, I have always thought the only funny thing about them was the fact that they were ironically delivered by a person named Blackman."

On October 10, 2021, *Hey Hey It's Saturday's* 50th Anniversary was screened by Channel 7. Despite his being a fixture on the show for many years, Kamahl's invitation to the event appears to have been lost in the mail. Even when faced with the snub, he claims that he would have gladly participated if asked. But maybe the programme's producers had other ideas. They acknowledged Kamahl's many years on the show with a mere split-second image amongst a montage of pictures of hundreds of other artists who had appeared on the show during its history. The snub, whilst evidently ungracious, was consistent with some of the treatment he had experienced for many years, so it wasn't entirely unexpected. Kamahl said, "You know, I have never been capable of being disrespectful, so when on the receiving end of such treatment, it genuinely confuses me. However, the resurrection of the show in the 50th Anniversary special just made me reflect once again on some of the things that had involved me on the show over the years. A number stood out for all the wrong reasons.

It was obvious that they had got me on the show as some kind of comic foil. It was hardly subtle nor clever, but it appealed to a segment of their audience, so they milked it for all it was worth. I thought that by taking such treatment in my stride in good grace may show that I could rise above it all by not overreacting. I thought that by going along with it, by being a good sport, the audience may understand that we can laugh at ourselves and that we aren't all that different. I now realise that in doing so I may have been seen to be supportive of such treatment, which is wrong. When the 50th Anniversary special aired and it was being lauded by all and sundry within the business, I felt compelled to seek an answer as to why my career milestone was treated with such disdain. I wrote an open letter to Daryl Somers so that he could be given an opportunity to publicly explain his actions" The letter was published on October 13th, 2021, in several Australian mastheads, it stated:

An open letter to Daryl Somers

I would like to extend my warmest congratulations to you for the great success achieved with the Hey Hey It's Saturday 50th Anniversary show. The accolades that you received within the program were well earned and rightly acknowledge your place in Australian TV history. As an Australian entertainer, my being a part of that history for a number of years is truly humbling.

Daryl, having viewed the show, it was greatly evident that you fully understand the significance of career milestones for entertainers. It is therefore puzzling to me that in 1984 during my appearance on Hey Hey on the eve of my second appearance at Carnegie Hall, I feel that the show decided to set me up as the butt of a rather crude joke in preference to acknowledging my achievement.

The Carnegie Hall concert was my second sell out performance at the venue, I was being introduced by none other than entertainment legend Bob Hope and yet this was evidently not worth a mention. The fact that I had poured my heart and soul into making that concert a success made the stunt on Hey Hey that evening an incredibly dispiriting experience. As a supporter of Hey Hey I have to say that at the time, I felt let down by the show, and it is a disappointment that remains with me today.

My continued confusion at this treatment lies in one unanswered question that I would like to put to you. If I had been any other Australian artist about to embark on such a massive venture, would I have received such treatment? In a week where you are deservedly receiving such plaudits for your career milestone, I am left wondering why when you had the opportunity to

acknowledge mine you chose not to. As I have been known to say before, why are people so unkind?
   Kamahl

And as of today, these questions remain unanswered for me and remain a mystery.

In 2010, after a long absence, Kamahl was asked to return to television to make an appearance on *Spicks and Specks,* the popular music quiz show hosted by comedian Adam Hills. He said that he was apprehensive about agreeing to appear, fearing this may turn out to be a 'gotcha' moment where he was being set up as the butt of gags. He knew that the audience was a great deal younger than his usual crowd and the humour driven content was ripe for his worst fears to once again come to fruition. In addition to these fears, he had to deal with another significant and more physical issue. For quite a time, he had been suffering from profound hearing loss. He worried that he may not be able to keep up with the banter in a fast-paced music quiz comedy panel show, let alone make out any of the questions. He decided that the show had provided him with sufficient incentive to finally do something positive about his hearing. He decided to seek out professional help. He took himself off to a specialist and was fitted with the best state of the art hearing devices that money could buy. Quite a bit of money, as it turned out, approximately $8,000 for each ear.

Now armed with his newly regained hearing and against his better judgement, he agreed to the appearance. He maintains it was one of the best TV experiences he ever had. No clumsy humour, each guest was treated with great deference and respect, and they even got him to perform at the show's end. However, he was not to sing; he was to perform a spoken-word rendition of the show's title as penned by The Bee Gees in the early sixties. He recalls fondly, "It was an amazing contrast to so many TV shows, the cast headed by Adam Hills and their crew were all such a delight to work with. I felt like I was there as a genuine guest artist, not just a comedy prop, and the audience was so warm and welcoming. I guess it demonstrates that you don't need to use crass humour or lame slapstick to make an audience laugh. Being clever will win out every time. My only regret was that the hearing aids weren't such a great hit. No one told me that they could only help you hear the questions. I thought at that price they should give you the bloody answers," he laughs.

Whilst Kamahl has always had a strong following with mature audiences, he has never been averse to testing his popularity among other generations. In 1998, the *Rocky Horror Show* producers needed someone as a backup for the role of Narrator in their Melbourne season when cast member Red Symons was on breaks. He enjoyed his appearances so much and was so well received in the role that he would agree to take on the role for the Adelaide season on his own. He really warmed to the freedom to be able to deviate from the scripted format and ad lib. The production's cult-like following meant that they played to some hardcore fans who would see the show night after night. The crowd interacted so much that they almost felt like part of the show rather than paying patrons. This meant that they practically knew every single word sang or spoken in the show and, as such, knew who in the cast they liked and who they didn't. It also meant that the cast had to put their own stamp on the role they were cast to play to be liked. Kamahl's ability to engage audiences with his spontaneous wit was a big hit. It was practically a perfect production for him. The audiences were receptive, and he wasn't hamstrung by an overly rigid format.

If *Rocky Horror* was a bit of a break from his traditional environment, he was placed in another cultural universe altogether when he agreed to appear at the 'Big Day Out' in 2001. The brainchild of uniquely named stage producer Duckpond who managed the Festival's Lilypad stage. He took his idea to BDO promoter Ken West. The latter initially had to be convinced about how Kamahl would be received at the show. In a *Melbourne Age* article in 2004, Duckpond said, "Obviously we wanted him to be treated with respect, which I was sure he would be, but on that first day in 2001, it was fantastic. He got such an amazing reception from the crowd. When he walked into the amphitheatre, there was this spontaneous eruption of applause. It was just spine-tingling. He came out and sang 'The Impossible Dream'." As Kamahl says, "I knew that my music was hardly what they had come to see, I believe my appearance was arranged to provide some kind of ironic humour, but you know what? Nobody was disrespectful, no-one said anything other than positive things to me. They were just a wonderful crowd, and I had nothing but fun in the few years that I was with the show." From Duckpond's inspired thought in 2001, Kamahl would tour right around the country with the event for several years, always being warmly received. Kamahl looks back on the experience very fondly. The sight of a group of young women showing their eager and enthusiastic support, like their mothers, aunties, and grandmothers had before them, was also a highlight.

"At the Gold Coast, the response was unbelievable. I thought I felt like I was a pop idol or something," he laughs. "I saw 20 or 30 young ladies wearing Kamahl T-shirts and singlets that said, 'Kamahl, I love you, 'Kamahl, marry me' and, far more concerning 'Kamahl, I'm pregnant'. It was hilarious. I am not sure if it was that concert or the next one at the Gold Coast when I had travelled up to the show with host Adam Spencer, who is a delightful young guy and extremely clever. He is some kind of mathematics savant. When we were checking in for the flight, I noticed that he was flying economy. So I persuaded the crew to get him an upgrade so we could fly together. He is such a knowledgeable guy and a really great conversationalist. Still, I must admit when we got to his favourite subject, mathematics, he was talking way over my head.

"When we finally got to the Gold Coast, close to the venue, we encountered massive road works, preventing our progress. I opened the window and asked the road worker what was going on. The guy yelled 'Kamahl' like he had just met a lifelong friend he hadn't seen for years.

I asked politely, if there was any way we could get through, and he said 'of course' and moved the barrier and waved us through. Adam referred to me as Moses as he said I had managed the equivalent of parting the Red Sea. In 2006, I received an invitation from a young child who asked me if I would attend the wedding of his mummy and daddy. Daddy was Adam and his partner Mel were that couple. When I rang to congratulate him, he asked me if I would sing at the wedding, I agreed and told him that I would provide a song list from which he and Mel could choose, he said 'Could you sing 'Love Is In The Air'?' 'My response was, over my dead body!' I am sure he thought I was joking, but I had always had a problem with covering modern songs and really hated the idea, but somehow, he talked me into it. Interestingly I enjoyed performing it so much that I added the number to my repertoire from that time on. Like I said, he is a very clever fellow Adam Spencer."

Being linked to an older demographic is something Kamahl has accepted. However, it has never prevented him from surprising and confounding those who have tried to pigeonhole him. He has time and time again shown no inclination to stay in any particular entertainment lane. He is driven hard by a desire to be accepted by all. The urge is so pronounced that when he has to, he can launch a charm offensive on cue with all types of audiences, irrespective of gender, race, orientation or walks of life. Therefore, it stands to reason that his appeal can also be multi-generational as he reasons that people are just people after all. It was quite a surprise for him when in 2000, he was approached by Anthony Field of The Wiggles to be a part of a DVD project. The Wiggles are a unique Australian children's entertainment phenomenon. "I was in my sixties at the time, and I was being asked to be involved in a kids project? My kids were already adults, and I hadn't even become a grandparent, so the Wiggles were not featured high on the Kamahl home playlist. You may even describe my condition as suffering from acute WDD, Wiggle Deficit Disorder.

"I initially ignored the request mainly due to my lack of knowledge of who I was dealing with. I thought nothing more of it until I was approached a second time and given a polite but reasonably short deadline to make a decision. When pressured on the timeline, it really got my attention. I decided to do some research on the group and take the time to review their material. Straight away, I thought it was fun, imaginative and obviously very engaging. They were colourful, upbeat, positive and extremely popular with young kids and parents. Even more impressive to me was the laundry list of big-name local and international high-profile artists who had worked with them before. It was pretty incredible. I persuaded myself that it would be a good idea, and that instinct proved 100% correct. They were tremendous people to work with who genuinely loved what they did. And so was born the Brown Wiggle or as they prefer to call me the Tuxedo Wiggle," he laughs.

Kamahl's performance, accompanied by a giant green dinosaur named Dorothy doing 'Sing With Me,' proved extremely popular. The age-old adage about not performing with kids and animals had been shattered. That is if you can classify a green dinosaur with a hat on as an animal. So a whole new generation of Kamahl consumers was invented.

Kamahl says, "You know far too many people in my industry become a victim of their own ego. They obsess over what they will and will not do. They get so swept up in themselves and end up living in continual fear of the unknown. My view is, if you project a positive image and are genuine in your desire to entertain people, your image will only be enhanced."

A great example of Kamahl taking things in his stride when the unexpected crops up happened one evening in September of 2007. Kamahl was at his home entertaining long-time friends and fellow Variety Club devotees Grahame and Sue Mapp. The dinner party was quite a regular feature at Taj Kamahl. Both he and Sahodra are great hosts who love entertaining. To top it off, she is a highly accomplished cook of traditional Indian food. Like many gatherings at his home, this particular evening was a light-hearted casual social affair filled with conversation and laughter. However, proceedings were briefly and abruptly interrupted by a buzz from the front door security intercom. As no further guests were expected, Kamahl responded to the intercom. It was a young man who said, 'Hi, my name is Chris. Is this where Kamahl lives?' After nervously answering in the affirmative, Kamahl made his way to the front door to investigate. When he opened the door, he was confronted by what appeared to be a young newlywed couple dressed in a bridal dress and dinner suit. They were also accompanied by a small ABC TV film crew.

Satire program *The Chaser*, notorious for their audacious pranks, had decided to run a skit on how newlyweds could scam freebies just by relying on the goodwill of others toward them. Within the sketch, the couple had received free drinks from a liquor store, free meals from a five-star restaurant, free cinema entry, among many other things. As a finale for the skit, the program had decided on simply gate-crashing Kamahl's home at the end to try to get him to sing the 'bride's favourite romantic song. Despite his having no prior warning, far from 'turning out the hounds' to shoo away the interruption to his dinner party, he actually welcomed the couple and crew into his home. He introduced them to Sahodra and his guests and gladly then took on the task of singing the requested 'And I Love You So' as the 'newlyweds' slow danced in his lounge room. He reflects on the incident by saying, "I had no idea what was happening, but one thing for sure, I knew it was all a bit of harmless fun and far be it for me to be a stick in the mud. The way I looked at it, I could have overreacted and been indignant, acting like it was some kind of gross invasion of my privacy. I could also deal with it for what it was, a funny, harmless piece of television. Either way, I reacted. I am pretty sure that the show would have run it anyway. After all, an entertainer losing their mind on TV could have been just as funny for their audience. Besides, it gave my dinner guests another laugh for the night, one which I am sure made a memorable evening even more memorable."

Kamahl's attitude throughout the years has not shifted from the day he emerged from furtively rehearsing 'Nature Boy' under a blanket on his school's oval. He has always believed that an audience is an audience. Whether it is a theatre crowd, a TV audience, a group of people or an individual, it is his time to shine when it's showtime.

12

A jumbo hit

Tell me said the elephant
Tell me, brothers if you can
Why all the world is full of creatures
Yet we grow in fear of man
Tell me said the elephant
tell me why this has to be
we have to run from man and hunter
never safe and never free

People kill without regret
although they fly by jumbo-jet
let the word all may remember
Let the children not forget.

Gentle is the elephant
Pulling loads and everything
we love to hear the children laughing
when we're in the circus-ring

Happy was the elephant
Happy was his jungle life
and then they came, the cruel hunters
with their rifle and their knives

In 1975 Kamahl's tradition of unexpected opportunities continued. This time it came in a highly unlikely pachyderm proportioned package, 'The Elephant Song'. Initially entitled 'The Elephant's Plea', it had been written by Dutch composer Hans van Hemert in response to a request from the chief of Holland's TV Network AVRO-TV, Ger Lugtenburg. It was a most peculiar request. Lugtenburg asked Van Hemert how he would like to write a song about elephants for Frank Sinatra. The song was intended as the musical finale for a TV special for the World Wildlife Foundation. The WWF had as its patron HRH Prince Bernhard. He was a passionate conservationist keen to use his social standing to draw attention to the plight of elephants in the wild. The song, Lugtenburg explained, was to be performed by Sinatra at a televised gala launch before the Prince and Queen Juliana that the following summer. For a Dutch composer, this was a job that was impossible to refuse, and therefore he accepted the challenge immediately.

When the music had been completed, a lyricist named Gregor Frank was commissioned to apply the words to bring the song to life. Once this was achieved, they reached out to Sinatra to check his availabilities and preparedness to perform at the event. Who could have foreseen the failings of this plan? It would appear that the team in Holland had massively overestimated the allure of participating in the event to Old Blue Eyes, who was interested in neither the song nor the occasion.

Lutgenberg was facing two issues, he was without a singer, and he was running out of time.

Hans Van Hemert, in an attempt to rescue the project and ensure his song would see life, reached out to an old friend, Piet Schellevis, VP of Phonogram International, to see if he could recommend an artist with the voice and 'grandeur' to perform the number in a royal gala event. Just to add another level of complexity to Piet's challenge, Hans stated that the artist would have to be in Holland within twenty-four hours and block out all engagements for the following two weeks. Shellevis asked for a bit of time to take all of this in and promised that he would see what he could do. In less than one hour, he forwarded several albums to Van Hemert's home. This was highly fortuitous for Kamahl. He had an excellent relationship with Piet Schellevis from when he was working on the label in Sydney. Although he cannot prove it, he believes that Piet ensured that the album on top of that pile was the one belonging to Kamahl.

Kamahl, at this time, was becoming quite frustrated with his lack of progress in Britain. He had become a popular live performer on BBC2 playlists. Still, he had yet to achieve anything like a major breakthrough in Europe that he worked so hard to achieve. He had resolved that he would take up the matter with his old friend and VP of Phonogram, Piet Schellevis. Before he could, Piet had called him. He was asked if he could get on the first plane headed to Amsterdam to meet with the composer and TV Network Chief. Before he could make that call, he was in for a colossal surprise… The Dutch team had heard Kamahl's voice, knew it was what they wanted for the song and were determined to go ahead.

Not having listened to the piece, he politely said that he would like to reserve judgement until that had happened. A follow up meeting with the composer the very next day at which the song was played to Kamahl. He loved the song but was quite uncomfortable with the lyrics. It is not that the lyrics were wrong per se. It was just that when translated from the original Dutch into English, they had lost some of their meaning. The clock was ticking very loudly at this point as the recording deadline loomed large. It fell to the composer to inform his young lyricist that his words would need to be replaced by someone who had English as a first language. Frank luckily was philosophical about the problem at the time. He states, "I was told that Kamahl had been chosen and that he wanted changes to the lyrics and that the reason was that it would require someone who had English as a first language. If I said no to the rewrite, the song could not be recorded. If I agreed, I would get only half the residuals. I knew that Lugtenberg was pressed for time, so I made a business decision to do it. With hindsight, that may have been quite a naïve decision, as I never knew how big a hit it would become, but then again, no one did."

Having agreed to find a new lyricist for the song, Kamahl returned to London with two problems. He was working with a really tight deadline, and he had no idea who he could get to write the lyrics. As soon as he arrived in London, he called harmonica legend Larry Adler. Kamahl had met Larry socially sometime before and respected his views immensely. Adler had been around the British entertainment scene for decades and knew just about everyone in show business. Adler, without hesitation, recommended Roger Woddis. Kamahl, with even less hesitation, rang Woddis. He arranged to meet him in a Leicester Square pub the following evening, which was imperative as he had to be on a flight back to Amsterdam the next day. They came together for their hurriedly convened meeting in the crowded and noisy pub. Kamahl had to sing directly into Woddis' ear to be heard over the other patrons. To say the least, it was not a conventional meeting, and Kamahl reflects it may have looked quite like he was serenading a romantic interest. When Woddis said to Kamahl after only a short time, "I think I have the gist of it", he wasn't exactly filled with confidence. Good to his word, within a couple of hours, Woddis was on the phone with the first couple of lines, a short while later again with more lyrics. Finally, just before midnight, he came back with the chorus. Kamahl was relieved and extremely tired, confident Woddis was going to deliver precisely what he needed. He told him not to call again but instead meet him with the rest at Heathrow first thing in the morning with the completed lyrics.

Minutes before boarding his 9am flight the following day, Roger Woddis met Kamahl at the boarding gate with an envelope containing the final piece to 'The Elephant Song.'

Meanwhile, back in Amsterdam, Van Hemert was in the studio completing the musical arrangement in anticipation of Kamahl's arrival and the vocal track recording. Neither had worked together before, so there were reservations on both sides about how this would work out. The potential for this to go horribly wrong was significant. The composer had no idea if his singer would immediately grasp the arrangement. The singer had not heard the final instrumental arrangement. There was a lot of tension when it came time to lay down the vocal track. Van Hemert recalls "After this first few bars, I was reassured, the voice felt like a warm embrace, and I knew it was going to be good". Unfortunately, Kamahl's voice, having endured three crazy days without much rest, didn't want to go beyond that first few bars. It was gone. Nothing at all was coming out of his mouth. He was mute. The thing that could go horribly wrong did. Much panic ensued.

A singer Van Hemert knew quite well, Lenny Kuhr was married to a former Israeli Army doctor, Gideon Bjalistock. Gideon's surgery was thankfully very close by. Urgent phone calls were made, and Kamahl was despatched to the good doctor, who injected him with cortisone after inspecting the damage. He was back in the studio two hours later, with his voice totally restored. Kamahl recounts, "I think it was simply fatigue. I had been running around on pure adrenaline. I was like a man possessed trying to get this whole thing to happen. I had started to feel about the significance of this recording and what it may mean to open up a new market and audience for me. I had neglected what one needs to do every day to be healthy, a lesson well learned."

'The Elephant Song' was released on June 23rd in a slow sales period for music, early summer. The song's release had been held to this date by the request of AVRO-TV to use its recording as a trailer for Prince Bernhard's documentary, which was to screen six days later.

The song entered the Dutch charts at the 7th spot to everyone's great surprise and delight, blasting past a raft of international smash hits. Within a week, it hit number one, where it remained for the next six weeks.

As it happens, the chart success of 'The Elephant Song' was not the only triumph Kamahl would experience in Holland. His album release in July also charted at number one. To crown these achievements would be the performance of the song at the Royal Command gala launch. It received a standing ovation not only from the large crowd but from Queen Juliana and Prince Bernhardt. His European breakthrough had arrived, not through the United Kingdom as he had always thought it would, but from singing a song about an elephant in Holland.

Holland has always been an exceptional place for Kamahl, where to this day, he still has a highly active fan club. Another single was released in October that year, *Chanson D'Amour,* which would chart at number 10.

His work with the World Wildlife Foundation was also acknowledged when he was presented with a silver elephant figurine at a gala function at the stately Muiderslot Castle in September 1976.

Kamahl's chart success readily translated into a touring hit with sell-out crowds in Amsterdam, Rotterdam and Tilburg.

"When I look back at that period, it seems almost surreal as the whole thing came from left field. Firstly the opportunity is presented with the narrowest of windows to make it happen. When I needed lyrics, Larry Adler managed to pluck Roger Woddis out of thin air. My voice disappeared only to be rescued by Dr Gideon. We recorded the song, and it just went crazy… all of this coming from a song that took me only three minutes forty seconds to sing," he says.

It was crazy indeed. It not only provided Kamahl with the international record success he had always wanted, but it also raised much-needed funds for WWF's conservation work. As a dedicated conservationist, Kamahl had always been a great supporter of the WWF and their work.

He was to follow up 'The Elephant Song' over the next few years with two further hits produced as fundraising vehicles for the WWF, 'Save the Oceans' and 'Save the Whale', written by Van Hemert, Roger Woddis and of course Kamahl. He remembers being invited to a function a day after his birthday to commemorate the release of 'Save The Whale'. He says, "At the function, which was well covered by media, they presented me with a huge cake for my birthday. Believe it or not they had made it in a giant whale-shaped with a gelatinous topping. They were trying to get me to cut the damned thing which I refused to do. You can just imagine the photographs of me sticking a huge knife into the image of a whale," he laughs. "Sometimes even the most well-intentioned people can do the silliest things."

Kamahl also became a firm friend of Dutch royalty. He was invited several times to perform for them at high-profile gala events and was a guest at the Palace on many occasions.

Meeting Royalty also managed to help Kamahl do something extraordinary for his ageing father. He wrote to the Prince enquiring if it were possible to provide recognition from the people of the Netherlands to his father for his role in saving the lives of Dutch POW's during the war. He decided against mailing it to the Palace, as he deduced that it would be handled by many administrators and protocol police. Kamahl chose to hand the letter to the Prince in person on stage during a Royal Presentation. Kamahl's stage attire really didn't lend itself to an inside pocket, so he had it tucked into his trouser back pocket. When the Prince arrived, Kamahl shuffled about with his hand to retrieve it. There was an awkward but thankfully brief security moment as the burly guard beside the Prince looked set to pounce if a weapon materialised from under Kamahl's kaftan. When he produced the envelope to great relief, it was gladly accepted by the Prince. To Kamahl's great delight, the Prince did indeed oblige with a letter of commendation to his father. He was finally recognised for his bravery all those years before.

Based on the tremendous success with the single and album in The Netherlands, Phonogram was keen to release 'The Elephant Song' in the UK. They had negotiated a royalty for the World Wildlife Foundation. They packaged the single with 'One Hundred Children' on the flip side under the title *It's My World Too*. The rerelease did not receive a great deal of commercial success, something that Kamahl had sadly grown used to in the UK. It was October, and whilst the record company was doing its thing with the record, Kamahl went back to where he did enjoy success. He continued on with his Talk of the Town season, which was drawing to a close by this stage. At one of his last performances, he was approached backstage after the show by Elisabeth Skovdam. She introduced herself by saying, "I'm from Phonogram Denmark, and I can make you a star in Denmark. Can we have lunch?" Kamahl was taken aback by her direct approach and somewhat sceptically agreed to meet the next day at a local Italian restaurant. Skovdam explained at lunch, she had been made aware of 'The Elephant Song's success in the Netherlands. She believed that if he would come to Copenhagen for a week's long promotional tour with media appearances, she could get him a number one hit. She went on to say that her boss had approved her making the approach and had even signed off on her proposal but had told her that he had no belief that they would sell more than a few records. Kamahl was surprised but nonetheless greatly impressed in such faith being shown in him. Unsure if it was her kick the door down approach or his own pride in the product being challenged, he was up for it.

Within days of his promotional visit, Denmark had a new number one on its charts. This spread to a number two in Sweden, a number three in Norway and a number four in Finland. Elisabeth Skovdam's faith had paid off handsomely for Phonogram and left more than a bit of egg on the face of her boss.

After this, he was contacted by a company in Germany who were keen to hop on the 'Elephant' cart. Unfortunately, they were insistent that the song be re-recorded in German. "Having quite a bit of operatic training, I was used to singing in German, but the song just didn't work in that language. I also feel that quite unlike Scandinavia politically, Germany was less attuned to progressive issues like conservation at that time.

Hence, the record failed to set the world alight. Ossie Drechsler, one of Philips Records senior people, told me that I sang with the best German accent he had ever heard. Whilst that was nice to hear, it meant very little when they didn't buy my record."

Kamahl, possibly still riding the massive wave of Netherlands and Scandinavian success, took a relatively relaxed attitude to the German experience. He wrote it down to a missed opportunity from the record company who had made a critical mistake of insisting that the language was more important than the song itself.

Kamahl's European sojourn interestingly provided him with a connection to his much younger years. As a young boy in Malaysia, he was acquainted with a young girl named Sothie Durasame. Sothie was from a highly respected Sri Lankan Tamil family much like his own. Unlike his Hindu parents, however, the Durasame's were Christian. He only remembers this because he got his first acting role playing Joseph opposite her Mary in a Nativity play when eight or nine years of age. "Sothie was a really nice kid. However, I am ashamed to say that I went through almost my entire youth resenting her awfully. She was one of those high achievers that did extremely well at everything. No matter what she turned her hand to, she was just brilliant. Consequently, my parents, in what I assume was their ham-fisted attempt at motivation, continually used her as a shining example of what I wasn't: studious, dedicated, and committed. The case of 'Sothie has just passed her exams with high distinctions, what are you doing just scraping by? Sothie just got moved ahead a year, she is leaving you behind and so on?' So, without this poor girl even knowing it, she became a kind of nemesis to me. When she was inevitably packed off to finish her schooling in London, I actually thought they may let up. Still, no, it continued as she, of course, was successful, completing her studies in London, and the news kept coming back home. I was leaving a lot to be desired in career progression, a mere entertainer just getting by. I was getting Sothie'd by long-distance."

Many years later, Sothie, now a successful concert pianist, had married and settled down with a man named Louis. He was a Dutch national with Sri Lankan heritage who was an engineer with the Shell Oil Company. They had settled in his hometown of Rotterdam. Kamahl, at this point, was himself a very high achiever, having gained fame and familial approval for the career that he had forged out of nothing in Australia. "Through our families who remained in close contact in KL, Sothie managed to communicate to me that she would like to catch up next time that I visited Holland. As it happened, I was touring a short while later and arranged to catch up with her and Louis for dinner at their home. It was an enjoyable time for a couple of reasons. Firstly it was nice to see her again and to see that she was happily married to a really great fellow, but more than this, it killed the one-sided feud that I had been having in my own mind all of those years. I finally realised that my resentment was entirely due to her success being used as a cudgel by my own family to motivate me. It wasn't that she had been a high achiever to spite me, she was just a talented person, and that should have been a joy for me. It just goes to show what can happen when you allow others to frame someone in a certain light."

One of the more amusing highlights of the evening was Louis' revelation that all of his workmates had nicknamed him Kamahl. Louis' workmates had given him the nickname Kamahl as he was the only high profile Sri Lankan, that they knew of.

Several years later, Kamahl was asked to perform at a birthday celebration in Kuala Lumpur for Sothie's younger sister Gnanan. She was a few years younger than them and had, like Sothie, been an academic high-flyer. Her chosen profession was medicine, where she had become a distinguished doctor on her way to becoming the Head of Haematology at a prestigious hospital in Malaysia. The event was a somewhat formal affair with over 500 guests. "I was delighted to perform for my 'home' crowd and family once again. When I saw Sothie and Louis, however, I was struck by the fact that he was in a wheelchair and seemed very frail. I learned that he was in the late stages of aggressive terminal cancer. It was so sad. I remember him being seated up front and catching a glimpse of him during the ovation. He obviously couldn't stand but was applauding enthusiastically from his chair and was tearing up as he smiled broadly. I found out later that he died early in the new year. Such a great shame, I still keep in touch with Sothie from time to time just to see how she is doing, and I am very pleased to say that there isn't a hint of the silly resentment that I inappropriately carried with me for those years."

13

A high tea

There is no trouble so great or grave that cannot be diminished by a nice cup of tea.

Bernard-Paul Heroux

Kamahl was always an odd choice as a spokesperson for a tea company. While he was exposed to the almost mythical benefits of tea drinking throughout his entire life, he has never been a tea drinker himself. In fact, he always was and still is a dedicated coffee man. This may come as a bit of a surprise for those who have associated Kamahl's name and image with the Sri Lankan tea brand Dilmah for many years. Even more surprising for many Australians to learn just how short his association with Dilmah actually was. He appeared on the TV screen for a mere three years, from 1988–1991. It is a testament to the effectiveness of the use of Kamahl in those early campaigns that many still recall his presence. The campaign saw Dilmah become a serious competitor in the hot beverage market and gave them such a great communication platform for years afterwards.

"My manager at the time, John Hansen, was approached initially to see if I would be interested in doing the commercials. He told me that they were looking for a recognisable brand ambassador to front the ads that would help them lift awareness in Australia. Apparently, my name came up, as did John Farnham, who was going through a career resurgence at the time. What John Farnham and I had in common as presenters remains to be seen, but who am I to question the wisdom of the gurus of advertising? I have to admit I was not keen at all and said no to Hansen. He managed to persuade me that it would be a good fit and would allow me to maintain my profile whilst being paid for the privilege. Reluctantly I agreed to take the meeting with their ad agency to review what was being proposed. I'm not sure if their head creative genius had ever read *How to win friends and influence people,* but I was told that he had said, 'I don't drink tea, and I don't like Kamahl but somehow bringing the two of them together is as logical a union as a horse and a cart.' I was never sure if I was meant to be the horse or the cart in his scenario; however, I was absolutely convinced which part of a horse he was. They told me that the ads were to be shot in Sri Lanka. I was to provide a voice to some vision of me being driven through tea fields, and I was to sing the backing track, a bespoke jingle for Dilmah. It all sounded straightforward enough, although I would have to say the financial benefit was far less than I thought it was worth. I am sure far less than the public would ever believe."

Dilmah is very much a family business based in Sri Lanka. It was founded in 1988 by patriarch Merrill J Fernando and run by him and his two sons Dilhan and Malik. The company's name is, in fact, a combination of the two boys' names. Like most family businesses, the purse strings are tightly controlled. They are not prone to frivolous spending, and very few decisions of significance are delegated to underlings. When it came to the image of the company, this was even more, the case. Any meeting or discussion relating to the advertising, creative content, execution, and costs were all strictly family-controlled.

"I am sure that the ad agency when they suggested me for the campaign, thought that they were making a suggestion based upon pure logic. You know a Sri Lankan company needing a personal face in Australia? They figured Kamahl is an Australian of Sri Lankan descent hence a perfect fit. It was a suggestion that ignored just how complex a culture like Sri Lanka really is. Certainly, I am ethnically Sri Lankan, but I am a Tamil. The Fernandos are Sinhalese, so there is a vast difference in our backgrounds, religion, and social standing in Sri Lanka. Horse and cart analogies aside, this was not as great a fit as our mate in the advertising agency had thought. The most obvious social implications related to the fact that the Sinhalese are the dominant ethnic group in the country and, as such, tend to have most of the power and wealth. In this instance, the Sinhalese owner of a tea empire was hiring a presenter from the Tamil community, the same community that had historically provided his field workers and labourers. Although never overtly raised, I always felt that Merrill was always in the background of negotiation of fees and contracts as he never really viewed me as anything other than the hired help. At one stage, well into the relationship, I was alerted that Dilmah ran the campaign without my permission in countries not covered by my contract. Whilst compensation was eventually paid, it was only my pointing it out that made payment happen. I also had no idea how long the ads had been running as I only had their word that this was a one-off mistake. At the risk of sounding immodest, this was a brand that had practically no recognition in the country before my profile was added to it. It was a hugely successful launch that saw them capture a significant slice of the market, lifting it to being the number two tea in Australia. Being the keen promoter I am, if I present for a brand, I will always go the extra mile to look for opportunities to push it. For example, during our association, I would send the product to on-air personalities who would plug Dilmah without any charge, which all added value to the relationship and the awareness of Dilmah. If I was sending a gift basket to anyone, Dilmah Tea was always present. I take my role as a brand ambassador very seriously. If I add my name to something, there is an expectation that I support it one hundred percent. I even sent the product to the Royal Family in Holland at my own expense." Kamahl added so much value to the company, believing quite reasonably that this would be a long-term relationship. He was, therefore, most surprised when he was informed after three years that he would no longer be required. "I was disappointed, to be honest, as I felt a bit used and underappreciated, but that is the way things go. I held no ill will toward the company or the family for that matter. They made decisions that I am sure they felt were in their best interests. I even agreed to appear in an ad they ran to celebrate their twenty-fifth anniversary in 2013. I do sometimes ask the question if they hadn't had such a successful launch if they would have made it that far".

One interesting side issue coming from the production of the original Dilmah commercial that sticks in his mind was an incident at Nuwara Eliya. This is a town near the plantation where the first ad was to be shot. A young English guy had been assigned to chaperone Kamahl when he was on the shoot to provide him with any assistance he may require whilst travelling. One of his tasks was to arrange for accommodation at a grand hotel in the nearby town. Kamahl recalls, "This young fellow who travelled with me was a very nice, very pukka young English guy, extremely helpful and attentive. When we arrived at the hotel, one of those really grand colonial places that you only see in movies, we checked in, and I was taken by a bellboy to my room. When I reached the room and saw that it was a straightforward, no-frills affair. I thought, oh well, so be it. I was disappointed that it wasn't a suite, but I wasn't about to play the precious star and ask to see the manager. When it came to work, I had been in much worse places over the years. Then just when I started to unpack, there was a knock at the door. A couple of hotel staff accompanied my English companion, who was very contrite and apologised profusely, saying there had been a mix up with the rooms. I was to be taken to my suite, which had been mistakenly assigned to my assistant. Hotel staff had assumed that the white person they were checking in was obviously of greater social standing than I and would naturally be assigned the suite. When I got to the actual room I should have been given in the first place, it was very grand and really opulent, totally different to the original. It may sound like a small mistake, but I had actually been racially profiled as the lesser important of the two of us. This was in my own ancestral homeland just because of my appearance. I have often joked that I never needed to go very far at all to find racism. It was always there in front of me."

His visit to his ancestral homeland had been a bit of an eye-opener for Kamahl. On the way back to Colombo he needed to make a phone call to his friend Tanya Shand, then the Australian High Commissioner to Sri Lanka. The Shands were good friends, and he had agreed to stay with them whilst in town, and he wanted to inform them of his estimated time of arrival. Mobile phones in the eighties were not at all commonly used. They were sized like a giant house brick and required a massive charging case. The mobile network infrastructure was sparse, meaning poor signal in metropolitan areas and zero in regional locations. Public phones were practically non-existent in the very rural territory they were travelling through. Someone in the party suggested they drop into a small community bank en route. There, they kill two birds with one stone by exchanging some currency whilst requesting us their phones. It sounded like a perfect idea to Kamahl, and a bank was located fairly shortly afterwards. Kamahl recounts. "When I walked into that bank which was staffed entirely by Sinhalese workers, I felt as welcome as Bonnie and Clyde. There were security guards armed with massive weapons everywhere, all seemingly on red alert at the sight of a Tamil. The staff were quite rude and officious. They seemed extremely keen to have me out of there in short order. Having spent a good proportion of my life being regarded as different to others, I know those looks and that attitude. I just hadn't experienced it from people I wouldn't have expected it from.

Interestingly when I informed the person behind the counter that I needed to contact the Australian High Commissioner, the attitude changed immediately. I was introduced to the manager and politely ushered into his office to use his phone. I suppose it just shows what happens when society conforms to a social structure that defers to status. There will always be someone perceived to be higher up the ladder. It was as if I had played a racial trump card by introducing an officer of a white government, a senior one at that. Sri Lanka is a beautiful country, and I mostly enjoyed my trip but the unrest between the Tamils and Sinhalese at the time of my journey was quite unsettling for me."

14

The kamahlcoholics

Spread love everywhere you go. Let no one ever come to you without leaving happier.

Mother Teresa

In any lengthy career in show business, it is not unknown for an artist to gain a following that sticks with them through thick and thin. Kamahl is definitely no exception to that rule, having accumulated a significant loyal following both at home and abroad. One such dedicated fan is Marianne Mellema from the Netherlands, who started a Facebook Fan page many years ago. The page, which she respectfully sought Kamahl's permission to start, is updated lovingly and diligently. It features practically all you would ever need to know about Kamahl's career and music. She has catalogued his songs on the site and has shared his career highlights and thoughts with various quotes and video clips. Her dedication over the years has been exceptional.

Starting in the seventies when she was just thirteen years old. At the height of Kamahl's popularity in her home country, she first saw him appear on Dutch TV when promoting his number one hit, 'The Elephant Song'. When asked what it was about Kamahl as a performer that has made her such a stalwart of support, she says, "He is great. I think his singing is beautiful. His live performances are just incredible. I have attended every concert in my country other than the few just too far from my home. Mostly wherever and whenever he has appeared in Holland, I have been there for the last few decades. One concert really stands out for me in particular. He performed with a large choir in the Der Aa-kerk, a large historic church in Groningen. It was a stunning performance and a magical evening. When the show finished, one of the choir members came to me and said, 'I have enjoyed watching you all evening because you never stopped singing along to all of the songs.' I was so surprised that one of the performers had been watching my performance. It made me very happy." Marianne has collected many things over the years. Still, none are as treasured as the pictures she has had taken with him. "My first meeting with Kamahl was in 1994. In a church in Maassluis, I was so happy to see him in real life after being such a big fan for over 19 years. Then I was going to meet him in person. My husband was with me, and he says he had to keep me calm. I was so happy I wanted to fly over the pews. It was an indescribable feeling, my idol…his music and voice supported me in good and bad times. My mother allowed me to join the fan club when I was still young, and I am still grateful to her. When I first saw him on television, I was so deeply moved by that beautiful voice… It was amazing," she recalls.

"When I first became interested in Kamahl, there were no online forum platforms back in the seventies. We had a fan club newsletter called *Kamahl Fanclub* from 1976 to 1982. It grew so much it started to circulate outside of Holland. So the name changed to the *International Kamahl Fanclub*. At the height of his popularity in Europe in the seventies, this fan club was massive. It had thousands of members who would exchange stories, articles and information on him, his tours, recordings and other general interesting facts. There were so many of us who were very active. He was a huge star with a following as big as any I have seen before or since." When asked which of the many songs she would say was her very favourite, she says with little hesitation, "'Rainbow'. It is such a beautiful song about racial harmony."

Kamahl's fan base in Australia was no less dedicated and organised by Eve Cain. In the seventies, she had formed the *Friends of Kamahl*, which had members right across the country and ran for decades. Like their Dutch counterparts, they shared stories and information. They were invited to send fan mail to a PO box which was tended to by Eve and provided directly to Kamahl. Some years after the club started, the responsibility was taken over by Vivienne Green. Both ladies always diligently ensured that Kamahl got his mail. In one letter he received, a fan told him that her husband had become so enraged with her continued playing his music, he had hurled her tape deck to the ground smashing the machine to pieces. She responded by threatening to take their children and leave forever if it wasn't replaced immediately. According to the fan, her husband had sheepishly complied with the demand.

Dennis Smith recalls, "Kamahl was always a big hit with the ladies. Some were incredibly dedicated. In 1974, after a week-long booking at Melbourne's Dallas Brooks Hall, Betty Elden, the wife of a highly respected member of the city's business community, turned up with her daughter and sat in the front row for every performance the whole week. Both Betty and her daughter were huge fans, and after the final performance, they invited Kamahl and me back to their home for coffee ... all totally harmless. Basically Betty poured coffee and chatted, and the daughter played Kamahl's latest album not terribly rock'n'roll. Well, not until one o'clock in the morning when suddenly John her visibly irate husband appeared in the room dressed only in his pyjamas. He stomped over to the stereo, grabbed the album off it and flung it out the window like a discus. Without uttering one single word, he glowered at us, turned on his heel and departed upstairs back to his interrupted slumber. I guessed he mustn't have shared his family's taste in music."

Even though Kamahl's concert audiences always seemed to be overloaded with oestrogen, many husbands and boyfriends initially were reluctant attendees. They however became begrudgingly engaged by the good-humoured banter and skilled performance. It would be fair to say, even though very few may have rushed out and bought a kaftan, their attitude toward Kamahl as a performer and celebrity had warmed. He was known as a really safe bet for a generation of men wanting to impress their better half with a date to show their partners that they were in touch with a more romantic side.

Whilst it has been a few years since Kamahl last recorded, his extensive back catalogue still sells well and attracts followers from all around the globe. For example, he received a recent email from Sussana Tarjan, the daughter of Jerome Moross, a famed American composer most remembered for his iconic soundtrack of the Hollywood Western classic *A Big Country*, for which he was nominated for an Academy Award. She was writing in her capacity as the curator of her father's incredible collection. Sussana expressed her great admiration of Kamahl's version of one of her father's songs 'Lazy Afternoon', which was also one of her favourites. Someone evidently posted the song on the official Jerome Moross Facebook fan page. Her email read:

Greetings Kamahl,

Your version of 'Lazy Afternoon' was profiled on the Jerome Moross Facebook page recently, and I wanted to let you know how much I loved it. Thank you for including it in your album.

While I was listening, I thought that another song, 'Ridin' On The Breeze' from Ballet Ballads, would be perfect for your voice and style. It's from an earlier show my father wrote with John Latouche.

If you check out the www.moross.com website, it is on the recording titled 'Windflowers.' It is written for a baritone, but it is sung by a tenor on the recording. I hope you will check it out.

Thanks again for your interest in my father's music.

Best regards,

Sussana

Kamahl was so surprised to be contacted fifty-two years after he recorded the song with a compliment and suggested other pieces that would suit his style. He says, "It always amazes me that after so many years, someone would take the trouble to reach out with such a lovely comment. I recorded 'Lazy Afternoon' way back in 1969. Yet, fifty-two years later, I received feedback from the daughter of the actual composer. It is not only flattering but really quite humbling. To know that she was so moved to contact me after all of these years. As performers, we are so lucky to have a permanent record of our work. Long after we are here, there will be something that people once again will remember us by and causes them to think of us so fondly. After receiving her note, Susanna and I had a call in which she shared some great stories with me about her father and his collaborations with superstars like Streisand and many other incredible artists."

The Kamahlcaholics are a highly protective bunch, as was evidenced in 2007 when a report emerged in the *Sydney Telegraph* that Kamahl had been killed in an accident involving electrocution. Kamahl was actually touring in Malaysia at the time, so the story was allowed to get a little currency before Sahodra started receiving a flood of tribute cards and flowers at their home which alerted them to this story. When Kamahl was finally contacted, it emerged it had been either a case of mistaken identity, a hoax or just a plainly stupid rumour. Frustratingly, the story could've easily have been verified if the reporter had a little more energy, as Kamahl remains one of the most accessible stars in the country. Kamahl has never met a pun he didn't like, so he delighted in responding to the *Telegraph*, "That's a shocking rumour if you will forgive me for making a joke," Just like Mark Twain before him when he had said in similar circumstances many years before, "reports of my death had been greatly exaggerated."

His fans' commitment to Kamahl is part of a long-term reciprocal relationship. During an appearance on the *Pete Murray Show* on BBC Radio 1 back in the seventies, the show took a call from a fan in a small town called Pitlochry in Scotland. Pitlochry is located near Perth in the Scottish Highlands and is way off the beaten track for entertainers. The caller opined how much of a great fan she and her friends were and how it would be great if Kamahl could ever see his way to perform in her town. Kamahl had never heard of the city much less locate it on a map. He wasn't even sure how to pronounce its name. Determined to not disappoint his followers however, he committed on the spot to do a performance. This commitment was arranged and followed through. A concert was held at the Pitlochry Festival Theatre to packed house a few weeks later. His grateful fans presented him with a canteen of cutlery with bone handles to show their genuine appreciation. "They were great people and even gave me a special round of applause for getting the pronunciation of their town name correct," he reflects.

Another far-away place that Kamahl developed into a long-lasting relationship was Hawaii, specifically the Royal Hawaiian Hotel. He performed for an annual season with a cabaret show for many years. During these many tours, he became acquainted with a couple who attended every performance, Toki and Percy Anzai. The couple had met in Hawaii years earlier when Toki, a Japanese migrant, had met Percy, a statuesque blonde Canadian lady. Despite their diverse backgrounds, the two shared an interest in the beauty industry. They would combine this interest and successfully build a multiple outlet businesses throughout the islands. One of these outlets was a salon in the Royal Hawaiian Hotel itself. Whilst many entertainers have a mindset of keeping fans at arm's length and have an almost obsessive desire to maintain a private life, Kamahl has a totally different approach. He has no issue with people becoming his friend, "To be perfectly honest, I have never really sought to have that much privacy in my life. For me, what you see is pretty much what you get, so there are no dark secrets to shield the world from. If people like my music, my shows and like me, and I like them, I think that is a great start to a friendship. I struggle with drawing an arbitrary line between fans and friends. I always hope that people can be both. Toki and Percy never missed one of my shows, and they became great loyal friends of ours. They retired to Reno some years back, and unfortunately, Percy passed away back in 2007 which was very sad. I still talk to Toki regularly."

15

That fine line between pleasure and pain

We cannot learn without pain.

Aristotle

O ver the years Kamahl has at times been beset by a number
of potentially career threatening maladies that could have
brought his career to a premature end. For anyone to be
incapacitated temporarily with any illness or medical condition is a major
source of frustration and annoyance to them. For an entertainer, being
laid low by anything at all, the impact seems devastating. Firstly they have
to deal with the fear that the condition may be long term, or even worse,
permanent. There is something far worse however that they have to deal
with. Being forced out of the public eye, being de-staged, left without
their audience and the applause.

In the late seventies Kamahl had started to experience pain in his lower
stomach region when performing. Although not acute initially it was
nonetheless troubling and highly distracting particularly when singing
at the extremes of his range. As is the case with many men, he views
doctors as only useful when a limb is likely to fall off and they are needed
to reattach it. He therefore suffered in silence and soldiered on until the
pain became too much. When he finally did seek help, the news was

predictably not great. The diagnosis was that he had an inguinal hernia. This type of hernia occurs when tissue, such as part of the intestine, protrudes through a weak spot in the abdominal muscles. Whilst he was a little relieved that it wasn't something far more serious, the prognosis gave him little to cheer about. He would require surgery at some point in the near future and he was cautioned about exerting himself. When you make a living which requires significant use of your abdominal muscles on a nightly basis to push out notes both deep and high, this was a problem. As at this point his career was starting to climb and time away from it to have an operation and convalesce meant time off, time he could not afford. Therefore in his mind it was clearly not an option, not to him anyway. He did what many do, he equipped himself with a truss, a supportive undergarment designed to keep the protruding tissue in place with a strategically positioned pad. When worn the pressure of the pad provided some relief to the discomfort. Whilst such devices work they don't treat the hernia at all. He recalls, "I just couldn't allow that damned hernia to slow me down at that point, I resigned myself that the operation was absolutely necessary but that I would deal with it in time but not now. There was a funny moment with that truss, once when I was on a trip to Nashville the security guys at the airport pulled me up for a random check of my luggage. The guy ran across the truss and pulled it out asked me what the padded part in my 'underpants' was. I was very embarrassed and self-conscious about it and ridiculously blurted out that it was a tampon! To this day I have no idea why that was the first thing that came to mind, but it must've sounded so weird to the security guy he just handed the bag back to me with a really puzzled look on his face and waved me on." Kamahl also claims that when he performed at Carnegie Hall he had a microphone in his left hand whilst his right was in his pocket pushing the hernia in place. "The audience were none the wiser thankfully. It may have taken a little bit of the gloss off the performance if they had realised the man crooning romantic songs to them was holding his insides in to prevent them from falling on to the stage," he laughs.

Finally succumbing to the pain and Sahodra's insistence the operation was booked and dealt with permanently. The hernia whilst it was painful he believes it was nowhere near as scary as his next medical problem.

In 1979, he was shaving and noticed that his face was swollen on one side and he was experiencing significant numbness in his jaw. A quick self-analysis determined that this was some type of deep-rooted dental issue. He got himself off to the family dentist as soon as he could thinking that he would walk out of there that same afternoon totally repaired. After preliminary x-rays the suggestion was put forward that he may be having issues with his bite. Much to his dismay, he was informed that the issue required far more than mere dentistry. This was a case for far more specialised attention. His dentist therefore suggested that he see an orthodontist as soon as possible. A referral was written, and a booking made for a consultation later that day. In that time, the discomfort had been increasing, possibly exacerbated by the stress of the unknown nature of the cause. During this consultation he heard the specialist's dreaded words, it was not problem with his teeth, his gums, his bite or his jaw.

In fact, all were in fine shape. Kamahl returned to his dentist and was referred to a neurosurgeon. Whilst Kamahl is not generally a worrier, when being told that he may have a problem inside his head, his heart sank, and he couldn't help but think the worst. Driving his Roll Royce on his way to the Macquarie Street neurologist, he noticed a ragged individual riding on a rickety old pushbike. "When I saw this scruffy looking guy who looked down on his luck, I couldn't help but think that I would trade spots with him right now in a heartbeat, I was convinced I was headed into the worst possible news." He was sent off to St Vincent's Hospital for brain scans and it transpired that the scans would show nothing life-threatening. However, the specialist confirmed that he had the symptoms of Bell's palsy, a condition that causes a temporary weakness or paralysis of the muscles in the face. Although still the subject of ongoing research on the causes of the condition it is believed by most medical experts to be a viral infection. The infection inflames and puts pressure on the nerve that controls the facial muscles. It can be mild, or it can be severe. One thing for certain, it was far from conducive to either singing or being seen until it passed. Kamahl's doctor informed him that it was just one of those things that had to be waited out. Generally, the symptoms would pass within a few weeks and would resume to normal after that. He says, "It was incredibly uncomfortable as not only does half of your face feel like it is about a foot lower than the other, but there are also things that you just can't do. Your speech is slurred and one of your eyes is frozen open as the lid loses its function. I had to put drops into it constantly. Of course I had to wipe my schedule for weeks ahead including a season at The Talk of The Town in London. The doctor told me that I would be laid low for at least six weeks. It was truly awful, I had to hold my lips up to even speak, and the dribble?? One thing the doctor did mention was that I would know the worst of it was over when I could whistle again. Strange advice I thought as I had never been a great whistler before but nonetheless I took it on board. It truly isn't a disease for anyone with the slightest bit of vanity as when you look in the mirror you see Quasimodo looking back at you." Several weeks after his diagnosis, Kamahl sat up in bed at three am and started whistling, much to his delight. He was so excited that he woke Sahodra to demonstrate his impromptu bird impressions. Whilst she was naturally relieved she would've probably preferred if he had waited to accompany the birds themselves a couple of hours later rather than do a solo act in the middle of the night. What followed was twelve weeks of therapy at Sydney's Adventist Hospital so that he could make a full recovery. Bell's palsy would go on to play an interesting role in his life some years later in a most unexpected way. He had been invited to one of those celebrity lunch functions that entertainers are compelled to attend by those who advise them. He found that he was to be seated next to George Clooney, also a guest at the function. Whilst this no doubt may have delighted most, if not all of the female attendees, he struggled to think of anything he could possibly have in common with the Hollywood icon. Little did he know that George had had his own experience with Bell's palsy in his life. "We chatted on for ages about our experiences, he turned out to be a really great guy. Who knew we would have anything in common, other than our both being ageing sex symbols of course," he says with a loud laugh.

Kamahl's third health crisis was in 1982 and this time it gave him one of the greatest fear of all as it temporarily stole from him his means of living. Early that year Kamahl had released his *25th Anniversary Album* and as per usual he was looking for any opportunity to promote the release. He had agreed to appear on an ABC Radio program hosted by Peter Ross. As usual he wanted to leave a big impression and decided that he would perform a substantial piece for the audience to showcase his skills. He reasoned that since this was an audio appearance and a kaftan creates little impression on radio the bigger the piece, the better. The song he was to perform was Handel's 'Hear Me Ye Winds and Waves' from *Julius Caesar*, a very demanding operatic piece. In those days, Kamahl's preparation ritual was to simply turn up, no warm-up, no throat protection, he would literally just get to the show and sing. During the performance he remembers that it felt like something just gave way, it didn't affect the performance at all but the sensation he felt gave him pause for concern. He quickly got over it however and resumed his promotional tour in earnest. A few weeks later he would find himself atop a lighthouse being filmed for *The Today Show*. He was to sing 'Born Free' and managed to get all the way through the number without much incident until he had to push that big finish. Once again he sensed the same sensation that he had noticed at the ABC shortly before. Still unfazed by this development he proceeded to set out on his Queensland tour. Shortly into the schedule it became clear that he had damaged his voice. Seeking out professional advice from his doctor, he was sent off on referral to a speech pathologist who diagnosed the damage. He had suffered a prolapsed false vocal cord. The treatment he was prescribed hit him hard. He was told to stay home for six weeks and relax his voice. Not using his voice was like telling a long-distance runner to crawl. It was a bitter pill, but he was persuaded to swallow that pill or face permanent damage. His therapist chided him for his non-existent warm up before performances, telling him that just like an athlete's muscles, vocal cords required training to stay in shape. He had six weeks in rehabilitation where he would attend sessions designed to improve the damage with corrective vocal exercises. When fully recovered he swore that he would always exercise his instrument prior to performing, irrespective of the size, length or scope of the show.

Quite soon after Kamahl's recovery from the prolapse his most significant health scare emerged. It would eclipse all that went before it in both severity and significance. Somewhat chastened by his false vocal cord prolapse he had been very mindful of exposure to any illness that would jeopardise his voice. It was therefore of concern when Sahodra had noticed a swelling, a lump on his throat. Ever the optimist, he reasoned that he may have just over developed a muscle from all of the singing over the years. However if that were the case it appeared that it was in muscle growth hyperdrive. Soon, his shirts were needing to be replaced on almost a monthly basis because the collars were only meant to fit Kamahl's neck and not an ever-growing passenger. He realised that he had to face the music and headed off to the doctor, who in turn referred him to an endocrinologist. The news wasn't good. He was diagnosed with the aptly titled Graves' disease, an autoimmune condition that causes the thyroid to swell up to twice its normal size. The most notable symptoms include disturbed sleep and irritability. The remedy was medication that would control the condition of the thyroid. This treatment worked to a point but was by no means a cure for the condition which he would go on to suffer for a further nine years. In 2003 as part of his maintenance of the condition he was referred to another specialist who matter-of-factly advised him that he needed to have an operation. When asked if the operation could have had any lasting effect on his voice, the good doctor quite dismissively stated that it was quite likely that he would have significant changes to deal with, or as he put it. "With an operation like this, it is extremely invasive, and damage can result, it is like a drum. When you alter the skin of the drum, after you adjust it, it's likely that it will never sound the same again." Kamahl was shocked by the almost casual manner in which this specialist had dealt with a threat to his livelihood and decided to ignore his advice and seek another opinion. Thankfully the second specialist had a vastly improved bedside manner and whilst still recommending the operation, a thyroidectomy, he gave Kamahl an easier feeling about placing his glands in his hands. In basic terms, a thyroidectomy involves having the throat cut open and the removal of bits that shouldn't be there. It isn't as some may deduce by the name a removal of the thyroid gland. It is a complex and delicate operation due to its proximity to the vocal cords. As terrified as he was to even contemplate a failed procedure, he gritted his teeth and allowed his surgeon, Professor Leigh Delbridge, to work his magic. Kamahl emerged extremely sore and sorry and headed home for recovery. "Getting my voice back to normal was a tedious exercise requiring daily therapy. It was almost like learning how to walk again." He was filled with a dread that his voice may never sound the same again, but little by little it started to return and improve. He had been given strict instruction from the doctor that he should avoid exerting his voice at all for at least six weeks. Kamahl took this strict advice literally and had arranged a double booking the very day that six weeks elapsed. A show at the Rosehill Exhibition Centre followed later that evening by performing at a close friend's wedding. "I really shouldn't have done either but, it all went fine, and the voice was back to where it was, and six weeks is six weeks after all" He says, "I was so grateful to the Professor and his team who literally saved my voice. It is a very tricky piece of surgery and quite a number of people have been nowhere near as lucky as myself with the outcome. Julie Andrews for example had the very same procedure around the same time as I did. She evidently lost most of her four-octave range, effectively most of her singing voice. I shudder to think what I would have been like if that happened."

Within each of these health issues, Kamahl claims to have to have learned a valuable lesson. To never take your health for granted and listen to the experts, they know what they are doing. "I am very stubborn by nature so changing my mind on things is always a challenge, just ask Sahodra! However when it comes to health, there is just no point in listening to your own counsel. Doctors will always know more about any ailment that you have or find floating around on the internet. Ignoring my symptoms almost cost me my whole career before it really took off, so ever since I have learned where I should place my trust, and that is to trust in science."

The most persistent health issues that Kamahl has faced in his life date back to 1972. He was in Rio de Janeiro at International Music Festival where he had reached the finals. Maurice Guardrio an executive from his label Phonogram, had offered to take he and Sahodra sight-seeing during one of his rare breaks from the competition. They gladly accepted and he duly arrived along with uniformed chauffeur in a grand old shiny black Humber Super Snipe. It was quite luxuriously appointed and built like a small tank with lots of metal and chrome. Riding in it was like sitting in a mobile lounge room from another era. As they were returning to their hotel in the heart of Copacabana a motorcycle was attempting to pass them. Their driver was either unaware of its presence or simply didn't want to be passed. Kamahl, having some experience of the driving standards in South America favours the latter. When the motorcyclist ran close to the back of a line of parked vehicles, he swerved out in a last-ditch effort to get around. The chauffeur reacted by also swerving taking the car up onto the median strip and out of control. Before the brakes could be applied effectively, their momentum was swiftly and suddenly halted head on by a very tall palm tree which was more than a match even for the seemingly invincible Humber Super Snipe, which was looking anything but super at that point. Evidently the couple of tons of metal and chrome had met its match. Sahodra luckily escaped any serious injury, as did the driver who had a couple of bruises and scratches, Maurice was not so lucky however, he had a nasty deep wound to his head, the result of contact with a metal attachment to one of the hand straps he had been holding onto. For his part Kamahl had suffered a bad whiplash leaving him in need of treatment. Luckily the local hospital was just a short walk from the scene of the accident. Whilst the whiplash was treated and medicated, allowing him to continue with his performance later that day, it had left him with a back condition that persisted throughout his entire career to this present day. Since that day in Copacabana, on every subsequent tour, major concert or practically anything requiring him to be on his feet for any length of time, he required a precautionary trip to the chiropractor. As he puts it; "I have been so lucky to have found some terrific chiropractors over the years … I swear that these people perform miracles and if they hadn't worked their magic it would have been impossible for me to have worked mine," he laughs. He claims that his current chiropractor, Larry Whitman is a genius. "I suffer terribly from sciatica which can come on quite unexpectedly, although even waking up these days is a bit unexpected." He laughs, "Larry is my saviour, he gets me up and running in no time, well maybe running is a bit of an exaggeration, but you know what I mean."

Kamahl has always had great faith in the professionals who advise and treat anything that has been sent his way. During the challenging days of the corona virus he has become dismayed at the reluctance shown by many in getting vaccinated. "Despite my inherent reservation and total dislike for needles, I gladly got down to the GP and had my shots.

To me it is more than a personal medical decision, it is a community responsibility as it isn't only yourself you are protecting. It is your friends, your relatives, your neighbours and the rest of the community you live in. I would always urge people to get their medical advice from someone qualified and not some nut on the internet."

16

The two subjects to avoid at dinner

Those who believe that politics and religion do not mix,
understand neither.

Albert Einstein

Anyone who has viewed Kamahl's highly active Twitter account will testify that he does not shy away from sharing his opinion on any subject, large or small. He realises that he may ruffle more than a few feathers from time to time. Still, this does not prevent him from sharing as he recognises the unique experiences that he has had in life has led to informing an interesting perspective. He says, "I am always happy to share my opinions. That is not to say that I am dismissive of the views of others, far from it in fact. I respect anyone's opinion just as long as they respect my right to voice mine. When I was growing up, I had to fight very hard to be heard, to have a voice, so once liberated from that I refused to go unheard." His views on both politics and religion are quite a surprise for many. He is totally unaligned with any formal body of either subject, refusing to pigeon-hole himself into a faction of either discipline. He is his own man and makes his judgment on the issues based on a considered review of the facts. "My life has been a really long journey. Along the way I have seen so much and learned so many things. These experiences have very much influenced my attitudes and beliefs. I see the obvious failings and frailty of tribalism, blind faith and having a closed mind to new ideas. So I reject falling into the type of thinking that leads to acceptance of simple dogma," he states.

As a young person, Kamahl was immersed in an environment where religion was a significant factor in daily life. Religion was all around him and it informed most if not all decisions made by his family. Led by his father and uncle, who were devout Hindus, they attended Friday night temple and participated in all festivals and social activities relating to their belief system. They strictly and unflinchingly adhered completely to all teachings. Kamahl, for his part, conformed obediently and without question, mainly because questioning was not an option available to him within the world he then lived in. However, within himself, he equated the strict and pious constraints that were the norm in his home as stifling and restrictive. It provided no room for critical thinking, free thought and even less for open discussion. He continually wondered if his family's complete commitment to their faith had not possibly contributed to some of the practical challenges they had faced when he was a youngster. Once away from home and the boundaries, he felt faith had placed upon him, he gradually drifted from Hinduism until he felt separated from it almost entirely. Once in Australia, he was now in a culture bound by a different set of rules and attitudes. He observed that these rules were far more secular with only a passing reference to religion. He realised that he was entitled to question and not just accept rules imposed by the teachings of ancient texts. He could now form his own objective opinions, which to him as an eighteen year old was wildly liberating.

Kamahl remains highly respectful of those adepts of whichever religion they subscribe to. He feels that they are purely attempting to connect with a purpose in life and seek to explain its meaning the best way they know how to. Over the years, Kamahl has had many great friends who are devout within many different belief systems. He claims he is pleased that it provides them with reassurance comfort and meaning to their lives. He has on many occasions recorded spiritual songs and performed in many churches and cathedrals over the years. He can readily understand the connection that people have with their faith as he has witnessed first-hand the joy that it evidently provides them. He states, "To me it is science that holds the answers as it deals with facts that are properly researched and relies on those facts being proven. The role of science continually evolves in informing us, enlightening us and providing explanation. Many religions on the other hand, adopt a worldview wedded to knowledge from when far less was understood about life. Back then, the answers to that which couldn't be explained was in many cases invented by religious leaders and endorsed by their cohorts in power to suit some agenda. Much of this fabricated mythology went on to become enshrined in many religious practices.

These myths have become like unquestionable proof points that we are meant to believe just because it is written. To many, their beliefs are more important than knowledge. To me, it is a very dangerous thing to give precedence to faith over proven fact. My own life, for example, has been filled with examples of inexplicable miraculous coincidences, but it certainly doesn't mean I am compelled to believe that they have resulted from intervention by some mysterious being or omnipotent power guiding my fate. But this is my belief, and I don't expect everyone to share it. Whilst I think that faith is a highly personal and individual issue, I refuse to lose friends over it. I will say, however, that of the over ten thousand religions in the world, most of which claim to be the only true one, it never seems to occur to any, that if it is only they who are right, everyone else must be wrong."

His gradual separation from Hinduism was definitely not the last time Kamahl had to question those who saw fit to save his soul. In the late fifties, an attractive young lady named Carlene Berg in Adelaide saw fit to try to save his soul. He was well on his way to allowing this to happen until he found himself on their third date back at the same venue as the previous two, the Church of Christ. He recalls, "At the time, I thought that I could win her heart, but she made it clear she was more interested getting me to give my soul to Jesus rather than what I had in mind, which was significantly less spiritual. It all seemed a bit Faustian but in reverse. After nobly trying and failing to connect with what was being taught at the Church, I realised there was no future in a relationship as the third wheel with Jesus. I was a little more than heartbroken by the unrequited aspect of the relationship."

Whilst the coupling was not a tremendous romantic success he had hoped for, it was not without its benefits. Carlene's father Lloyd was a chef and a keen amateur musician who played many instruments. Upon hearing Kamahl's voice, he would suggest performers that he thought he should see who would help in broadening his music education. Lloyd was very keen to ensure that Kamahl made the most of his talent and always pushed him to ensure he did something with it. He recommended Kamahl enter *Australia's Amateur Hour*. The show was a top-rated talent programme, like an early day equivalent to *Australia's Got Talent* only on radio. In the absence of TV, Radio was still the dominant entertainment medium of the day, with families gathering around the gramophone each week to hear their favourite shows. *Australia's Amateur Hour* was initially made in Sydney but would later be broadcast from all major cities.

Dick Fair, with a staff of six, travelled for eight months a year to audition some five thousand people and rehearse the ten needed for each Thursday live performance. The weekly winners then would be narrowed down to being regional finalists to appear at the Grand Final in Sydney at the end of the season. Practically the whole nation tuned in to the live broadcast each week. Kamahl, still lacking confidence as a performer, vacillated about entering, so much so that Lloyd put him in his car and drove him to the radio station. Once he was there, he felt overwhelmed by the environment with the images of big-name recording stars all over the walls. Kamahl refused to fill in the entry form. He says, "Lloyd grabbed the entry form from me and filled it in for me himself. They are pretty determined people, those Christians", he laughs. Later that year, he competed on-air and represented South Australia at the Grand Final in Sydney. "It was a fantastic experience I don't actually remember who won. I know it wasn't me though," he laughs.

In 1959 whilst working as an architectural intern at the practice of Mr Brown, a prominent Adelaide architect, he was provided with the opportunity to take lodgings with him at his impressive family home in an exclusive Adelaide suburb. "It was a large, impressive home with beautiful furnishings. The home had a huge window looking across lush parkland to the city, as I recall. Indeed, it was a very nice address, and I was quite excited to be away from the modest boarding house type digs that I had called home for the past few years. As impressive as the home was the actual accommodation itself was far less than spectacular, a kind of jerry-built shed halfway down the large sloping bank of a garden and a good way removed from the house. It was almost like a shed from a building site only painted. Picture a granny flat built by someone who hated their granny. Mr Brown, at this stage, was in his late middle age. He lived with his wife Beryl and their three children, one of whom grew up to be a South Australian Premier, Dean Brown. Old Gordon was an imperious fellow and had a rather authoritarian presence. Within the first day of my arrival, I was informed of the house rules. He explained to me that he was part of a thing called Moral Re-armament, and whilst I lived under his roof, I would be expected to conform to its practices expressed as the four pillars or 'absolutes' as they referred to them: Absolute Honesty, Absolute Purity, Absolute Unselfishness, Absolute Love."

The Moral Re-armament was an international moral and spiritual movement that, in 1938, developed from American minister. It was a movement that has long been viewed as highly political and interventionist. Members were encouraged to proactively become involved in commerce and government. They were instructed to further the anti-socialist agenda.

This was somewhat of an obsession in the 'reds under the beds' era of the nineteen fifties. A famed actress, whose family were deeply involved in the movement, described the MRA as a dangerous cult claiming that she required therapy after leaving the movement at 22. She also claims that trauma contributed to the failure of her three marriages. She has also claimed that her sister battled with mental health issues for years after her departure, directly attributing her membership as the cause.

Kamahl, who had just gained a small taste of freedom from religious zealotry, was far from happy to immerse himself in yet another form. Immediately his thoughts turned to planning his departure. "All that praying all the time, if anything it was more stringent and extreme than what I had grown up with. They also believed in confession, but they didn't confess to a priest. Instead, they confessed to one another about which of the four absolutes they had neglected to diligently observe. At that point, I literally had nothing to confess to them. I lived in a shed on a bank like a monk and went nowhere except to work. By far, the most awful thing about the confessions for me was that I had to listen to the head of the household. He was also my boss and landlord, confesses to me his impure thoughts about his unsuspecting secretary. It was all very awkward indeed."

After three months of living like a monk in a jerry-built shed, albeit one with a nice postcode, Kamahl had his own epiphany. Indeed, he had seen the light, as Brown had talked about. It was shining a bright light on the route away from that stifling, puritanical environment. Kamahl's whilst grateful for the hospitality he had been given, felt that he was being used as some kind of patriarchal missionary project. There was no way that he was prepared to play that role, not for his boss nor anyone else for that matter. His attitude began to foment into an evident lack of enthusiasm for the MRA cause.

Moreover, he was convinced of only one absolute and that was he had no appetite whatsoever to tackle the looming red menace through prayer and purity. At breakfast one morning, he announced that he needed to leave. He told a clearly shocked Mr Brown, "Mr Brown, I had a vision last night in which God spoke to me, he said 'you must absolutely leave this place!'" To Kamahl's great relief, this disclosure led Brown to ask him to find somewhere else to live. Even though he was faced with limited options and very short notice, he willingly and gleefully departed.

His lack of enthusiasm for politically motivated religion has continued throughout his life. In more recent times, he has been outspoken about what he sees as the toxicity of American politics leading up to and beyond the Trump era. "Evangelicals supporting a morally reprehensible character like Donald Trump just reek of hypocrisy. It would be comical if the implications were not so serious. The man has no morality about him at all. Yet, he is embraced by people who are supposed to be of faith. They tirelessly campaign for him. How can anyone ignore what they must see with their own eyes and hear with their own ears just to promote their own agenda? To me, the whole thing is quite sinister. It has even allowed some extreme evangelist leaders to use bigotry and racism whilst clothing themselves in morality and respectability. They influence their followers to be fooled into following such a flawed human being…to me, it is not very Christian at all, I would have thought. One can only hope that as information and education increases, the fear and superstition that currently attracts people to some of these beliefs will become less significant."

Whilst holding strong views on a broad range of political and social subjects, Kamahl's beliefs are not guided by any specific party-political dogma. He is probably best described as a political agnostic. He finds it amusing that he has often been labelled quite incorrectly as a closet conservative and has been aligned with the Australian Liberal Party. This, he speculates, is possibly due to his older audience appeal. People in this demographic tend to lean more toward conservative parties. Therefore it is assumed that is where his own allegiances lie.

He has had great friends who have represented both sides of Australian politics over the years. He honestly believes that they all seem to share a genuine desire to serve the community's best interests and enter political life to attempt to do just that... He says, "Politicians are interesting people, people that I think we sometimes hold to impossible standards. I have known very many over the years. They have come from both major parties and some independent. Practically all of them got into public life with the noblest intentions. Some of them really deliver on their promises whilst others are just not as competent as they thought they were. Of course, some are just downright corrupt. At the end of the day, they are mere people, and people are far from perfect. When we place people on a pedestal, we are bound for disappointment. That is not to say that we don't have the occasional great person who emerges from the pile who inspires progress and achieves great things. I just wish that it happened far more often than it currently does. I think particularly now, as the world faces huge existential challenges, none more than the Environment. This issue affects every man, woman and animal on the planet, so we really need positive and thoughtful leadership. Unfortunately, we have seen the rise of opportunists with empty rhetoric who are seeking to exploit the crisis for their own gain."

Kamahl does have some political heroes and quite a few villains, as is evidenced by his very active Twitter feed. His complete repudiation of demagoguery and the apparent renaissance of nineteen-thirties style far-right populism has been dramatically influenced by his own life experiences as a marginalised person. He naturally finds more in common with those who look to heal the wounds of societal differences rather than those who seek to exploit them. He sometimes despairs that some of the greatest minds are dissuaded from entering leadership in civic life because of the apparent shortcomings that exist within it. Kamahl says famed physicist Neil de Grasse Tyson is a prime example of the type of person he would love to see run for high office in the United States. He says, "He has an amazing intellect, is not bound by stupid political dogma. His knowledge would allow his decisions to be made on substantive factual assessment rather than the influence of donors, religious dogma or industry groups. I remember seeing his analysis of Van Gogh's painting 'The Starry Night' once. He puts forward a theory that the painting was not just the product of Van Gogh's mind. Tyson says it actually depicts a massive atmospheric disturbance. He explained this view in such a way that he made even the most complex of issues clear enough for the most disinterested layman to understand. That skill of making the complex comprehensible is a wonderful gift, one that sadly most of our political leaders seem to avoid like the plague."

On politics in general, he believes that there is a need to be more considerate of issues that address the needs of society rather than the wealthy or powerful special interest groups. He says "I think that there is nothing more powerful in life than the love and compassion we have for our fellow humans. Those that realise this fact and work toward promoting this need to be our future leaders. People who use the irrational hatred of others by using fear which can lead to violence, need to be reckoned with because when they try to seize power there is a massive cost. Based upon experiences in my own life, my belief is that the extreme, will always fail in the long run. This is mainly because people at heart are inherently good, and goodwill always prevails over evil."

Kamahl doesn't believe that the use of mean-spirited rhetoric is exclusively reserved for people on the extreme right. He believes that plenty of examples of bully tactics are used to make a point on all sides of the political spectrum. He believes that there needs to be far more civility in public discourse in general with far less combative posturing. In 2004 Kamahl's friend and well-known composer/musical director, Mike Harvey, a man he describes as a handsome version of Beethoven, released his musical *Eureka*. He says, "Mike is one of the really great talents in Australian Music. He has worked with the very best in music and is a terrific composer. In 2004 he wrote the piece *Eureka,* adapted from a book written by Gale Edwards and John Senczuk. The story is based on the Eureka Stockade Rebellion of 1854 in the goldfields of Ballarat. The musical referenced an actual Australian historical event of significance drew a lot of attention, particularly as its release timed with the one hundred and fiftieth anniversary of the event itself. I attended the opening evening and have to say it was one of the most enjoyable and entertaining musicals that I had seen. The music, as expected, was great, and the cast performed magnificently. The show business media critics seemed to be very much of the same mind as they were very complimentary of the show. What followed that positive critical reception was laughable. Germaine Greer and a posse of like-minded accomplices set about denouncing the show over its historical inaccuracies. No doubt Greer is obviously a well-educated and learned person and I am sure she is very knowledgeable about Australian history. That being said when did anyone go to a musical for a history lesson? Does anyone really use *Miss Saigon* or *Les Misérables* as an authoritative piece on the respective conflicts from which they took their themes? I am reasonably sure that *Hamilton* has never been held under the microscope that *Eureka* was. If it were, there would have had to have been some radical recasting. Poor Mike had done such a tremendous job with the music and had produced such an entertaining piece of work."

Of those he really looks up to, Kamahl rates Barack Obama, who in 2008 rode to victory on the single-minded proposition of 'Hope' as one of his heroes. He was inspired to believe that maybe the United States had turned the corner on the things holding it back for so many years, such as racism, abuse of civil rights and inequality of social justice. With his election and subsequent re-election, it appeared that the United States had started the process of healing from the self-inflicted wounds of hate and was genuinely embracing progress. "Obama first inspired me when I read an essay in *Time Magazine* by Hugh Sidey. The piece was about this young African-American Junior Senator invited by John Kerry to do the keynote address to the Democratic National Convention in 2004. His speech, which he had penned himself, was inspirational. It was really the beginning of his ascent to the Presidency. The praise he had received for the address was so significant that it established him as a potential leader of the Party. As the momentum grew, I was in awe of the fact that an African American could rise to such great heights in the not-too-distant shadow of the Jim Crow era. It was truly amazing."

In 2007, awaiting a flight to Singapore, Kamahl followed Sahodra into a bookstore and picked up a copy of *The Audacity of Hope – Thoughts of Reclaiming the American Dream*. He claims to have been overwhelmed by its content. "It wasn't just the eloquence of the writing. The manner and tone in which he clearly articulated racism, celebrity and prejudice by being different. It was as if he actually knew me and the struggle I had felt being an outsider in a largely Anglo-Celtic society. He even shared some of my heroes, Nat King Cole and Paul Robeson."

Needless to say, Kamahl was an immediate convert and followed the Obama presidential campaign with a passion. He even went to sign up for an organisation called 'Obama for America' online. Evidently, a 25 minimum donation was required to join the campaign. He was so inspired he donated $100 without hesitation. "It was my first ever political donation, and within an hour, I received a note from the great man thanking me for my kind contribution to the campaign. Now I knew it wasn't from Obama himself, but it had his name on the bottom of it, so that was good enough," he says.

"A funny thing is that the donation itself was never ever charged to my credit card; this was even though I received a ton of correspondence from the organisation for years after."

In 2010, Kamahl attended a fundraiser in regional Victoria for a scout hall destroyed in a fire earlier that year. He provided a copy of one of the letters he had received as an auction item. To Kamahl's great delight, it raised $500, significantly more than a signed copy of Paul Keating's biography. Never having been a fan of Keating, who he had always regarded as quite an intellectual snob in his own opinion, made the achievement all the sweeter. His opinion of Keating was formed whilst attending the Mahler concert one evening some years before at the Sydney Opera House. He was seated in a box with Gough and Margaret Whitlam and, encountering Paul Keating on the way out, was met with a stare that could only be described as incredulous. He asked, "What are you doing here?" Kamahl recounts, "Judging by his tone and expression, it was as if in his mind, I was not entitled to be there. I felt that it said a lot about his character."

The Obama letter he had donated for auction was indeed quite significant. It far penned just before delivering his historic victory speech at Grant Park on November 5, 2008. It read:

Dear Kandiah,

I'm about to head to Grant Park to talk to everyone gathered there, but I wanted to write to you first.

We just made history. And I don't want you to forget how we did it.

You made history every single day during this campaign – every day you knocked on doors, made a donation, or talked to your family, friends and neighbours about why you believe it's time for a change.

I want to thank all of you who gave your time, talent and passion to this campaign. We have a lot of work to do to get our country back on track, and I'll be in touch about what comes next.

But I want to be very clear about one thing… all of this happened because of you.

Thank You

Barack

For all the genuine affection that he holds for Obama, he has never bought into the notion that heroes are entirely without spot. He offers, for example, his great disappointment in things that Obama did not deliver on. The failure to end the military conflicts started by his predecessor, the inability to close Guantanamo Bay, to name but two. However, his one stand-out incident that soured his perception of Obama the mostwas Flint, Michigan. In April 2014, during a budget crisis, to save money, Flint, Michigan had changed its water source from Detroit Water and Sewerage Department to the Flint River. This decision resulted in a public health crisis as the drinking water for the city became contaminated with lead and Legionella from the new source. This was seen nationally as a shameful decision whose fall-out is still with them today. Obama somehow allowed himself to be involved in an apparent political stunt to prove that the supply issues had been resolved.

Whilst addressing the city at a gathering, he coughed, paused thoughtfully and rather clumsily requested a glass of water to clear his throat, which he took and then sipped. The point of the stunt? To add substance to the rhetoric, all was now well with the supply. Unfortunately, despite all the assurances, things were far from well, and Flint's dangerous water quality issues remained. Kamahl thought the stunt unseemly for a man of Obama's stature. As far as he was concerned, it was a dereliction of duty to the citizens of Flint, most of whom were low income, working-class and his strong supporters. "Heroes, unfortunately, can sometimes disappoint. No matter what they have achieved in the past, they can become complacent and take the people they are meant to serve for granted. I thought that this was the case, which, whilst profoundly disappointing for me, it would've been devastating if I were poor, black and living in Flint. I suppose the thing they say about idols is true… they do have feet of clay."

Disappointment aside, Kamahl still regards Obama as one of the most significant political figures in his lifetime. He says, "His journey was so inspirational to millions, me included. It's a story summed up beautifully in the title The Audacity of Hope, Obama's second book. It is something that all of those who are marginalised, repressed or ignored, these people can personally relate to. His story gives so many a tremendous inspiration."

Kamahl was delighted to meet Obama at an official reception in Canberra in 2011. New South Wales Senator John Williams and Kamahl had been friends from their first meeting back in 2009. He enjoyed the Senator's company, straightforward manner, and deep commitment to charity. When Williams asked Kamahl if he would appear at an event at a local club in Inverell to raise funds to construct a 'Men's Shed' in the town, he agreed without hesitation. The concept of the Men's Shed appealed to Kamahl greatly. It provides a facility for older men to get together, work on individual or group craft projects and discuss their health issues. John, aware that Kamahl was an Obama tragic, offered to see what he could do, if he could get him an invitation to the reception. Kamahl, whilst thankful for his friend's ambition, decided not to get his hopes up too high. He says, "After all this was the leader of the free world, and I am a mere entertainer, I was convinced that there would be a list a mile long ahead of me to get that invite."

Good to his word, Senator Williams came through with the invitation. Kamahl would be attending as the guest of his friend on November 16th, 2011. When he arrived at Parliament House, he was shown to Senator William's office. Kamahl had a three-hour wait alone before cocktails were served. He, therefore, had to find ways to amuse himself. He resorted to singing to pass away the time, anything and everything that came to mind, including, at one point, the Star-Spangled Banner. He reflected, "I wish that I had been able to sing that night. I had previously for George W Bush several years earlier. Still, I was just happy to get the invitation to be there at that point."

Once the evening had started and guests were seated, Senator Stephen Parry approached Kamahl. He said, "You are going to meet the President".

Initially, Kamahl thought the Senator was joking. He says, "I remember saying, of course Stephen and pigs might fly. However, I could see in his eyes that he wasn't joking."

Kamahl later discovered that the President had been taken on a tour of Parliament House earlier that day. When he passed Senator John William's office, the party was treated to a stirring rendition of 'The Star-Spangled Banner'. Obama had remarked that he would like to meet the singer. Kamahl had sung for yet another President without even knowing. He reflects, "I think I was about 699 out of 700 to be introduced to him, but I really didn't care. This was already much more than I could've hoped for. When we were taken forward to be presented, we all stood in the queue and shuffled to the front. I vividly recall Queensland Premier Anna Bligh was ahead of me. She did seem to be taking an eternity, so obviously, it was something weighty, quite possibly the Queensland flood crisis. Eventually, she moved away. It was my turn. Just as I was about to move forward, a man stepped between us and announced, 'The President is about to have dinner. Could you please all take your seats?' There I was a couple of feet away, and I was going to be denied. I was gutted but remained until someone told me to go away or security men in reflector glasses crash tackled me to the ground and dragged me off. I closed my eyes and braced for impact. To my surprise, when I opened them, there was Obama with an outstretched hand and a beaming smile."

After a brief, polite word or two, the meeting was over, and he returned to his seat. When he got to the table, John Williams said, "Take a look at your email." He saw a picture memorialising his meeting with one of his greatest heroes shaking his hand. Kamahl remembers what he said to him just as the photo was taken. "Before I leave you, Mr President, I want you to know that you've always left me spell-bound and sometimes tear-bound."

Kamahl believes that the inspirational void Obama left may yet be filled by his current favourite American political figure, Kamala Harris.

He sees Harris as a powerful and eloquent speaker. This massive intellect has managed to elevate her to the Vice Presidency based upon merit and not unearned privilege. "She has a tremendous presence and is a great intellect. I really believe that she will be a great president one day, and I firmly believe that it is about time for the best person and not just the best man to run that country. I made this point to Rupert Murdoch early in 2020 when we spoke. Harris was still one of the delegates standing to be the nominee for the Democratic Party Presidential candidate. He agreed that the strongest Democrat was indeed a woman, to my surprise. Still, he believed that that was Elizabeth Warren, who he is greatly impressed by. For clarification, my support for Ms Harris is because of her glittering credentials and track record, not because she has a name that sounds very much like mine. Although the last part is definitely an added bonus", he adds with a laugh. As she has now been hoisted to the very top of her party's presidential ticket, it would appear his observations are quite prescient. "I have my fingers and toes crossed that she becomes the first female President of the United States, for her to be part South Asian too is just remarkable to witness this in my lifetime, I'll be sure to remind Rupert of my prediction", Kamahl reflects with a grin.

In the 2016 American Election, he took greater than usual interest in the nominees. This was primarily due to his wanting to see how Obama's successor would measure up. He reasoned Obama had left considerable shoes to fill. Even though the last six years of his presidency had been frustrated by his party's failure to give him the legislative power required to push for his reforms. Poor showings at both the 2010 mid-term and 2012 general elections meant Obama had to operate with minorities in both houses for the bulk of his term. This meant he was continually blocked by the Republican majority in Congress, Senate or both. Hillary Clinton was to secure the Democratic nomination, something that Kamahl was quite comfortable with. He reasoned that it was another progressive move for the United States, first a man of colour then a highly qualified woman as President. Kamahl also admired her intellect and the credentials she had brought to the job. He felt her staunch loyalty to her husband during his controversial term in office was admirable, even though many took a totally different view. "There was a bit of the Tammy Wynette about that whole thing. She certainly stood by her man. Whether he deserved the loyalty or not is highly debatable. Still, loyalty is definitely something that I personally value a great deal, so regardless of her motivation, I thought that her loyalty was to be commended."

Interestingly, one thing emerged during the lead up to the election that soured his support for her entirely.

Whilst she was a court-appointed defence attorney in Arkansas in 1975, Hillary Clinton (then Rodham) successfully represented Thomas Alfred Taylor. He had been accused of the rape of a 12-year-old girl, Kathy Shelton. Whilst the man was acquitted, it was widely believed that this was a miscarriage of justice. In the lead up to the election, this story was relitigated in the media. Footage emerged of a young Clinton appearing to be in high spirits during the trial, even laughing. The clip was pushed entirely without context, hoping that it would dehumanise the candidate. The tactic was quite successful in consolidating the negativity. It also made him question his initial assessment of Clinton.

"It may have been that as I too had been abused by adults at a similar age to the victim and felt largely unprotected by adults. It resonated with me and turned me off her as a candidate. She was a court-appointed attorney who was still quite young and inexperienced in projecting her image. As Sahodra reminded me, Clinton was there as a lawyer and had to do the job she was getting paid to do, namely, provide an accused man with representation under the law. Of course, she was correct … as usual."

However, his reservation for the Clinton candidacy did not readily translate into support for her opponent Donald J Trump. He readily admits that he knew very little about the man until he thrust himself onto the political stage in 2015. He knew of him, but not much about him as his career to that point held little interest to Kamahl. He knew that he was a tycoon and had a TV show where he played the hardly challenging role of a business tycoon, but that was probably about it.

For Kamahl, that changed dramatically the more he got to see him and what he learned left him cold. That changed yet again during his presidency. Now he is not only outspoken on his distaste for Trump. He sees him as a man who was wholly consumed by his own gain from office, He believes that, to Trump, it was never and not about serving his country in any way, shape, or form. He genuinely worries about the societal implications of Trump's elevation in 2016 to a job which is arguably the most powerful in the world. "In my view and this is only my opinion, Trump is a truly awful human being who cares about nothing other than himself.

"I realise that many people my age are quite conservative in their thinking and do not share my views on this man. I suspect it comes from being fearful of new things and new ideas. That fear of change allows them to align with anyone who plugs into that emotion by saying that he can somehow reverse the clock and take us back to a time when they felt more in control of their lives. Of course, it is nonsense, but it provides a strategy for an unabashed charlatan like Trump. The pace of change in the world provides people like him a gilt-edged opportunity to exploit fear of that change for political gain. In many ways, the same fears were exploited using the same playbook by Nigel Farage in Britain with his ridiculous UKIP movement and before that by demagogues throughout history. Exploiting fear when people feel vulnerable due to financial hardship or an irrational feeling of loss of inherent privilege is appalling. They mobilise ignorance against those who are always the easy targets, different nationalities, different religions, people of different colour, different sexual orientations. The usual suspects, I suppose you could call them. A leader like Trump speaks against the 'other' for them, giving their insecurities political legitimacy. Their irrational fears and are validated and allows them to blame the 'others' for everything, promising to either eradicate or curtail supposed privileges that are supposed to be being threatened."

Kamahl maintains that he knows this fear really well, not by sharing it but by being the object of it from a young age, when he too was an 'other' himself. "When I see this type of fear, it reminds me of my early days in Adelaide. I remember when my fellow Asian schoolmates and I witnessed white kids with fear in their eyes running away from us, mocking us, throwing things at us. Sadly, those kids were simply indoctrinated by adults, believing that people who weren't like themselves had evil intent or weren't as intelligent and therefore worth less than them. They were genuinely not wilfully ignorant, the same could almost be said of their parents, who must've been the source of their fear. Courtesy of the White Australia policy, generations of Australians had such little exposure to other cultures and other races. I am so thankful that we live in a largely tolerant and accepting society here in Australia. It wasn't always that way, perhaps, and certainly there is much improvement still needed, but the advances we as a country have made in such a short time, in fact in my life within this society relative to much of the world, make me proud of that advancement and hopeful for the future."

Kamahl says that he despairs the rise of autocrats throughout the world. "I could hardly be labelled as a left-wing radical. I am not at all, and neither am I a conservative. I do not believe that politics is as simple as picking a team and slavishly following it wherever they may go. I have, over the years, had great friends on both sides of politics, and those friends all shared one common attribute. They are great people, people of character. They may well have differing views on achieving what they believe in. Their heart is in the right place, and they are prepared to thoughtfully debate issues rather than the ad hominem garbage we see too often. We should always tolerate everyone's differences, whatever they may be, with respect and not insults.

Regrettably, America, the biggest democracy in the world, this is now practically never the case. They seem engaged in a cold civil war, and like in most wars, truth has been the first casualty. It is their role as the supposed leaders of the free world that makes me fearful about the tribalist path that they are currently on. I have become a little obsessive about what is going on there and sincerely hope that we never allow ourselves to push our country down that same path."

Any reading of Kamahl's Twitter account will leave you with no doubt that he cares about many issues. He has always been an environmentalist, a supporter of human rights, social equity and helping the disadvantaged both at home and abroad. He pulls no punches when voicing his opinions stating, "I have plenty of opinions on most subjects. It seems to be the conventional wisdom that when you arrive at an age, you are too set in your ways to embrace progressive thoughts and concepts. Therefore, you are thought by many to no longer have the right to a voice. Having gone through my early years mostly silenced, I will be damned if I would ever allow that to happen again at the other end of my time here on Earth. My Social Media accounts provide me with a great opportunity to give my opinions, and I enjoy taking full advantage of that opportunity. If people agree with me, that is great. If they don't, I respect their right to have another opinion as long as the same respect has been afforded me in return."

Kamahl has become disturbed by the increase of what he describes as vile muck spreaders pushing ridiculous conspiracy theories on Social Media. He feels that older site users are often being duped into distributing dangerous information. Conspiracy generators like the American Q.Anon movement are garnering support for some of their most outlandish ideas by using shock and fear. He says, "A lot of older people are spending an increasing number of hours per day scrolling through things on their Facebook Newsfeed. They grew up reading traditional media, as flawed as it may have been. The media has always, no doubt showed bias sometimes but it still operated in a regulated environment and had to have a basis of fact to run its stories. No such regulation exists in the digital social media world it appears. As a result, some people afford misinformation a greater level of trust as it may be telling them what they want to hear. They are telling this audience not to believe what they see in the traditional media as they are a part of a sinister world-controlling cabal." He believes that these conspiracy-based groups deliberately target older audiences on sites like Facebook. He believes they will generally pass something on without too much questioning as they generally receive information of concern from someone they trust like family or friends. The topics of these groups, of which Q.Anon appears to be the most active, exploit well-established fears in the older demographic groups such as the collapse of society being brought about by progressives, the threat to religious freedoms, the diminishing of their race by interlopers or 'others', child sex trafficking through paedophile rings, an evil Illuminatis manipulating World Order to their own wicked agenda etc. "It is all such nonsense. All of which would be laughable if I didn't see the more sinister side of it. The tragic consequences that belief in something like this can bring can be catastrophic. In a really sick way, they have mastered bringing together the very worst aspects of fear which they wrap in religion and politics to produce a putrid pile of dangerous disinformation. Most recently, they are even risking people's lives by misinforming them of the COVID 19 virus. Encouraging people to ignore health experts, questioning the need to take appropriate precautions and encouraging people to refuse vaccination. All of which will end up costing lives."

In his own words, Kamahl has become a little 'obsessed' with the sinister undercurrent of lies and distortions of fact that characterise quite a lot of politics today. He says, "In the US in particular, the truth seems to be of little value, and facts seem to now have flown out the window. The truth is being replaced with dark conspiracies that have just enough plausibility to gain traction with a substantial population who are prepared to believe practically anything."

Even though he is aware of the type of misinformation being spread he has even been a victim of it on occasion, "Only recently, I received a tweet from someone I knew who forwarded an article posted on Twitter. This story reported the crowning of a 'man' as the winner of Miss Nevada 2021. It stated that a 'dude' had entered a beauty contest for women and had won. My incorrect reading of the article was that it had been some kind of a prank designed to undermine and mock the competition. More out of amusement than outrage, I stupidly retweeted the clip without questioning the information I had been provided. Twitter being the pretty unforgiving arena it is within minutes tipped bucketload of backlash all over me. When the facts were pointed out to me, I then did my research. The story emerged that the winner Kataluna Enriquez is, in fact, not a 'dude' as the piece stated but a transgender woman. I actually felt pretty silly and a little bit of a bully.

"Here was a young person who had been the victim of a great deal of abuse in early life. She is a migrant of colour who had bravely stood up to enormous adversity to not only succeed but become a positive role model for her community. I was horrified that I could have contributed in any way to the ridiculous outrage against her. The Twitter criticism I received was warranted as I had acted thoughtlessly, and I certainly take it on the chin to seek to rectify my position. Of all the criticism I rightly received, one in particular really stung me. It truly brought home the consequences of my behaviour more than anything else. It was an email that I received from my own dear 16-year-old granddaughter Izzy. She told me in no uncertain terms that I was not only wrong but that I should be more thoughtful in what I post in future because my actions have an impact and influence on people."

Kamahl's granddaughter Isabelle wrote in her email:

Hi Grandpa,

That's transphobic. She is not a 'dude', she is a woman. This is not okay, and not respectful. Even if this was a joke, it is not funny. So much is wrong with this. I do not want you to lose fans over this. You are a public figure; you should be setting a good example.

Love,

Izzy

Why hateful misinformation spreads on social media so quickly he offers, "I really love my social media, but I don't understand why there is so much anger and hate within it. Hate is such a powerful emotion, it's a hungry beast that has to be fed continually for it to keep alive. However you know there is a French philosopher named Jean Rostand who summed it up perfectly using just three words when he said, 'To hate fatigues' and I agree with that. All the energy required to feed that hungry beast, must soon exhaust. Surely people will tire of feeding hate. I truly hope that day will happen sooner rather than later."

17

Friendship

Friends are never earned, they are a gift from the loving God,
and they are precious beyond human evaluation. You dare not
take them for granted, or they will drift away like smoke and
the warmth of their caring will vanish like the chill of the
endless night.

Glen Campbell

Before Kamahl's trip to Rio de Janeiro in 1972, there were dramas on the home front to deal with. Kamahl had wanted Sahodra to accompany him on the trip, and she was far from keen to do so. Having only given birth to Rani around a year and a half before, her acute maternal instinct proved a significant and worthy opponent to Kamahl's wish to have his wife by his side. As it happened, providence would intervene, courtesy of the Cain family. Eve and Len Cain were not only neighbours, but they were also long-time fans. Eve would in fact go on to be the founder of the Australian Kamahl Fan Club. Kamahl had met the couple years earlier when performing in *Follow the Sun* at the Doncaster Theatre in Sydney, early in the seventies, he would reencounter the couple as they attended three of his shows on consecutive nights. Kamahl recounts, "Len and Eve were great supporters and came to many of my shows in 1970. When we moved to St Ives, we became neighbours

ABOVE: Pictured here in New York 1976 with Mae Boren Axton the 'Queen Mother of Nashville' and writer of Elvis hit 'Heartbreak Hotel', Piet Schellevis head of Polygram and a Polygram US executive.

BELOW: Party time at the Royal Hawaiian, after a Kamahl gig. Pictured here are Kamahl, Sahodra, *Hawaii 5.0*'s Jack Lord, multi-award winning producer Allan Carr of *You Can't Stop the Music* fame, Sammy Davis Jr and his wife Altovise.

ABOVE: Kamahl with great friend Sir Donald Bradman at the Don's home in Adelaide.

BELOW: As he likes to put it, Kamahl pictured with other mature sex symbols, George Clooney and Hugh Jackman.

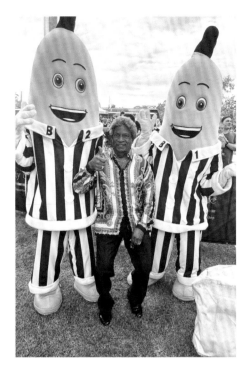

CLOCKWISE FROM ABOVE: With the Bananas in Pyjamas at a Christmas Concert for the Ryde Rotary Club in 2022; Kamahl with Charlie Teo at a fund-raising event for the famous brain surgeon's charity foundation, Kamahl with his long-time friend and collaborator, Musical Director Kenny Powell; Pictured with two Dallas Cowboys cheerleaders and legendary American comedian Milton Berle.

Kamahl in his sartorial splendour through the years. He has always believed firmly in the saying that "people listen with their eyes", so style has always been a part of the Kamahl experience.

CLOCKWISE FROM ABOVE:

At a Rotary International award ceremony. As a recipient of the organisations highest honour, the Paul Harris Fellowship, Kamahl has always valued the role he has been able to play in their great community work.

Another album release in 2014.

Being honoured by having his 1973 concert poster, included as part of an art installation at the Sydney Opera House 50th Anniversary.

Here receiving an award from long-time friend, great philanthropist and business leader Grahame Mapp. He is the person who recruited Kamahl into a long relationship with Variety Club.

TOP: Unveiling his very first kaftan at his Sydney Opera House Concert in 1973.

ABOVE: Kamahl was a regular at the Chanel 7 Perth Telethon for years, pictured here manning the phones again.

LEFT: A big supporter of staged musicals, here at the Sydney premiere of *Wicked* in 2010.

TOP: Curtain call at The Royal Command Performance in Adelaide, 1981.

ABOVE: Kamahl walking in Hyde Park in 1975 with long-time family friend Zel Redford.

LEFT: Speaking at Government House at a Variety Club function.

BELOW: A recent performance of Tom T Hall's *100 Children*, a children's advocacy anthem which he first recorded in 1970.

ABOVE LEFT: Performing at Carnegie Hall concert in 1976.

ABOVE RIGHT: As he appeared as The Prisoner in *Journey Out Of Darkness*, in 1967.

BELOW LEFT: Performing at his concert in Amsterdam in 1976.

RIGHT: The last in a long line of Kaftans featured recently in concert.

and then we became terrific friends. They had three young kids, and we found ourselves socialising quite often before too long. When I discussed the Rio trip with them and said how much I would have liked to have Sahodra there with me, but she couldn't bring herself to leave the kids. Without taking a breath, they offered to take care of the kids in our absence. I was delighted to accept their generous offer, anticipating that Sahodra would likewise share my enthusiasm. I was far from being right on that score, she took the news like we were playing poker, and I had just laid down a royal flush. Her reservations aside, I worked on her and still managed to persuade her to accompany me, but she wasn't exactly thrilled about leaving the kids even though it was with our friends, the Cains. Even before leaving, it seemed she couldn't wait for the trip to be over so that we could head home."

In 1975 the relationship dynamic with the Cains would be changed significantly and suddenly by tragedy. Len died as the result of a massive heart attack. It was surmised the likely cause was the strain of running the family business. Cain Confectionery had been struggling financially for quite some time. It was believed the stress he had in dealing with this had taken its ultimate toll. The suddenness of Len's demise had left Eve with limited resources and struggling with three kids to raise all on her own. The two eldest children, teenagers Liz and Peter, were highly gifted figure skaters who had been selected to represent Australia at the World Junior Championships in 1976. Like all amateur athletes, they were required to self-fund their attendance and participation. Kamahl and Sahdora decided to fund the sibling's trip to ensure that the grieving kids had one less disappointment to face.

The young pair not only represented Australia at the Championship, but they also did so with distinction winning Bronze medals. Both children would have long and distinguished skating careers as competitors and the country's leading coaches. In this capacity, they still both play vital roles in the sport. Eve Cain took to charitable work and was responsible for

Kamahl being introduced to the work of *Save the Children Fund*, which he would support for many years.

Kamah has consistently rated a person's character as the most significant factor in determining where and to whom he gave his personal approval and support. This was very much the case in 1994 when he first met Dr Brendan Nelson AO. Brendan had been the National President of the Medical Association, a role he took on at the age of 34, the youngest person ever appointed to the position. The AMA and the Federal Government were engaged in a challenging relationship on many issues during this time. His appointment to the high-profile position resulted in him having a public platform and the media attention that went with it. He was articulate and very forthright in his views. He did not appear to match the conservatism that the Association had become renowned for. His ideas were both contemporary and progressive. Nelson said at the time, "Doctors should lead the way in showing that national progress can be made, by placing the welfare and consideration of other human beings ahead of their own." He even took a strong position on the failings of his own profession, with an excellent example, his fearless stance on Aboriginal Health. He said, "Doctors need to ask themselves how a person can be well when they've been denied their land, their hunting grounds, their citizenship, their freedom and even their own children. Of course, Aboriginal people's health has suffered when you look at this litany of misery". He lobbied the government on issues like the size of the Medicare Levy and its permission for cigarette manufacturers to advertise. In his role, he had been highly effective at contemporising what many had regarded as a dusty old institution, giving it a significant voice within society. In 1994 he was persuaded by his mentor, Dr Bruce Shepherd, himself a previous President of the AMA, to relocate from his practice in Hobart to Sydney and stand for pre-selection in the safe Liberal seat of Bradfield. Bradfield may have been a safe seat, but it had been tightly held by incumbent David Connolly for over twenty years, so winning was a massive challenge.

Kamahl, as a constituent of Bradfield, was intrigued by this young upstart doctor who'd decided on a career change to politics. Brendan was a highly unlikely Liberal in so many respects. He was the son of a staunch Union operative and ALP member, had been a former member of the ALP himself for a couple of decades. Additionally, up until 1991, Brendan had been business partners with David Crean, the brother of former Labor leader Simon Crean, a State Labor frontbencher himself in the Tasmanian Government. Of all things that marked him down as different to the blue rinse element of the pre-selection committee, however, was that he wore a diamond stud in his left ear. For these folks at the time, that stud may as well have been a twenty-six-inch wheel rim dangling from his head. With his interest piqued in this quirky character, Kamahl attended Brendan's first public meeting in the electorate to see what he had to say. He not only liked what Nelson had to say and how he said it, but he also became a staunch supporter and, reasonably soon after that, an ally and friend. Nelson recalls, "It was one of those meetings that one has to front as a politician when standing for pre-selection. Most of them are pretty dry affairs, but what made it much different was the presence of Kamahl. I remember him sitting front and centre. Of course, I knew who he was immediately and was taken with his attentiveness and genuine interest. After the meeting, I had a chat with him. He generously offered his support there and then." Kamahl recalls, "Brendan was an outsider challenging the status quo, and that appealed to me. After all, I am an outsider and know what it is like to work against the odds. He projected sincerity and intelligence as a man, two very underrated attributes. In fact, they're practically unheard of in his profession."

Brendan, against all odds, became the Member for Bradfield and would also go on to hold the high-profile portfolios within the Howard Government. He headed Education, Science and Training from 2001 to

2006 and Defence from 2006 to 2007. Following the electoral defeat of
the Howard Government in 2007, he was then elected as the Leader of
The Opposition defeating Malcolm Turnbull in a 45–42 result.

Brendan says, "After knowing Kamahl now for almost thirty years, I
still have no idea if he has any political allegiances at all. He voices his
support and criticism for both sides of politics. He is committed to issues
rather than teams, which I can understand completely. As a friend, he
had always stood by me privately and publicly when it mattered the most.
I could always count on him. I will always have the greatest of respect for
that. He's an incredibly generous person who'll always go out of his way
to do whatever he can for a friend."

Brendan reflects, "I remember going through my divorce back in the
nineties and was looking for a place to stay. Another great friend of
mine, Doug Thompson, stepped in and told me that he was more than
happy to offer a flat at the back of his property to afford me some time to
organise my life. I gratefully accepted and stayed there for a few months.
He naturally refused to contemplate any suggestion of compensation for
his kindness. Doug, an extremely wealthy man, makes selecting a gift
for him almost impossible. Doug did have one major passion outside of
his business, and that was his love for Australian country music, but far
more specifically, it was the country music of Slim Dusty that drove his
passion. He had every one of Slim's ninety-six albums and had attended
every one of his shows that he possibly could, but the one thing he hadn't
done was meet the man himself. I decided, therefore, that I had to make
this happen somehow. There was only one problem, I had absolutely no
idea how to do that. Without too much hesitation, I rang Kamahl. He
said immediately, leave it to me, and within barely a couple of hours, he
had arranged a meeting at Slim's St Ives home. Needless to say, Doug was
thrilled to meet Slim and committed to being there in a heartbeat. That
simple act of generosity on his part saw that introduction lead to those

two men having a long-term friendship. Doug would become the prime driver of an enduring legacy to his dear friend, the Slim Dusty Centre in Kempsey. The multi-purpose arts facility features a theatrette, museum and a recording studio that encourages and supports young country music artists. Kamahl's ability to bring people together in friendship to me is one of his greatest gifts."

During Kamahl's time at Yarranabee Road, Darling Point, whilst staying with the Murdoch's, he was introduced to a whole new world of people from many walks of life. One dear old friend, Zal Redford, was a fascinating character who was a frequent visitor to the home. When Kamahl met her, she was already toward the end of her middle age. Never married, she had arrived in Sydney from the country many years before and had settled near the city in Elizabeth Bay. It was there that she became friendly with a couple in a neighbouring apartment. Kamahl recalls, "When Rupert and Pat first arrived in Sydney, they rented an apartment in Elizabeth Bay for a couple of years. After that, they settled in Yarranabee Road. Zal, a close neighbour in Elizabeth Bay, was a great and supportive friend to Pat. Even at this early stage, Pat spent a lot of time alone whilst Rupert was practically working around the clock. Zal had great positive energy. She was humorous, a great conversationalist and companion. When they moved, Zal decided on selling up also, departing the Eastern Suburbs altogether and bought herself a magnificent waterfront property on the Northern Beaches. Despite the distance, she still managed to pop up all the time in Darling Point at almost every function or gathering, no matter how big or small. I suppose living mostly on her own, she liked the company and was energised by the environment."

As Murdoch's marriage eventually fell apart, it was almost fated that Kamahl and Sahodra would take over as Zal's couple friends. It was as if they had been awarded her in the Murdoch divorce settlement, not that they ever minded. She was fun to be around, she was knowledgeable, and she had a genuine affection for Kamahl, Sahodra and subsequently Rajan and Rani.

In the late eighties, Zal's age started to make the Northern Beaches home too much to handle. She was now a quite elderly single lady, so she sold up. She moved herself to the Mowll Retirement Village in the quiet leafy surrounds of Castle Hill. Sahodra, in particular, would visit her very regularly, and Kamahl would accompany her as his schedule would permit him to. On one of these visits, he learned that one of the other residents at the Mowll Village was none other than Mrs Nancy Gunn. Nancy was Rupert Murdoch's redoubtable long-term Executive Assistant who had long since retired by this time. This was the lady that had provided Kamahl with those highly beneficial letters verifying his student status for The Department of Immigration for years. He has always enjoyed a great relationship with her and was extremely grateful. Upon discovering her whereabouts, he had to make a point of visiting her. He remembers, "It was so wonderful to see Mrs Gunn again. She had been such a great ally to me. I hadn't seen her in such a long while that I confess it made me quite emotional. I gave her a big hug, and we both shed a couple of tears. I stayed with her, chatting for ages about old times and was brought up to date about her family. Her son, John Gunn, was a writer of some note, and she had a grandson who had become a musician. Inevitably we started to talk about how remarkably well Rupert had done for himself and how other family members were. This led her to ask me if I had ever met Dame Elisabeth Murdoch, the family matriarch. I replied that I hadn't, to which she said that she believed that I should and that she would arrange it. In next to no time at all, I was scheduled to pay Dame Elisabeth a visit her Cruden Farm Home at Langawarrin, an hour or so outside of Melbourne."

Kamahl would have a long friendship with Dame Elisabeth, whom he describes as a national treasure. He says, "We were instantly great friends. She was such a warm and welcoming person, and whenever I could visit,

I would. She even had a picture of me on her desk, which I took as a great compliment."

In 2009 a long time good friend Basil Sellars rang him to ask if he had any suggestion for nominees as his successor for the Sir Roden Cutler Medal. The medal is awarded annually to a person in the community. Basil himself, a great philanthropist, had accepted the award the previous year with some humility. It was a great honour to be recognised by the organisation founded by Sir Roden, a man of such epic stature who was broadly acknowledged as a tireless and selfless contributor to over a hundred charities. To receive the medal named after such a man was indeed a great honour, and Basil rightly believed it was a form of public recognition not to be taken lightly. Basil and Kamahl shared several things in common. Both men were immigrants to Australia, both attended the King's College in Adelaide, both shared a great passion for cricket, and both excelled in their chosen career paths. This bond is most apparent regarding philanthropy and commitment to the community. When Basil reached out to Kamahl for advice on a recommended nominee for the Sir Roden Cutler Medal, he understood the significance of the advice sought. He knew that his friend needed to nominate a person who would be totally worthy of such an honour.

Kamahl had no hesitation. He recommended Dame Elisabeth Murdoch. With Basil's agreement, he suggested that he sound out Dame Elisabeth on his behalf to gauge her interest in being put forward, which he did as soon as possible. When he spoke to her, he informed her of Basil's intent to nominate. She agreed to consider suggesting that both Kamahl and Basil travel down to Victoria to meet with her at Cruden Farm for lunch the following week. Following their luncheon, Basil emerged from this meeting with an absolute conviction that Kamahl's recommendation was entirely appropriate. She had agreed to accept the medal. Without much ado, Dame Elisabeth was nominated, and the judging panel signed off on the prize shortly after that. Dame Elisabeth Murdoch was named the Sir

Roden Cutler Medal recipient for 2010. Following her presentation of the medal Kamahl wrote to Dame Elisabeth:

Dear Dame Elisabeth,

It was indeed a pleasure to speak to you, albeit briefly last week.

As I mentioned to you on the phone, I lunched with your fellow recipient of the Sir Roden Cutler Medal, Basil Sellers, two days ago and needless to say reminisced fondly over the times we were together with you at Cruden Farm, for the presentation of your medal and the earlier visit for a most memorable lunch.

Time is so fleeting. It seems like it was only yesterday when I fortuitously met Rupert and Pat on the night of the News Ltd Christmas party in December of 1958 in Adelaide . But for that chance meeting and subsequent friendship with them, my life as I know it may never have come to pass. I remain forever grateful to your generous son for being able to remain in Australia and pursue the career I couldn't have dreamt of.

Along the way, it has been my privilege to know various members of the Murdoch clan, not least of them, your most wonderful daughter, Helen, who I think of every day. I miss her more than I can say. Most of all it has been an honour and privilege to know you and to have sung for you and enjoy your continuing friendship. I have always admired the strength of your character and principles and values and tried to emulate them, but not as successfully as I might have wished. However, you remain an enduring and endearing role model and we as Australians are indeed lucky to have you.

With warmest regards,
Kamahl

Kamahl remained a great friend of Dame Elisabeth for the duration of her long life. In fact, he performed for her at her gala 90th Birthday celebrations at her request. He says, "She was an unabashed fan, and it was totally mutual. She was such a strong-minded and eloquent person with a great sense of fairness and decency. I missed out on performing at her one hundredth birthday celebrations. Evidently, the family had decided on going with a tenor that evening, so they flew Jose Carreras in from Spain. I heard later from her son-in-law, Geoff Handbury, that she had actually fallen asleep during the Carreras performance. I couldn't help my ego from thinking it was both a critique and a way of showing her disappointment at the real deal being overlooked," he laughs.

The time that Kamahl had spent touring rural Victoria would provide him with yet another Murdoch connection who would become very dear friends, Helen Handbury and her husband, Geoff. Helen's maiden name was Murdoch, and she was the eldest daughter of Dame Elisabeth and Sir Keith and big sister to Rupert. In the forties, she had met Geoff when both were pursuing their respective successful careers in Melbourne. Despite a long successful career in Media ownership, Geoff's primary interest was working the land. Having been raised in the country, he was always destined to return to it one day. Helen shared his passion, having spent many years herself in the country. The couple, therefore, mutually decided in the late seventies to return to living on the land full time and eventually settled in Hamilton near Horsham, where they spent the rest of their lives working on the land while raising their four children. Geoff still retained media interests by owning a dominant portion of the commercial radio licences throughout regional Victoria.

One of the first things they did when moving to the town was to purchase and re-open the Hamilton Abattoir, thus providing over 80 much needed full-time jobs for the townspeople. The couple were legendary philanthropists, with many of their activities being fed through anonymous donation. Helen was a Director for CARE Australia for a lengthy period. Both she and Geoff were highly active in their support of regional development through funding education programmes, the arts, health programmes and the construction of much-needed facilities within the region.

During one of his early Victorian tours, Kamahl recognised one of the people queuing up for an autograph after a concert at the venue at Horsham. It was none other than Helen. Kamahl thought it spoke highly of her character. Despite her wealth and social standing, she was just the same as any regular patron, neither seeking nor demanding any special treatment whatsoever. "She was a wonderful human being. Both she and Geoff were so incredibly generous. They were tireless philanthropists who gave so much to their community and a wide range of worthy Australian charities. I was very privileged indeed to know them both for so many years. I used to stay with them most of the years I was touring in Regional Victoria, and they were such wonderful hosts. I would also make sure that I had the time in the schedule to catch up with them whenever they were in Sydney. Sadly Helen succumbed to cancer in 2004 after beating it many years before. She was only 74. Geoff did survive until 2019 when he too passed away at the age of 94." The Handbury's lifelong commitment to charity work continues through the Geoff and Helen Handbury Foundation. The couple established the organisation many years ago as a vehicle to support the many causes they were involved in.

In 1993, whilst touring the US, Kamahl found himself in Los Angeles having to make a clothing purchase on Rodeo Drive. The acquisition was necessitated by two things. Firstly, he was keeping a promise to Dame Elisabeth Murdoch to give her a copy of his latest album which he decided to drop off at Rupert and Anna's relatively new Murdoch home. The couple had moved to the West Coast following the acquisition of entertainment entities to add to the Fox Group. The second more pressing issue was that the hotel he was staying at had had a massive laundry malfunction with his trousers. In fact, they had practically destroyed them. The Hotel management, full of contrition, informed him that they insisted upon replacing the trousers inviting him to head to Rodeo Drive and pick out a new pair. They would cover all costs. He accepted their apology and their more than reasonable offer of compensation.

While he was trouser shopping, he also took the opportunity to browse some of the other great stores located in the street. In one such establishment, a gallery specialising in high-end objet d'art, he chatted with the store owner, a rather pushy LA socialite type. Discovering that Kamahl was from Australia, she asked him if he knew Bryce Courtenay. He remembers being quite amused that Americans thought that Australia was such a small place that everyone from there must know everyone else. Sadly, however, he had to disappoint her. The woman went on to say that she had been holding a large piece for Courtenay, an elegant glass model of an eagle and unfortunately, she had misplaced his details and, as a result, had lost contact with him. Evidently, Bryce had been there to make the movie version of *The Power of One*. The gallery owner assumed that he would return to pick up the item after showing some interest in it before his departure. As the movie had recently been released to great fanfare, he had been feted in tinsel town as the next big thing. Hence the store owner was very keen to continue an association with him. Kamahl half-heartedly decided to humour the lady by saying that he would broker contact upon returning to Australia. She was so persistent he feared he may not get out of the store otherwise.

"When I returned to Australia, I found Bryce's contact details and gave him a call. We made arrangements to catch up for dinner, and I raised the subject of the eagle sculpture. He responded by saying, 'Yes, I remember that sculpture,' and that was it. Nothing else was said about it, no doubt much to the disappointment of the intrepid gallery owner. I reasoned that she may be a pushy sales type. But I certainly was not, not on behalf of some overly aggressive trinket peddler anyway," he laughs. Both enjoyed the dinner and chatted cordially for hours about shared and unique experiences of being FBAs (Kamahl's term for foreign-born Aussies).

"He told me that when he left South Africa, his friends and family gathered at the small railway station. They felt that they needed to send him off with a song. The dilemma was what to sing. They didn't want to do anything British as they were in Boer heartland, and the Boer War, whilst long gone, had not been erased from memory. They didn't want to sing anything in Afrikaans either. Bizarrely they decided upon the 'Battle Hymn of The Republic', the American independence anthem. He asked me if I could record a version for him. He often used to refer to the story in his public speaking engagements and would like to have the song played at a point in the presentation. I was delighted to accommodate his request with a no-frills version. In a quid pro quo, I asked him to write me a foreword to my 1995 biography, which he did magnificently," he recalls.

While the two exchanged the odd note from time to time, both were slaves to hectic schedules. They didn't catch up again until 2012. "I was shopping one day and ran into an old friend, Margaret Hamilton. It was unusual seeing her there as I knew she didn't live close by. It turned out that she was catching up with friends for lunch that day, one of whom, she explained was going through a hard time as her husband was critically ill with gastric cancer. I enquired who that was, and she informed me that her friend was Christine Gee, who I had known professionally for quite some time. Still, I hadn't been aware before this that she was married to Bryce Courtenay. She went on to say that he was apparently going into surgery quite soon, but the prognosis was far from encouraging. I had heard in the media that he had been having health issues, but I must admit I hadn't thought that it was anywhere as serious as I found it to be." Kamahl rang Bryce as soon as he got home to give support for the impending surgery. He felt Bryce seemed pleased to hear from him and quite upbeat for someone in such circumstances.

Kamahl shared his recent experiences, amongst which was his work on what was to be his new release *Yesterday Today and Tomorrow,* a triple CD. Kamahl even suggested recording a spoken piece, a poem of the same name he had written but wasn't really happy with. He indicated that Bryce may like to take a crack at it himself, a challenge he was hoping may provide a welcome distraction from his treatment. "We agreed to have dinner at the Point Piper Club, close to his home, which we did a short time later. On the evening, he was accompanied by Christine, his brother-in-law and wife and another friend. It was an enjoyable affair, all very convivial. However late in the night, Bryce turned to me and said, 'When I go will you sing the 'Battle Hymn of the Republic' at my funeral?' I was a bit confronted by his almost calm resignation to his fate, but obviously, I agreed. How could I possibly refuse? I did my best to change the subject to more pleasant matters. He asked me if I could sing for them, which I did falling back comfortably on good old 'Nature Boy'." Despite making plans for another catch up shortly after, Kamahl was not to see Bryce alive again as he died only a short while later. After his death, Christine contacted Kamahl telling him, "We hope you forgive our indulgence. Bryce has included you in his acknowledgements for his new book *Jack of Diamonds,* due out in December" Kamahl says, "Not mind? I was absolutely honoured"

When the funeral took place at St Mark's Church, Darling Point, it was attended by over 300 family and friends. Kamahl reached out to the organisers before the funeral to ensure that he could fulfil the promise he had made to his friend. Evidently, Bryce's publishing company, had assumed responsibility and had already arranged for another singer to perform the number. Not to be deterred, Kamahl joined the rest of the congregation in their collective rendition. With his booming voice, he was undoubtedly heard above the group. He says, "It may not be how I planned to perform it, but I performed it nonetheless." Following his last dinner with Bryce, Kamahl received a note from him it read:

To Kamahl,

At a recent Sydney dinner, I was given the rare honour of having Kamahl sing to our private gathering of family and friends. In addition, he recited the Gettysburg Address and believe me, you could hear a pin drop. The other diners, waiting for staff and our fellow guests, were transfixed, and some shed a tear. The dinner was transformed into a heartfelt journey that reached deep into our souls and resonated as we reflected on our collective lives travels. We were drawn into the emotion of the moment and could feel the pulse of life running like a river across the dining table. The magic of this occasion will never be forgotten, as it was unexpectedly one of the most memorable evenings of my life.

Kamahl has graced our land for decades, and he is unquestionably a national living treasure. I also wish to pay tribute to Kamahl's unfailing efforts over many decades to give back to those less fortunate. I am a storyteller, and Kamahl's remarkable life is probably worthy of a novel should I get the time to write it as I approach my 80th year."

Warm Wishes

Bryce Courtenay

Kamahl states, "To receive such a beautiful note from one of Australia's great creative minds was so precious to me. I will keep it forever as a testament to a man who, even though he was dying, had the grace and class to pen it."

Kamahl has indeed enjoyed many interesting relationships with prominent Australians over the years. Just like in any walk of life, some relationships lead to great friendships spanning decades whilst others are, to put it politely, challenging. His relationship with broadcaster Alan Jones, it would be fair to say, has been a bit of an emotional rollercoaster. "I met Alan at a Variety Club function in 1988. He was kind enough to donate his time to perform as an after-dinner speaker. A few guests encouraged Alan to perform a mock race call of the Melbourne Cup. He agreed with one condition. Guests at the table needed to donate $100 per head to Variety. As we were all dedicated Variety supporters at the table, I was on board. My fellow table guests agreed immediately. Alan did this party piece, and I went to introduce myself and thank him for his efforts for Variety. We had a conversation and seemed to hit it off quite well. We shared a lot of mutual acquaintances and so forth. He suggested that we should have lunch sometime. I agreed, and the invitation was sent via Alan's assistant only days later. We met at his Newtown premises which he lived in back then. The building was quite an impressive industrial conversion located right in the heart of the inner city. He had arranged an excellent meal, and we had a lengthy and amicable chat. He is a big music fan and knowledgeable about an era I am extremely familiar with, so there was plenty to talk about.

From this lunch, we would maintain quite regularly contact and someone who became a regular at many of the social engagements and gatherings over the next few years. After a while, I realised how difficult he was to maintain a relationship with. He and I have had many ups and downs over the years, to be honest, more downs than ups. It is remarkable all things considered that I ever had anything like a friendship with him, given the fact that our views on most things are at opposites. Still, I have always been able to see beyond rhetoric and bluster, particularly when someone can do incredibly positive things. Undoubtedly, he has been a great supporter of many of the charities I have been involved with. I will always be grateful for the assistance and professional support when it has been forthcoming. It is almost impossible for me to reconcile how someone capable of generosity can hold such extreme views. I have always tried to see the best in people, so I focus on the positive. I tend to view such things as quirks."

There had been a situation at 2GB which had led to an intense period between Kamahl and Jones previously, and both had been invited to appear together at an event to commemorate John Howard's thirtieth year in politics. It was scheduled only a few weeks later at Sydney's Hordern Pavilion in front of an audience of several hundred VIP attendees. To make matters worse, on the eve of the event, the letter story had been reported in the high circulating *Sydney Morning Herald*. It appeared right on the front page under the headline "Jones scolds old mate Kamahl". The story detailed the rift and had included a copy of the letter in its entirety. Kamahl, whilst embarrassed by the revelation, felt that the information was far from damaging to him or his reputation. He suspected that Jones would be livid. He was right.

On the evening of the Howard function, Jones was acting as MC for the event, and Kamahl was to sing the National Anthem. In practically every similar situation, it would be customary for the MC to introduce anyone performing on the night. Whilst this is precisely what he did do throughout the event, there was one notable exception. Jones allowed music to be Kamahl's only introduction to the stage. He evidently decided that he could not bring himself to offer any words. "On reflection, I think I may have made matters worse myself when I received that letter. I read it out to an audience at another show I was performing just before the Howard event. I was understandably angry at him for sending such a note, more than that, I was disappointed that Alan had such an outburst based on the hearsay. He never sought to hear my side of the story.

Somehow, we managed to get back on speaking terms after a while. However, it was a function of work bringing us back together rather than any great wish on my part to continue a relationship.

What was remarkable is that he agreed to host the launch of my first biography, *The Impossible Dream,* in 1995! I am pretty certain that he won't be anywhere near the launch of this one," he says with a broad grin.

One of Kamahl's most enduring friendships was with legendary entertainer Bob Hope and his wife, Dolores. After their meeting in London in the early seventies, Kamahl went on to work numerous times with Hope, whom he regarded as the ultimate mentor. There was literally nothing in show business Hope hadn't done. He was a comedian, actor, singer, dancer, and author and had a career that spanned nearly 80 years. If there was anything Bob Hope didn't know about show business, you could guarantee it wasn't worth knowing. For Kamahl, there was no question Bob couldn't answer nor advice that wasn't incredibly valuable, and he was never reluctant to share what he knew. Bob Hope continued to tour and perform deep into his old age, officially retiring after his ninetieth birthday. Kamahl had already appeared in a couple of Bob's US specials by this time. So when Hope toured Australia in 1978 to do a TV special, it was natural that Kamahl was engaged on the bill. Dispelling any suggestion that the booking was an old-friends act Hope, when interviewed at the time, stated, "I wanted to bring Kamahl's performance to the States". The TV special *Bob Hope Down Under* was produced in Perth by Chris Bearde. Chris was an Australian who had gained a strong reputation in Hollywood writing for Rowan and Martin's Laugh-In, a substantial international show of the early seventies. Bearde was to work with a little known writer named David Letterman. The show had a big-name lineup supporting Hope. It included TV stars Florence Henderson of *Brady Bunch* fame, *I Dream of Jeannie*'s Barbara Eden, and Charo, a comic actress who played a zany, fast-talking Spanish stereotype. At the time, this was a great lineup of stars guaranteed to appeal to both local and international markets, particularly the US market. In addition to the US performers and Kamahl, the popular Four Kinsmen, Miss Australia Gloria Krope and Maryanne Davidson, a six-year-old, antipodean Shirley Temple act who had recorded two songs, 'Tell Me a Story' and 'I Love My Daddy'. She was so overloaded on sweetness viewers risked developing type two diabetes. Kamahl was genuinely excited about the opportunity that the show presented. It was guaranteed to showcase his talent to a massive audience both home and abroad. The news got even better when Bob Hope approached him to ask him if he would be comfortable opening the show. Comfortable didn't adequately explain his feelings on the matter. Thrilled would've been an understatement. "My only disappointment was that Bob and Chris Bearde banned me from wearing a kaftan. They seemed to think that the US audiences would think I was a magician. It was a minimal compromise to be a part of something this big. I was sure that I could accommodate them." There were numerous rehearsals in the lead-up to the show, which was very necessary for a live audience program that ran like clockwork. Bearde and his Director, Dick McDonough, reminded Kamahl that he was to be there for ten minutes and not one second more when given his opening spot. When he was still out there twenty-five minutes later, the production teams blood pressure rose. As Kamahl left the stage, the assistant production manager angrily said, "What the f**k do you think you're doing? I said all you could do was ten minutes!" Kamahl calmly replied, "But I only did ten minutes. The guy spluttered that was more than ten effing minutes. I said, oh, I'm sorry, I must have forgotten to allow time for the applause. The guy really didn't appreciate my joke, but Barbara Eden, who overheard the exchange, certainly did. She fell about laughing, saying she didn't believe what she'd just heard."

Kamahl had been a big hit with the audience and clearly was in his element. "It was a great experience, and Bob paid me a lovely compliment when he said, 'How dare you be so good in my show?' which, coming from him, was very high praise indeed."

A few months after he had reached his one-hundredth birthday, Bob Hope died peacefully in his Los Angeles home after a short bout of pneumonia. Kamahl reached out to Dolores to offer condolences from both he and Sahodra. He continued to maintain regular contact with Dolores for her remaining years. She, like Bob, would go past the hundred-year mark and, like him, would retain her sharp wit and humour right up until the very end. In 2010 when Kamahl was in Los Angeles, he called to speak with her the day before he was scheduled to leave the US.

Dolores was delighted to hear from her dear friend. She even suggested that he delay his departure for a day or two to stay with her at her home. As Kamahl hadn't seen Dolores for many years, he felt obliged to comply with her generous request. When he arrived at the palatial home at Toluca Lake in the San Fernando Valley, he was informed by staff that Dolores was resting but would catch up with him at dinner. He was shown to the guest house, a magnificent home in its own right. A few hours later, he was told by staff that dinner was imminent and asked if he could make his way to the dining room in the main house.

Kamahl remembers the meeting, "I went to the dining-room, which was quite a stroll from the guest house. When I got there, Dolores still hadn't arrived. The room overlooked the rest of the property. I saw someone pushing a wheelchair containing Dolores from quite a distance. The closer she got, the frailer and smaller she appeared. Even though she was well past her hundredth birthday, I was still shocked at how much she had deteriorated from the last time I had seen her only a couple of years before. When she arrived in the room, she immediately said, 'Kamahl, I can't see you because my sight has gone, and you will have to wait to speak to me until I have my hearing attached.' She was blind and deaf. I am so glad she couldn't see the look of concern on my face, as I am sure I had not managed to contain my expressions of concern. Once she was settled at the table and had her hearing, quite a large and elaborate machine device placed on her head, we talked as though nothing had changed at all. Her mind was still powerful. Our conversation was just as it always had been. As I looked around the room, I noticed many framed pictures with Bob and her across the years. A couple of pictures caught my eye, particularly when she was a young singer before marrying Bob. She was quite the beauty and, to all accounts, gave up a very promising career after their being wed. I asked her about her career, and she told me how much she loved it and remembered it fondly and would give me a recording. She did give it to me before I left a couple of days later.

When I got home, I played it. I was very impressed with how beautiful her voice was. I even asked radio's Bob Rogers, who was on the air back then, to play it for his audience without naming the artist. Evidently, the station received many calls inquiring where they could buy a copy of the recording whilst it was still playing. More calls were received after he announced who the artist actually was. It just goes to show that time doesn't diminish true talent. I was so sad to learn that she passed away some months later at the grand old age of 102. Both she and Bob were wonderful friends."

In 1958 the famous American bass-baritone William Warfield was touring Australia, and Kamahl was lucky to be introduced to him during his tour with the South Australian Symphony. A significant opera performer, he is best known for the cinematic version of *Show Boat*, playing Old Joe, the role initially played by Kamahl's idol Paul Robeson. He performed 'Ol' Man River' in this role, a song that was a cornerstone of Kamahl's own act. Kamahl attended his concert in Adelaide and sat three rows from the front with his then-girlfriend Carlene Berg. Getting to meet him was a far more complex exercise than meeting either Nat King Cole or Paul Robeson had been. Henry Krips, the Symphony's conductor, was overly protective of his guest soloist and would wave away any approach by fans. To Kamahl's great surprise, as he and Carlene were leaving the theatre Warfield, called them out and gestured for them to return.

Warfield asked Kamahl if he had been to the previous day's performance. He could remember seeing him in the audience. This was one time Kamahl was genuinely grateful to be the only black face in the white audience. Warfield generously invited Kamahl and Carlene to a reception held in his honour the following day at the Australia Hotel. Kamahl attended the reception eagerly, filled with questions about performing, how to project his voice and a myriad of other technical matters. "William's voice was compelling. I was in absolute awe at his strength of delivery, and I wanted more than anything to be able to emulate his performance," he says. The great baritone encouraged Kamahl to follow his tour around Australia, and he would be happy to share his knowledge. Kamahl followed him to Sydney and Melbourne and was provided with lessons in his downtime in borrowed studio space at the ABC. Kamahl remembers during one of their sessions, the great man asked him, "Are you camp?" Kamahl, who was totally unfamiliar with the term, just responded, "No, I am Ceylonese."

Kamahl says, "William was a fascinating person. He had served in military intelligence during the war and immediately afterwards in Germany. He was apparently fluent in German, which he had developed whilst studying opera. However, his skills were not fully used due to segregation within the military. A classic case of the stupidity of prejudice. He was a great singer and had been married to another. His ex-wife was the gifted soprano he met whilst playing the lead roles in *Porgy and Bess.* Sadly they had already separated by 1958, but they would remain close and work together for years to come. When I first met him, I was eager to pick his brains as outside of Paul Robeson himself, there were few such credentialed bass-baritones around. He was most generous with his time and thoughtful in his advice," he says. The men maintained friendly contact through correspondence and a met up when geography permitted for many years.

In 1984 when Kamahl was touring the US, he received an invitation to attend the gala performance in Aaron Copland's Lincoln Portrait at Central Park. William told Kamahl that he had arranged everything for him, including transport. "I was blown away by his generous hospitality. He told me that he had arranged for a limo sent to my hotel and said that he hoped I didn't mind sharing the limo with Lauren Bacall. Did I mind? Of course, I didn't mind, but unfortunately, I was so star struck and yet embarrassingly so ignorant of her career history. I found it hard to strike up any meaningful conversation as we rode to the venue. She was charming and, even at her then sixty years of age, quite a stunningly attractive woman. As we were seated together in the VIP section, we took our seats close to a massive speaker stack. Sometime early into the performance, one of the speaker's drivers exploded, causing quite a panic. Bacall looked at me and just said one word, 'Run!' I suppose when anyone hears any kind of bang in New York, everyone is hard-wired to do a Usain Bolt impression. Let alone being told by Humphrey Bogart's girl." Evidently, when the source of the noise was identified, the audience reclaimed their seats, and the performance continued.

"It was a wonderful experience made possible by William, a wonderful friend. Aaron Copland was undoubtedly a musical genius, but I have always disliked him as a person. His mean spirited comments about Ralph Vaughan Williams, the brilliant British composer being the root cause of my issue with his character. Vaughan Williams had penned one of my favourite all-time musical pieces, 'The Lark Ascending'. Copland had said, 'Listening to the fifth symphony of Ralph Vaughan Williams is like staring at a cow for 45 minutes.' I always wondered what there was to be gained from being disrespectful to a man with such a great legacy. It was so spiteful that I often wondered why any artist would say anything like that about another artist's work. I can only assume his motivation was jealousy."

Kamahl's friendship with Warfield would extend beyond his untimely demise in 2002 when he succumbed to severe neck injuries sustained in a fall at his home. Kamahl attended a concert, a recital by famous American soprano Kathryn Battle at The Melbourne Hall only months after his friend's death. "The concert itself was an absolute train wreck. She was a great talent with a wonderful voice, but she kept being distracted by petty annoyances mainly of her own making. Her accompanist Sharolyn Kimmorley, who I had performed with previously and was someone I had very high regard for. The show had barely begun when she stopped in apparent frustration with Sharolyn and continued to treat her like she was a novice student taking a lesson from a great teacher. It was totally cringeworthy. I have never sensed so much discomfort in an audience. When I was invited to meet her backstage at a reception, I went in full of trepidation at meeting someone who was evidently quite prickly. All I can say is if I was expecting her to be anything other than rude, arrogant and unpleasant, I was to be significantly disappointed. In my attempt at small talk, I mentioned that I was a friend of William Warfield. She basically snarled 'So what!' along with a coarse assessment of William's ability. I was so disgusted. I told her what I thought of her lack of professionalism on stage, disrespecting her accompanist, and her obvious nasty nature. Well, words to that effect anyway adding another word which rhymes with twitch. Although the audience attending that night didn't get to hear my angry spray, I know every single one of them would've applauded it more than her fractured awkward performance, including my dear recently departed friend who I am sure would've given me a bravo for the performance from wherever he was. I certainly know that when I met Sharolyn Kimmorley sometime later, she definitely concurred with my critique one hundred and fifty percent."

Despite some of the frustrations he encountered in London during the seventies, Kamahl would love his time in the UK. It was a great time. I got to witness entertainers at the peak of their powers, up close and personal. I got to know many when starting out who would inevitably become legends," remarked Kamahl. One notable example was Herb Kretzmer. Herb started his career as a little known South African writer… a respected journalist, and satirist. He had decided in the early sixties that his true passion was writing lyrics. Herb had a hit early on in his new career, a co-writing credit with David Lee for the novelty hit featuring Peter Sellers and Sophia Loren, 'Goodness Gracious Me.' Being quite an accomplished linguist, he also translated and modified the lyrics of Charles Aznavour's works, including the massive hit 'She' covered by many great artists. When Kamahl first encountered Herb, he was already well known and well regarded within the industry. His introduction came via his good friend Matt White, the doyen of show business reporters in Sydney. In 1967, Matt had written a glowing appraisal of Kamahl's performance in *Follow The Sun*. Although a Sydney based writer, he had originated from the UK. When he found out that Kamahl was headed to England in the early seventies, he said he must meet his friend 'Herbie'. Obviously, Kamahl was keen to get as many contacts as possible and gratefully took the generous introduction from his friend and acted upon it when he arrived. He not only met with Herb, but he would also work with him on several songs. A piece called 'You've Got To Learn' would become one of his favourites. Whilst Herb was very well respected in the entertainment industry, publicly, he was little known. That was to change significantly when contacted by producer Cameron Macintosh in 1984 to write the English version of the French musical *Les Misérables*. The musical was written initially by Alain Boublil and Claude-Michel Schonberg. The translation turned the two-hour production into a three-hour stage musical masterpiece that would break records all over the world. Kamahl recalls, "I was on my way to London from the States a short while after *Les Mis* was launched on the West End. I knew very little about the show,but I knew Herb professionally and socially. We got on very well, so I thought I would call my friend to congratulate him on his success when I landed. He was very pleased to hear from me. He was thrilled with the show's reception and said, 'Kamahl, it is unbelievable, I am literally floating on money right now.' He was gracious enough to send me a ticket for a matinee show. I could clearly see what all the fuss was about. I loved the show and shared his joy. It is really great to see someone you know, genuinely talented actually get the acknowledgement they deserve. It is even greater when they are such a great person. In October 2020, he passed at the age of 95. Herb Kretzmer left behind such a great body of work as well as some great memories," Kamahl reflects.

When Jack Neary brought Harry Secombe to Australia in 1971, Kamahl was introduced to him and Harry's manager Jimmy Grafton as part of the NLT Agency family. Kamahl had an immediate rapport with both men. "Harry was exactly as you saw him on stage, warm, genuine and very funny. Both he and Jimmy knew everyone and anyone who mattered in Britain's world of show business. Jimmy, in particular, was always full of great advice and seemed eager to provide guidance, which for me was priceless. Jimmy suggested that I get over to the UK as soon as possible because he felt that I was good on TV. In his words, I would be run off my feet with work." Buoyed by the positive feedback, Kamahl had Jack Neary reach out formally to investigate an appearance on Harry Secombe's eponymous TV variety show. Good to his word, Jimmy showed he meant what he said by getting the TV spot and arranged a series of club engagements and a booking at the Savoy Hotel. Ross Barlow, Kamahl's recording company boss, also set for him to meet with the top producer at the Philips label. Before he knew it, he was to be on his way to conquer Britain almost before he had any chance of developing cold feet. He agreed to take on the world, starting in London. It was decided Bill Marshall would accompany him and was doing his level best to keep Kamahl pump primed for the challenges ahead. The itinerary was drawn up, and the tickets were about to be purchased when ABC TV came calling with an offer he simply could not refuse, his own TV show that would run across two series and two years in his own name. For now, it appeared conquering Britain would have to wait. Luckily when his TV commitments were finalised sometime later, he did get to take that long trip. It seemed that all of the plans previously in place had simply waited in anticipation of his arrival, including the previously arranged engagements through Jimmy Grafton.

The Secombe show went live on a Saturday evening and had a massive viewing audience. His performance was met with a positive critical response. If not for the personal involvement of Harry and Jimmy, many of the doors he walked through would undoubtedly be firmly shut. Not only did Harry provide access to his own audience, but he and Jimmy would also drop by to see Kamahl's act from time to time at the Savoy. They added a much welcomed moral support and Harry's excellent star quality to the audience.

During one of Kamahl's tours, he and Bill Marshall would stay with Warren Mitchell, the great British actor. Warren had toured Australia with NLT several times. Warren was a tremendously well credentialled, serious actor. However, it was to be playing a TV character Alf Garnett, in the comedy series, *'Til Death Us Do Part*, which would bring him to the attention of millions. It would afford him superstar status through the UK and many parts of the English-speaking world. He was so successful and convincing in his portrayal as the East End cockney bigot that it would typecast him for most of his career. It limited the offer of more severe roles significantly. Not as many people may remember his King Lear, that would remember Alf, the cringe-worthy racist curmudgeon.

The irony of Warren playing a part that was so at odds with who he actually was is undoubtedly the hallmark of the great actor he was. Warren was a most generous host and threw open the doors for Kamahl and Bill to stay as long as needed. "Warren was a real gentleman and quite unlike his on-stage alter ego Alf quite a reserved man with a profound conviction about social issues. He had a concern that the role he played, who he'd made just as awful as writer Johnny Speight's intended, could act as a role model for real racists and xenophobes. That was far from the intention. The character was meant to show the preposterous face of bigotry, not be its poster boy. With Alf, he had almost become a prisoner of his own success. The typecasting thing is a real problem for great actors when the show's popularity becomes so great that the public demand more and more of it. Of course, they want to see their favourite character played only by the familiar person. The only upside, of course, is the financial benefit of being in gainful employment for almost as long as they can stand playing the part. I believe the same thing happened with the two actors in *Steptoe & Son*, Harry H Corbett and Wilfred Bramble. Both were extremely well-credentialled actors restricted to the TV series for years. In their case, it was much worse because the two men famously couldn't stand each other and yet stuck with each other for years. At least as a solo singer, you haven't that conundrum to deal with 'like it or lump itl, the audience either buys you for who you are or not rather than the person you are pretending to be, although it is not entirely unknown for singers to become overwhelmed by their image and in doing so lose themselves."

Kamahl could always turn chance meetings into acquaintances and acquaintances into friendships. Some of which would endure throughout the years… For example, Michael Feinstein, the multi-platinum-selling, two-time Emmy and five-time Grammy award-nominated entertainer, known as *The Ambassador of the Great American Songbook*, was possibly the premier interpreter of American standards. He and Kamahl crossed paths in New York in 1986 at the famous Algonquin Hotel. He remembers, "I met Michael when I was having drinks with a couple of friends one night at the cocktail lounge of the Algonquin Hotel in Times Square. For some reason, the bar was practically empty. Michael was sitting at the piano just playing like it was his regular day job. When he had played for a while, he came over to our table. He introduced himself and chatted with my friends and me. I was absolutely mesmerised by his encyclopaedic knowledge of modern American music. He went to play Nat King Cole's 'Blame It On My Youth' at my request, which he did brilliantly. After a long and most enjoyable conversation, we exchanged details. Shortly afterwards, I sent him a letter with a tape of a song I thought he should record. It was called 'New Words.' He responded with a wonderful note that was both gracious and extremely flattering. He referred to my inclusion on the B-side of my interpretation of Nat King Cole's 'Nature Boy'. The very song that inspired me to be a singer and that I had been performing since the early 1950s."

Feinstein had said:

"… The song 'New Words' is a beautiful song and I am going to try singing it – but the real treat for me was the second side of the tape with your beautiful, heartfelt recording of 'Nature Boy' which rivals Nat King Cole's recording in my book. Your voice is captivating and you sing everything with such an easy, smooth quality, how I wish I could do that."

Praise is always gladly accepted by Kamahl, but this was recognition from an accomplished artist, better yet a veritable walking encyclopaedia of the American music canon. It was a great affirmation. It practically obliterated all those mean-spirited critiques he had had over the years.

One long term friend is the famed violinist Beryl Kimber with whom Kamahl attended the Elder Conservatorium in Adelaide during the 1950s. Beryl was a prodigy who made her debut as a violin soloist at the age of 13. In 1958, she won the first distinction at the Tchaikovsky Competition in Moscow, where she studied with David Oistrakh. When finally back in Australia in 1963, she became a lecturer at the Elder Conservatorium. Along the way, she had met and wed Clemens Leske, who was similarly credentialed as his very talented spouse. For decades, the couple would become the mainstay at the Elder Conservatorium, where Beryl and Clemens committed their careers to teaching until 1998. The couple then retired and moved to Sydney to be closer to their son, Clemens Leske Jr, a highly gifted musician. Like his parents before him, Clemens Jr would become a great performer with all symphony orchestras in Spain, the United Kingdom, Singapore, New Zealand, Hungary and China. He is now the Senior Lecturer in Piano at the Sydney Conservatorium.

Kamahl maintained regular contact with the couple throughout the years. In July 2019, he was very disappointed to learn that Clemens had sadly died. Beryl asked him to perform the Lord's Prayer at the memorial service. Naturally, Kamahl agreed but confesses that he was a little overwhelmed as the audience was filled with earnest musicians and vocalists. "I was to perform a solemn and spiritual piece to an audience filled to the rafters with such magnificent musical talent. It was quite intimidating, but I had to honour my old friend's passing wish and support his life partner and my other lifetime friend. I have kept communicating with Beryl since Clemens' passing to check on how life is treating her. For a few months, I hadn't heard from her. I only recently received an email apologising for her lack of communication. Her mobility has been extremely restricted, the result of a massive stroke she had suffered. She went on to tell me in her note that she couldn't speak to me as the stroke had robbed her of her voice. What a great shame for someone who dedicated their entire life to making so many people happy with beautiful sounds. She is no longer be able to make any sound at all, sometimes life is really very cruel."

On the subject of injustice, one of the earliest and longest friendships that Kamahl formed in Australia was with a man he met in University, a person he would go on to regard as close as family. His friend, who he cannot name, due to ongoing legal proceedings involving a family estate dispute, we will refer to as MB, was very high achiever both academically and athletically. MB would achieve honours in his studies while concurrently representing Australia internationally in his chosen sport. He would go on to establish himself professionally becoming known as one of his industries great innovators.

Kamahl witnessed MB strive to support his younger siblings through great personal sacrifice. He would not only pay for the studies of his brothers but went as far as financially assisting them in setting up their own professional practises.

Sadly in 2012, his friend died due to a massive heart attack which totally devastated his wife and only daughter. The death set up a sequence of events that boggled the mind as his siblings and their respective families took the opportunity of his passing to profit. They took advantage of a cooperative family investment trust that encompassed all family holdings. This included all property and funds. It also included his late friend's business premises and private homes. This led to a lengthy, bitter legal battle spanning almost a decade. The resulting ruling has effectively left his dear friend's widow and daughter disinherited, penniless, and homeless.

Kamahl refers to it as a Greek tragedy of monumental proportion. He is outraged at the greed and depravity of his MB's brothers and their respective families. Kamahl has been tirelessly attempting to support his old friend's family by providing counsel and has helped to finance legal challenges. Whilst his efforts may prove Quixotian, he is determined not to allow this tragedy to continue. It is a testament to his view on friendship that he is prepared to throw the total weight of his support behind their plight. For Kamahl, it is highly evident that he believes that loyalty is forever, well beyond life itself.

Kamahl cherishes friendships and consequently places a very high value on them. He has however discovered that sometimes, they have come at a cost, both financially and reputationally. Although Kamahl's hearing has been significantly impaired by his choice of career and advancing age, it hasn't stopped him from lending a willing ear to the problems of others. This has sometimes made him susceptible to those with a hard luck story which occasionally has ended in the odd unpaid debt.

18

The royal 'We'

Something as curious as the monarchy won't survive unless
you take account of people's attitudes. After all, if people don't
want it, they won't have it.

Prince Charles

As a young brown kid growing up in colonial Malaya, Kamahl was critically aware of class structure and the politics of race. They were a dominant factor in Malayan society, culture and everyday life. In this world, there was a defined hierarchy that was strictly deferential to the caste system, the segmentation of society into groups whose membership was determined by birth.

Beyond his community, however, other structures existed that were defined by different racial groups. Of course, wealth was within all of these structures, which provided some mobility. In so many ways, the design of Malayan society was arranged in ethnic and religious silos. Each with its own structure and hierarchy and interaction between the groups is mainly transactional rather than driven by a national purpose. However, British colonialism was above and beyond all of the social systems of the country's various silos. The British ruled over the land and imposed their laws rigidly, greatly aided by a divide and conquer strategy. Above that whole heaving byzantine mess was regarded as the highest human level, the inscrutable ruling class, the King and his lineage. Of course, each of these groups had their respective God as supreme ruler. Being born into a complex social structure created by birth not worth develops a mindset, where one feels pigeonholed and accepts power system where rising above your station is seemingly impossible. When British sovereign rule disappeared in 1942 after the Japanese invasion an alternative system was introduced. Like their counterparts however, the Japanese were beholden not only to their country but to the Emperor, or Tennō as they referred to him. This title literally translates as 'the Heavenly Sovereign'. For Malays of all stripes, it was a similar but far more repressive alternative to the lives they had always led.

When Britain reclaimed its colonial overlord role, the financial hardship forced upon it by World War Two significantly impacted its capability to maintain an Empire. For a short time, it was the resumption of business as usual. No one in Kamahl's world thought to question British rule as their social construct was designed to reinforce everyday people knowing 'their place'. Cecil Rhodes, who established his legacy in South Africa, was an ardent British imperialist. He said of his countrymen, "Remember that you are an Englishman and have consequently won first prize in the lottery of life". Whilst the Malayan colony was geographically and culturally far removed from South Africa, the notion of racial superiority was in many ways identical to the vision that Rhodes espoused. National Independence was still some years away, and in Kamahl's mind, it had never been a consideration. Even when disrupted with a three-year absence, the colonial system had resumed almost seamlessly. When he departed his birthplace, independence was still some way off, and when it did arrive, it came only after a long and bloody civil war. When Kamahl arrived in Australia in 1953, it was the same year a newly minted and extremely popular young monarch, Elizabeth II came to the throne. Hence, he found himself in a new homeland, a nation where the monarchy had a substantial foothold. Whilst Australia in the nineteen fifties was undoubtedly a nation in its own right, it was still firmly entrenched in everything relating to an Anglo tradition. With a new, young and very popular monarch on the throne, support for the monarchy was objectively at its highest point, at least its most popular since Federation.

Kamahl recalls, "I remember in 1954 when the Queen toured for the first time, it was a huge tour in which it was believed that over 75% of the population had turned out to see her in person. I was part of the 75%. I was one of those cramming the streets of Adelaide, waving my Australian flag and hoping to get a glance of her as she was driven through the masses. The crowd just wanted to see her with their own eyes, and I can say that we actually felt privileged to be afforded that opportunity. Little did I know at the time that I would get to meet her in person in 1982. Actually, I have met most of the British Royal Family. Something that a kid from Brickfields would never in their wildest dreams believe was ever possible."

Kamahl's somewhat positive views on Royalty he confesses may be seen as unfashionable these days. He suggests that he has never been a republican and that could be due to the conditioning of his upbringing. However, he understands and respects many who are. He believes that possibly his positive attitude toward Royalty comes from having had such positive interactions with so many of them over the years. Most of those opportunities have been due to a connection through charitable work and what he sees as their genuine commitment by the great weight that their direct support provides. "My view is that being born into royalty is like being born into poverty. You really don't get a choice. If you are lucky enough to be born in a high station, you should use that fortunate accident to do good things and treat others with great respect. I see there is a net positive in having them. In my dealings with the Royal Family, they do both."

One aspect of Royalty he is not a big fan of is what he calls the protocol police. He feels that the rules they design to protect their masters and mistresses from the 'riff-raff' are more about their own ambitions. He recalls he met Princess Anne in 1974 after donating proceeds from his *Around the World* album to the Save the Children Fund, of which she was the patron. As is the custom, at the tea party function, donors present cheques from funds raised directly to the patron and are engaged in a short, polite conversation. He says, "She thanked me for my work, asked me where I was from, what I did, so on and so forth. I remember her being a really nice and very natural person. She even went so far as to tell me that she thought that I had a great voice. After a few minutes, she moved on to other guests. I was then approached by a very snooty older woman who rudely and abruptly asked me what the Princess had said to me. I replied, 'She said your place or my Palace?', it was obviously a joke, but she was not amused at all."

Kamahl's dealings with Royalty have been characterised by pleasant exchanges with the Royal person, bookended by brusque interactions with obsequious officials. They fawn upon the Monarchy whilst managing to be rude and arrogant to everyone else. He is confident that the monarchy is not the driver of this attitude. He suggests that they probably have no idea it is even happening. "You know there is an old saying, the Queen thinks the whole world smells of fresh paint because everywhere she goes, there is someone a few feet in front of her touching things up," he laughs.

One such instance was his first meeting in 1981 with King Charles III at a Command Performance in Adelaide, back when he was Prince of Wales. The country at the time was in the midst of an industrial dispute involving Qantas. The strike had greatly restricted the number of passengers able to fly around the country. As a result, Kamahl could not take Sahodra and the children to the concert. When doing the obligatory meet and greet with the Prince following the show, Kamahl was received most cordially, the Prince saying how much he had enjoyed the performance. "I thanked him and replied that I very much enjoyed the opportunity to perform for him. It was unfortunate that my family couldn't travel with me to see it. Prince Charles replied, 'that is a shame, there is a polo match I am playing in this Sunday in Sydney. I would be delighted to have you and your family attend if you can be bothered, that is?' Of course, I could be bothered. I packed Sahodra and the kids into the car that Sunday, and I was off to Warwick Farm. When we arrived, I noticed the Prince, as usual, surrounded by minders. He had had a fall in the tournament and couldn't play on. Much to his disappointment, he stood quite a distance away, champagne glass in hand and chatting with some people. He must've sensed my dark presence and headed over to welcome us. He spoke with Sahodra and both of the children as well. When he spoke with Rani, she point-blank asked him if he had my latest record. I was surprised but very proud of her pitching technique. When he replied he had not, she said Daddy would get him one. The Prince replied that he would very much like that. Shortly after, he was whisked away by a protocol policeman to have someone else get their rationed few minutes." Kamahl found out how to fulfil Rani's princely promise and despatched a copy of his latest album to the Palace. Several weeks later, to his delight, he received some very fancy looking correspondence, a thank you letter from Prince Charles, signed personally.

Whilst Kamahl has performed individually and collectively for the British Royals at one time or another. This is also true of the Dutch Royal Family. Following his involvement with the World Wildlife Foundation by way of his 'Elephant Song', he had actually become a long-term friend of Prince Bernhard, the patron of the Fund and was a regular guest for pre-Christmas drinks with the regent over a number of years.

One of his favourite memories through all of this regal interaction definitely is, however, one of his most recent. In 2018, Kamahl was to perform at the Invictus Games in Sydney. The Games, launched in 2014, promote the importance of sport and physical activity in rehabilitating wounded, injured and ill service members and veterans of military conflict. The patron of the Games is Prince Harry, Duke of Sussex.

Kamahl performed the poem 'Invictus' by William Ernest Henley as a spoken piece. His stirring rendition of the poem was delivered to a group of VIPs, including the Prince himself. Harry was clearly moved by the performance, as evidenced by him rushing to Kamahl on stage to congratulate him with far less reserve than is commonly associated with the Monarchy

Whilst meeting with Prince Harry was very much a treasured moment for Kamahl, getting to that point was characterised by the usual run-ins with the smothering level of protection. His involvement with the Invictus Games 2018 was, like many things, just by chance. He was aware of the Games coming to Australia and was keen to support them in the way that he knew best. Kamahl was very familiar with Henley's 'Invictus'. He loved the gravity of the words and their message. He was convinced that he could add the appropriate level of gravitas and drama. He tried to reach out to the organising committee on numerous occasions to volunteer his services for the opening ceremony. The organisers were initially reluctant to accept his offer, more or less ghosting him without response. He decided to take it on the chin and write it off as a missed opportunity until one afternoon in Parramatta when attending an opening ceremony for a new building. Kamahl can't precisely recall how he managed to be on the invitation list for this event. It was a multi-storey structure named in honour of Philip Ruddock, long-time Minister for Immigration. He couldn't help feeling the acute irony of the situation in his being invited, given his history with the Department of Immigration. Nonetheless, he dutifully turned up and was prepared for yet another of those public events wondering why he was there. When at the event, he encountered a young man named Adam Zammit, who evidently had something to do with organising the event. As it was a pretty dull affair, Kamahl was relieved to meet someone so full of humour and energy. He very much enjoyed the distraction that his discussion provided. During the conversation, it was revealed Adam was connected with the Invictus

Games. As Kamahl often states, his life is full of serendipitous situations. This was to be another as Adam promised to speak with someone on Kamahl's behalf regarding his performance at the Games. Within a few days, Adam was good to his word. He had raised the matter, and Kamahl was contacted to see if he could attend a meeting with the Invictus Games Organising Committee.

When he participated in the conference with what he describes as a table full of people in a board room, CEO Patrick Kidd asked to perform a read of the poem. After the read, he was informed that the Committee would like to take up his offer to perform the piece. However, they already had booked their speaker for the Opening Ceremony. They wanted him to perform it to a group of several hundred Games volunteers later in the week. Disappointed at missing out on the main gig, but ever wanting to please, he agreed to do it. He arrived at the event held in the ballroom of Sydney's Park Hyatt Hotel. He took to the stage without any guidance or introduction. "I was just left to my own devices. Really, I had no briefing other than turning up and doing the poem. I thought that maybe an introduction to the meaning and significance may be helpful, so I did my own introduction, followed by the poem and left the event," he recalls.

The following day he was contacted again by the Committee, who asked him if he could perform the piece yet again for a VIP event on the launch day of the Games. Kamahl ventured that he would provide a piece of original track music himself even though there was no real budget in place.

This was quite a bold move on his part. He had volunteered Rajan's services without conferring him first. To make matters worse, it was a really tough brief. He needed to write and record a backing track that incorporated both the spirit of the Games whilst providing a suitably dramatic backing to his dad's spoken-word delivery. To top it off, it was a volunteered piece. It had never occurred to Kamahl for even half of one second that Rajan wasn't up to the task. He was proved absolutely right, his confidence in Rajan's talent as a composer, and arranger was not misplaced, and he completed the job masterfully. The track was almost perfect. Kamahl had one minor issue with the piece, suggesting a slight pause be inserted at one part of the track. Rajan disagreed, and a small but tense stand-off ensued, "Rajan had done such a masterful job with the music that I felt terrible even making the suggestion. I just felt a small extra beat of timing inserted where I had suggested would actually make it perfect for my delivery. To his great credit, whilst he disagreed with my suggestion, he decided to play it to some people that he trusted. He then came back with a revised track accommodating my change. I was so proud of him because I believe that every good artist must always have the conviction to fight hard for their work … Great artists don't ever close their mind, even if that means accommodating an annoying old dad." On the day of the event, Kamahl arrived out at Homebush, the main venue for much of the Games, Rajan's music on CD in hand. He was ushered to the VIP Marquee, where he was to perform. He was deliberately early so that he could do a read through and speak with the audio operator. He was informed by the Hospitality Manager for the Games, Kim King, that this was not possible and that he needed to come back when he was required, over an hour later. They gave no suggestion on how he was meant to kill the hour. Nor did they offer to transport him somewhere else in one of the many golf carts present. He was simply dismissed as a distraction from their preparation. Homebush is not the friendliest of environments to kill an hour or so. The concrete and asphalt landscape in the heat of early Spring, is no place for a casual stroll, let alone for a man in his eighties. He figured he would head to the nearest venue providing shade and shelter. This was still over 800 metres away from the venue. So it was that he headed to the Novotel Hotel, where he was compelled to cool his heels alone in their coffee shop. He was feeling annoyed, and a bit like the 'hired help'… Worse still, he was unpaid help that had to provide his own backing track and transport and even pay for his own coffee.

Invictus

Out of the night that covers me,
  Black as the pit from pole to pole,
I thank whatever gods may be
  For my unconquerable soul.

In the fell clutch of circumstance
  I have not winced nor cried aloud.
Under the bludgeonings of chance
  My head is bloody, but unbowed.

Beyond this place of wrath and tears
  Looms but the Horror of the shade,
And yet the menace of the years
  Finds and shall find me unafraid.

It matters not how strait the gate,
  How charged with punishments the scroll,
I am the master of my fate,
  I am the captain of my soul.

William Ernest Henley.

When the time came for his performance, Kamahl quickly spoke to the sound engineer to start the track as he was entering the small stage area. Around five hundred were in attendance, quite a number designated appropriately as VIP. Kamahl had not realised until he completed the performance that the guy in his peripheral view with the ginger hair was, in fact, Prince Harry. "Immediately afterwards, Prince Harry walked towards me with his hands out, as if he was going to hug me, saying it was 'unbelievably powerful emotional and amazing.' I have to say it was definitely the most enthusiastic royal reception I had ever received. I was so surprised by his presence but more by his enthusiasm. I have to admit that I felt very awkward about the prospect of a royal hug. I am not sure whether it was my background conditioning about royalty and knowing my station, which made me feel that way. Still, I thrust out my hand for a handshake which was gladly accepted. I spoke with the Prince for a few minutes, recalling my meeting with his father years before. I had even brought a copy of the letter to show him on the off chance that I did get to meet him. Before that could happen, he was ushered away by Hospitality Manager Kim King, presumably for othermeet and greets that she deemed more important than me." Kamahl was highly annoyed and expressed his feelings in no uncertain terms in an email several days later. She responded to his questioning why he had been interrupted and was informed that it was due needing everyone to be seated for the Chairman's address. There were two points he took from this response. Firstly, Kamahl suggests that at delay of a few seconds at such an event, particularly one created by its most important guest would have barely been noticed by anyone at all, much less the Chairman. Secondly and without a doubt most amusingly, was the fact that the event was not a seated affair... there was not a seat in sight in the whole Marquee.

"It was just complete and absolute bloody nonsense. As if that wasn't bad enough, I finally learned who was to deliver 'Invictus', the person for whom I had been overlooked for the formal opening. I had imagined that they had arranged for someone with the ability to interpret this wonderful piece. Someone who could deliver it with the gravitas and drama, it occurred that the great Cate Blanchett, Jack Thompson or Geoffrey Rush or any one of the many great Australian actors could have been perfect. Instead, I discovered that this committee, in their infinite wisdom, had decided on Gladys Berejeklian, the Premier of NSW. Please don't get me wrong. I have no issues with Ms Berejeklian at all. I even think she did quite a remarkable job with the pandemic. However, with all due respect, she was totally wrong to deliver that piece. I totally understand that she is undoubtedly capable of delivering speeches in her role as Premier. Still, this poem is not a political speech about fiscal policy. It is a theatrical and inspirational piece meant to evoke a person's triumph against great adversity. Obviously, as Premier, she would be delivering a welcome speech, but why the hell would you get her to deliver such a powerful piece of prose, it was just an idiotic idea."

Of the recent Royal kerfuffle concerning Harry, Meghan and the Palace, he says, "Like everyone else, I really have no idea what caused such a rift. I would, however, also question the wisdom of doing an Oprah Winfrey tell-all interview to air such issues. For a family who is so protective of their privacy despite their very public position, it was bound to upset the apple cart... From my own experiences with the protocol police, I know there is confusion that they create when second-guessing the wishes of their masters and mistresses. That provides a fertile breeding environment for misinformation, misunderstanding and ill-feeling. They live in the most rarefied atmosphere. Because of that, there is always speculation and innuendo that can easily spiral out of control. Whilst I know very little of Meghan, I have some sympathy. I am sure that no amount of preparation could adequately condition an outsider for that life. Particularly a person without an entrenched understanding of British culture."

Kamahl confesses to becoming very emotional when hearing of the death of Queen Elizabeth II. "Several times, I had the very rare privilege of performing for Her Majesty and the honour of meeting her in person on those occasions. The first time I remember as vividly as if it were yesterday. It was at the Commonwealth Games Royal Gala Performance in 1982. That was not only one of my career highlights, it was a deeply personal affirmation, a validation of the choices I had made on my journey. Just to think that in 1953 I had been standing on the footpath in Adelaide with thousands of others hoping to catch a glimpse of the most important person in this society, a young black migrant kid in a very white world with no real plan on where his life was headed. Fast forward to 1982 after years of being provided with so many opportunities, in my mind, I had now bridged the gap between my beginnings in this society and was face to face with the person at the very pinnacle. It was such a remarkable progression that it had a deeply profound effect on me, more than words can express. She was an incredible person, with such natural grace and presence. It is really hard to put into words how her passing affected me but I am unashamed when I say that it moved me to tears."

19

What would I do without my music?

Words make you think a thought. Music makes you feel a feeling. A song makes you feel a thought.

Yip Harburg

One Saturday morning, Kamahl browsed through YouTube, looking for some orchestral music to help him launch his weekend. He ran across Beethoven's Ninth Symphony performance by Daniel Barenboim's West-Eastern Divan Orchestra. Kamahl says, "It was a piece of music I have heard thousands of times, but notably it was being conducted by the brilliant Daniel Barenboim. It instantly gave me a memory from my youth. I remember as if it were yesterday seeing Daniel in Adelaide when he was a young boy. He was a greatly celebrated prodigy around the world and was in Australia to perform with the Australian Youth Orchestra. He looked so young. He was quite short and slight of the build, which made him look much younger than he actually was, and if memory serves me well, he was even dressed in short pants. Like just any normal kid, he was standing there with his father outside Elder Hall at the Conservatorium in Adelaide. Little did I know at the time I had seen someone who would go on to be one of the finest musicians in the world. As I listened to him conduct Beethoven's 9th, I was suddenly overwhelmed by emotion, moved to tears by the performance's absolute power and pure beauty. I have often said that I am not a religious man. I have long believed that science provides us with our answers to practically everything. However, my deep spiritual reaction to music and beautiful words is an imponderable. These sounds and words somehow connect with me deeply and spiritually in a way even science cannot explain logically. What can lead some people to create, perform, and articulate material that genuinely connects with one's spirit? It is truly miraculous and mystifyingly inexplicable. I always feel a genuine pity for those who have not been touched by music, poetry and art. They are sadly missing out on some of life's great gifts."

It certainly isn't the first time in his life he has pondered the inexplicable power of music nor the last. He does remember the first occasion that he was held awestruck by music's ability to connect. "When I was still in school, we were taken to a recital. At that point, I was still not a great appreciator of music. As a matter of fact, I had hardly begun to sing. We had been taken to a performance of a piece called 'The Lark Ascending', a song that featured a solo piece on the violin. The soloist Harold Fairhurst was a giant of a man, not just in talent alone. He was actually a physical giant. When he stood to perform, I was struck immediately by his size. My memory may be embellishing his height, but I think he was almost two metres tall. I honestly thought that it may be a comic performance such as the size disparity of the performer and his instrument, which in his hands looked like a toy. It was almost like watching a bear on a tiny tricycle in the circus, he was so big I thought that he could've tucked a cello under his chin, and it would've looked less odd. When he started to play, I was in for a great surprise. I was totally mesmerised by the player's brilliant musicianship and the beauty of the music. It was one of my earliest introductions to Western music's power and great beauty. It remains today as one of my very favourite pieces. It also transformed my prejudice on how tall a musician should be. Evidently, they can and do come in all sizes" he laughs

Kamahl believes the power of music can ignite a passion so significant that it can alter the direction of a person's life. Kamahl, after hearing a famous Nat King Cole song in 1953, would result in his life literally changing from that day on. Somehow that song, 'Nature Boy', affected him so profoundly that it sent his very existence in a totally different direction. That one song ignited a fuse within him that would never be extinguished.

Kamahl always says that if a song is a sum of its parts, then to him, the most critical part of that equation is the words. Over the years, he was offered many great songs with great melodies and memorable hooks. Still, he passed on them when he could not connect with the message contained in the words. He believes that is possibly why he rates some of his spoken word pieces among his favourites. It is also why he developed some notoriety with writers for altering, or in his view, improving some of the lyrics in songs he has recorded. A classic example of this was the song, 'What Would I Be Without My Music'.

In 1976when leaving yet another successful trip to Amsterdam, Kamahl was surprised to be met at the airport by Jimmy Bishop, a senior representative of American music publisher April Blackwood. Bishop evidently had been alerted to Kamahl's increasing popularity in Europe and wanted to take advantage of this by having him record one or more of their catalogue of songs. Bishop had compiled a collection of six songs that he felt would be well suited. Kamahl thanked him, telling him that he would certainly give the demo tape a listen and get back to him if there was any interest. For Kamahl, one song really stood out, a number by Bruce Belland and Harry Middlebrook titled 'What Would I Be Without My Music'. On hearing the song, he knew he just had to record it, as once again, he could instantly relate to the story the song conveyed. 'What Would I Be Without My Music' poses questions about the trials of life on the road as a performer. The loneliness, emptiness, and how the only thing that keeps one going, to have the strength to struggle on, is the artist's deep love of music. The opening verse sets up a question:

Sometimes I stumble home at night discouraged,
dragging my battered dreams behind,
wondering´ if the battle´s worth the fighting
and why so many people´s eyes are blind.

Kamahl connected with the theme instantly as the song spoke to the very struggle he personally felt from time to time. After listening to it repeatedly, he thought that there was one change he just had to make. He changed the last line to … *and why are so many people so unkind.* His view addressed a couple of related issues faced by musicians, one that was very personal to him, the fear of rejection and being on the receiving end of cruel criticism. He made that change without seeking permission, and much to the writers' chagrin and recorded it when they found out. It turned out to be a more significant and more inspired change than he had bargained for. He was totally unaware of it at the time. He had just coined the catchphrase that would become part of the Australian vernacular for many years to come. The line found fame primarily due to a particular TV show using it and him as a punchline for many of their gags.

Kamahl says, "It is always the words that I connect with. In fact, there is one song that I recorded some years ago, 'Believe Me, If All Those Endearing Young Charms', purely because I loved the lyrics. I feel that Poet Thomas Moore's beautiful words were always a total mismatch with a song that just leaves me cold. On reflection, I should have done it only in a spoken word form because the lyrics are so evocative and poignant, and the melody lacks the depth in feeling that the words hold. I just love the story behind it. Apparently, Moore wrote it for his wife. The story goes that she had been badly disfigured by smallpox and was self-conscious about her pockmarked face. She refused to leave her bedroom for months. To lure her away from isolation, Moore wrote the poem for her. In it, he assures her that she was still beautiful to him, scars and all. When complete, the poem was pushed under the door, and she was evidently so moved by it that she emerged shortly after. Now I am not sure if this tale is apocryphal or not, but as it emphasises the power of great lyrics, so I am more than happy to believe that it is," he says. The lyrics that so moved him are:

Believe me, if all those endearing young charms
  which I gaze on so fondly today
were to change by tomorrow and fleet in my arms
  like fairy gifts fading away
Thou wouldst still be adored as this moment thou art
  let thy loveliness fade as it will
and around the dear ruin each wish of my heart
  would entwine itself verdantly still

It is not while beauty and youth are thine own
  and thy cheek unprofaned by a tear
that the fervour and faith of a soul can be known
  to which time will but make thee more dear
oh the heart that has loved never truly forgets
  but as truly lives on to the close
as the sunflower turns on her God as He sets
  the same look that she gave when He rose!

Kamahl was saddened to learn recently that his long-time friend and legendary country songwriter Tom T Hall had died. "Tom T Hall was a wonderful warm person. He was country music's consummate blue-collar bard. He had a great understanding of people, reflected in his lyrics. His songs were like small stories that were full of life and meaning. His ability to engage audiences with a song was unbelievable. For me, as someone who needs the words to connect me with a song, it made choosing a Tom T Hall song really easy. Altogether, I recorded seven of his songs, starting with, 'The World the Way I Want it' in 1970. Even if you only ever knew Tom from his Harper Valley PTA song, you could still appreciate his storytelling on that song alone. When I heard 'One Hundred Children' with its clear message of needing us to leave a legacy to all of the world's children, the next generation, it touched me. It is a call for adults to accept their responsibility to hand over a better world. To accept people from all nations just as we accept our own, care for the environment and stop stupid wars. I have always been a committed supporter of children's rights, and I am also an environmentalist and pacifist. Therefore the message ticked all the right boxes for me. Anything providing a positive message for children I will always wholeheartedly support."

Kamahl's own fractured and disrupted childhood has played a significant part in his determination to use his voice for those he feels have been robbed of theirs. A few years ago, Kamahl reached out to Tom through his management. He suggested a reprise of 'One Hundred Children', saying it could be reworked as 'One Million Children'. He explained that contemporising the song with a strong climate change message could help support Greta Thunberg's work. He recommended proceeds be directed to her organisation. He had Rajan work on a new arrangement, and he had made the suggested lyric changes to contemporise the message. To his disappointment, Kamahl didn't hear back from Tom's management. He believes they didn't share with their client. "I should have just contacted him directly rather than let some middle-man make the decision. He was a personal friend. I even stayed with him, his wife and what seemed like a dozen or so dogs at his ranch on a few occasions. They were both crazy about animals and had plenty of their own to prove it."

Kamahl's history of recording with British and American producers, composers and arrangers has been very positive, although, at times, he has found some of the idiosyncrasies a little unsettling. His collaboration with US legend Artie Butler is a case in point. Butler is one of the most respected arrangers and composers in the music business. Butler has been responsible for arranging over seventy-five hit records, playing on hundreds of other records, and receiving over sixty gold and platinum records. When it was suggested that Kamahl record his next album in the US, he was keen to collaborate with professionals with a list of credentials big as a mountain. Butler, in particular, stood out as someone Kamahl wanted to work with.

"Artie Butler was a music industry legend. His experience was unbelievable. He had worked with so many artists across multiple genres. I must confess to having been a little intimidated by his reputation. Our first meeting was in his luxurious LA home. I remember walking into the place and noting how pristine it looked. In one corner was a harp, and of course, his grand piano had pride of place. The other thing that stood out was a huge white shag pile rug. He was all about business, leaving little room for small talk. He had the list of songs that we were to do together, and he played through them all, and they all sounded great. The last number he got to, the classic Charlie Chaplin ballad 'Smile'. I loved that song so much, and predictably my favourite version was Nat King Cole's. I had envisioned an arrangement that was almost a replica, with my voice being practically the only difference. What he played me was miles away from that and, I thought, an uncomfortable stretch for my range. I was fairly straightforward in my view of the arrangement, but he insisted that we try it. I said that I wasn't comfortable with it and that it was hard to teach an old dog new tricks. He responded abruptly, 'I'm not asking you not to shit on the rug old dog, just to sing the song'. Reluctantly, I did his version but was never really happy with it until I received overwhelmingly positive feedback for it. I remember bumping into Harry Vanda of Vanda and Young fame. He was totally unprompted when he said it was the best arrangement of 'Smile' he had ever heard. High praise indeed from one of Australia's legendary writers and producers. I have grown to really like the version now. I have to say that the higher key Artie Butler chose to have me sing tested Bob Hope's generous assessment of the number of testicles I possessed. I had learned a valuable lesson from Butler, and that was when you are paying for the best, you are crazy to ignore them by thinking you know better," he laughs.

English composer Roger Cook also rates highly on the Kamahl list of quirky geniuses that he has worked with. Cook is possibly best known for his song 'Melting Pot' when he performed with the sixties band Blue Mink. When he moved full-time into song writing, he quickly had a monster hit with the New Seekers 'I'd Like To Teach The World To Sing'. The number was already a huge hit when released. Then it was given massive additional exposure when adapted to be an international jingle for Coca Cola. Cook wrote for many high-profile performers who had hits with his songs, including The Hollies, Cilla Black, Gene Pitney, The Drifters, to name but a very few. In the seventies, Cook had relocated to the US, settling in Nashville, the capital of country music and had great success with a string of notable hits mainly on the Country charts. Kamahl, before meeting Cook, had already recorded his song 'Miracles'. It was a cover of the Don Williams 1981 country hit, which had peaked in the Country Billboard Charts at number 4.

Kamahl says, "Roger Cook was a really strange sort of character. We caught up in Nashville at an arranged meeting at a hotel bar, we intended to discuss our working together. He made quite an entrance, dressed to the nines. He was wearing a very flashy suit with a big fedora hat and had a stunning blonde on his arm. He practically wore her like an accessory. Cook, whose appearance drew a lot of attention, wasn't one of the world's great communicators, mostly holding up his side of the conversation with yes or no or mumbled responses. I actually got the impression that he may have been more than a little bit affected by something he had prescribed by someone other than a doctor. As a means of breaking the ice a little, I told him about my having recorded 'Miracles' adding that I liked it so much that this was the reason that I had sought to work with him. He just mumbled a response indicating that he would like to hear me sing part of the song so that he could get a 'feel' for my voice. Without further ado, I launched into my best acapella version of 'Miracles' only to have him interrupt me angrily, saying, 'what the f**k did you do to the lyrics?' Evidently, I had used the wrong words in a part of the song where the line goes *We are not without.* Instead, I used the words *love will out.* Believe it or not, it was unintentional. Not only had I messed it up, but I had also actually already recorded it. It was incredibly embarrassing. Luckily he got over it enough to write 'We Love Each Other, Don't We?', one of my favourite songs. He was an extremely talented guy but very temperamental and hard to read."

Kamahl has an extreme fondness for a number written by Jimmy Grafton, Harry Secombe's genial manager. In the song 'When You Look Back On Your Life', Kamahl says, "It is a very sentimental father to son piece that poses great questions, the type that you ask yourself almost daily when you're reflecting on life and career." The love that Kamahl has for the song is also in no small part to the genuine affection that he had for both Jimmy and his great friend Harry Secombe. Without the two, many doors in the UK would never have opened.

Kamahl's never-ending search for songs has sometimes facilitated very interesting chance meetings too. In 1976, only a couple of days after his Carnegie Hall performance, he was urged by Piet Schellvis to head over to the US once again. Piet was a long-time friend and now a heavyweight with his label Polygram. Piet had provided an introduction to a top-notch recording label Platinum Records that was part of their organisation. The label was based in New Jersey, and Kamahl made the trip there accompanied by a couple of Polygram executives. He doesn't recall who they were or why exactly they were there but vaguely remembers one being a Dutch accountant. He welcomed their company as they provided travel companionship on the long drive

When he arrived at the studio, Kamahl took in his surroundings and realised that almost all of the acts that this label represented were African-American R&B artists. He says, "This was a serious label with some distinguished names and a great line up of songs, but they were hardly aligned with my positioning. I joked at the time that this was the whitest I have ever felt in my life." Kamahl nonetheless recorded several tracks with them, but none were ever released. He thanked them for their hospitality and their valiant attempt to get him on to the Soul Train, but he had reached the terminating station. He and his companions decided to grab a late dinner on the way back into New York. They arrived at a fashionable eatery and had barely ordered when he noticed an eerie hush falling over the wait staff and manager. A party had arrived and, he concluded from their expressions, that this was some type of unexpected VIP arrival. As it turned out it was. Jackie Onassis had entered the building accompanied by a sizable entourage, including one rather large Greek gentleman who seemed to dominate her attention and several security types that seem to never be too far away when people like they are out an about. Kamahl recognised her immediately, as did the rest of the restaurant patrons, not that there were many of them, as it was a quiet time of the evening for the restaurant. "I was determined to go and introduce myself and racked my brain on what to speak to her about. I stress speak to her because her companion didn't strike me as the type for small talk of any type. Then a lightbulb went off over my head. The Australian Ballet was performing *The Merry Widow* in Washington DC featuring Dame Margot Fonteyn. It was a very hot ticket, and I was sure that I could persuade my contacts to get her a couple of VIP seats. Nervously I approached the table and introduced myself, rather immodestly as someone who had just performed at Carnegie Hall a couple of days before. She didn't exactly sit up bolt upright to that revelation, but her interest was certainly piqued by the

Ballet suggestion. I chatted with her for several minutes, offered to get tickets to her and bade a fond farewell. I must admit that she was quite personable and easy enough to talk to. I did think that her legendary beauty was a little bit overstated. She was certainly an attractive woman, very skinny though, so much in fact that her sleeveless dress exposed a pair of very bony arms. I would have to say she was very well treated by the camera." Kamahl arranged tickets to be despatched to her the next day and received a kind thank you note. He was never sure if she ever did attend the show.

When touring in America, his good friends Judi and Sid Friedman suggested that Kamahl meet with a songwriter friend, Paul Vance. Vance had found chart fame some years earlier, with the novelty hit 'Itsy Bitsy Teeny Weeny Yellow Polka Dot Bikini'. It hit Billboard's number one spot when it was released some years before. To say Kamahl was less than keen was an understatement. After all, the guy may have had a hit, but it was a cheesy novelty song, but he was not that kind of artist. Judi wouldn't let it go. She was very keen to point out that Vance's song credits were far more significant than a one-hit-wonder from the past decade. Vance had worked with some of the industry's biggest names, including Johnny Mathis and Perry Como. He had also written the classic upbeat ballad 'Catch A Falling Star'.

Convinced by Judi, Kamahl took the meeting. "Paul Vance was a larger-than-life character who made his presence felt in any company. At our first meeting, I remember he cracked a joke that was extremely crude, not one for mixed company. I have never been prudish, but I was actually embarrassed at the language he used in front of Judi. I managed to suppress my distaste and gave him a hearing. He told me that he had this song that would work really well and played this number. It was called 'Hey There Lord'. Strange, the dirty joke guy pitching a religious song, I thought, but what the hell. The song's lyrics depicted a man making an impassioned plea to God about the fear of uncertainty over the world's plight. It was almost like a prayer asking for help. Now I am not a religious person, but I am quite happy to provide my voice to those, particularly concerning peace among my fellow man. I agreed to do it. Sid Friedman had this nice idea for the opening of the song. To set the tone of turmoil, he would record news items that were current to act as a dramatic entrée to my singing vocal. We recorded it that way, and it sounded great, but then I suggested diplomatically that the news items being current would date the song terribly. I suggested that to maintain the tone of the number, an alternative would be to have me recite the ten commandments instead of the news. It would create the necessary drama without losing the message. Surprisingly, Sid rejected his brainchild very well and agreed with me, as did Vance. We actually deviated from the original idea only using some and not all commandments, but the impact was the same." The song was a minor hit in several markets, particularly popular with American evangelists, a market Kamahl barely knew existed before receiving feedback. In Canada, DJ Wally Crowther told him that when he played the song on-air, his wife rang him to say that she thought the narrator sounded precisely how she believed God would sound. "I have been called many things in my time, not all of them good, but this was definitely the only time I have been mistaken for God. I was worried that I may end up in a demarcation dispute with James Earl Jones," he laughs.

In 1972, Kamahl heard Don Mclean's classic album *Tapestry* when he was in London. Whilst he loved the whole album, he knew when he heard 'And I Love You So', he had to record it. By then, he was working with Philips Records. This gave him a reintroduction to Fred Marks, with whom he had previously worked at Festival Records in Sydney. Fred introduced him to producer Johnny Franz who was very well regarded. He recorded several tracks for a new album called *About Falling In Love*.

The album would later be retitled before the release to *Love is a Mountain*. When discussing the project, Kamahl convinced the label that he should record the McLean song for the album.

While beautifully sung by the writer, the original had not achieved any great attention with a more significant market. Therefore, it was determined that with an appropriate arrangement, he could have a big hit with the song. Franz knew the right man for that job was Peter Knight, a musical arranger with a massive reputation and a string of hits to his name. Kamahl was delighted with the choice. He would record the song, but it never lived up to his own high-quality expectations. "Don McLean's version is so intimate and vulnerable. Unfortunately, between Knight, Franz and myself, we failed to capture the magical quality present in Mclean's original. To this day, I believe it is by far the best version of the song." Subsequently, the song would be covered by many big names, including Shirley Bassey, who enjoyed a reasonable hit with the song. Perry Como's release of the song achieved the most significant commercial success, giving the American a worldwide sensation. Kamahl says, "Como did do a great job, that is for sure. Interestingly he actually muffed the lyrics. They should have been *the book of life is brief, and once a page is read, all but love is dead*. Como managed to sing, record and release the song with the end of that line as *all but life is dead*. That was a massive mistake, not only for the singer but all of those people involved in its recording. How that could happen is totally beyond me, even allowing for my own minor gaffe with Roger Cooke's 'Miracles'. This was far more obvious as it changed the entire meaning of an essential line in the song. Yet no one pointed it out. Either his production team were incompetent, or they were too intimidated by their star to say anything. Either way, it was totally unacceptable. Don McLean himself was furious about his lyrics being incorrectly presented and once told an Australian audience in person just how annoyed he was. I met with him eight or nine years later at a function they had for him at the Intercontinental Sydney when he was touring. Such a delightfully modest and humble fellow. He didn't mention Como at the time. I suppose the massive royalties he earned all those years from old Perry's release, gaffe included, might have helped him get over it."

20

He ain't heavy...

Be the change you want to see in the world.
                                Mahatma Gandhi

Kamahl relates significantly to this quote from Gandhi, but of equal if not greater influence were the lessons imparted to him by his old friend and mentor Bob Hope. Hope was a celebrity with a genuine sense of obligation to the American public and the people who had given him his fame and fortune. He understood that giving back to the community isn't just a 'nice to do'… in his mind, it was a duty. He believed that those whose lives have been blessed must show appreciation for the support they receive by working for others less fortunate. As Hope put it very succinctly, "If you haven't any charity in your heart, you have the worst kind of heart trouble."

Kamahl, even before his meeting, Hope had always understood that he had blessings and opportunities that many in society could only dream of. He says, "My life has been abundantly blessed with many extraordinary situations which have given me so much. I have reached my ripe old age with relatively good health. I have a truly wonderful and talented family, I also have many great supportive friends. To top that off, I have had that rarest of opportunities, a career that has never been work to me and fans who, for whatever reason, have stuck with me for decades. I have always believed that I had to show my gratitude for these gifts by stepping up wherever I have been able to make a difference."

His own challenging childhood experiences have undoubtedly influenced his lifetime commitment to supporting organisations that promote the protection and advancement of children. Those experiences gave him an abhorrence of cruelty and bullying in all its forms. Having been a victim of cruel behaviour himself, he empathises with victims and those trying to elevate themselves despite the challenges they encounter. Providing his booming voice, talent, and ability to bring influential people along with him to those respected organisations dedicated to welfare has been a lifelong commitment. Those organisations have also benefited from having an advocate with a hard-nosed salesman's stubbornness and an inability to process the word 'no'.

Kamahl is also a dedicated conservationist and environmentalist who cares deeply about the future of the planet he has walked for well over eighty years. Many celebrities reflect upon their privileged life and decide to give something back for the fortune they have achieved at the end of their careers. Kamahl's commitment to charitable causes was always there from day one.

Dating right back to his very early career, there would be few good causes that he would refuse. Quite simply, if he could be there, he would be there, no matter how large or small the request. Even now, well into his eighties, nothing has changed. When it comes to good causes, he will pitch in at the drop of a hat. In early 2021, he announced the donation of his entire Gold and Platinum rcord awards to Variety Australia as auction items in a significant fundraiser for the group. The same things that symbolise some of the greatest moments in his career, he believes, are best put to good use rather than gathering dust on a wall. He says, "Of course I am proud of my achievements, but the gold and platinum records are merely symbols of them. The achievements will still stand, and no one can take them away from me. Putting those symbols to good use, to make a difference in young lives provides a much better and more satisfying outcome for me."

Kamahl's strict religious upbringing, whilst not a significant influence for most of his life, evidently still managed to contribute one major characteristic, a solid moral foundation. In the Hindu faith of his parents, it is observed that giving or *Dana* is an integral part of one's duty or *Dharma* as they refer to it. Each person in Hinduism has a *Dharma* toward family, society, the world and all living things.

He explains, "In the Hindu text *Bhagavad-Gita*, it speaks of three types of giving: Firstly there is a gift that is given without any expectation of appreciation or reward. It is beneficial to both the giver and recipient. Second, a gift is given reluctantly and with the expectation of some advantage. This is harmful to both the giver and recipient. Lastly, there is a gift that is given without regard for the recipient's feelings and is given at the wrong time. This can cause embarrassment and harmful to both the giver and recipient. The lesson is that the first option is the only path you should choose. While I have retained not much Hindu religion, I do subscribe wholeheartedly to the giving philosophy. I believe that it stuck with me, possibly because I grew up with people who practised what they preached. My family, particularly my father, were deeply committed to the welfare of their community. It often came at great personal cost to them. The best example was during wartime when my father took life-threatening risks at times to help others. I would like to think that in my own small way, I have tried my best to honour his philanthropic character to help others wherever I could. My philosophy in life is reflected in a quote from that great American reformer Horace Mann. He was responsible for providing state-funded basic education to Americans in the nineteenth century. He said, 'Be ashamed to die until you have won some victory for humanity'."

For many years, Kamahl had been performing by invitation at a number of Christmas carols events wherever it was possible for him to. These free events were generally organised and run by local service organisations and allowed fundraising by a donation from attendees for nominated charities, usually to support those less fortunate within the community. For years, one such event that he had performed at was named *Christmas Carols in the Common*. This was a concert run by the North Ryde chapter of Rotary International. Kamahl had long held a very positive disposition toward the organisation, having been involved in numerous fundraising ventures over many years. In recognition of his community efforts, he was presented with a Paul Harris Fellowship, Rotary's highest honour. Kamahl related readily to their philosophical principles and hands-on attitude to community support as detailed in their stated purpose of *bringing together business and professional leaders to provide humanitarian service and advance goodwill and peace around the world*. Kamahl says, "Rotary are a great contributor to society. My motivation has always been to be positive without being encumbered by political or religious agendas. Quite simply, they do good because it is a good thing to do, the humane thing to do, and for me, you can't get a simpler or more noble principle than that."

In 2004 after performing at *Christmas Carols in the Common* for some years, Phil Isaacs, the chapter president of North Ryde Rotary, approached Kamahl to seek further support for a fundraising effort to support ROMAC (Rotary Oceania Medical Aid for Children). The group provides surgical treatment for children from the Pacific region in Australia and New Zealand. It is supplied in life-saving or dignity restoring surgery which is not accessible to them in their home country. Phil recounts, "Kamahl had always been so generous by providing his time and support previously. When our chapter decided to mount a major support program for ROMAC, we thought that it was something that he may like to get on board with. As it happened, we had one young beneficiary of the program in Sydney at the time. A four-year-old kid called Mohammed from the Solomon Islands who'd just been brought to Sydney for a herniated brain operation. This condition had left him severely disfigured with a huge bulge protruding from just above his eyes. I asked Kamahl if he would like to meet Mohammed and his mother to see for himself how transformative the program had been in this young person's life. He agreed immediately and suggested that we meet him at his home. When we met, it was easy to see that both he and Sahodra were so deeply touched by Mohammed's story that he immediately agreed to do whatever he could. What I had in mind was a series of fund-raising concerts across New South Wales where we had people on the ground who could arrange ticket sales and venues. These concerts weren't only held in Sydney but right across the State in places like Dubbo, West Wyalong, Coonabarabran. It was a big commitment for him, but he never hesitated to make it. Further, he came up with a great enhancement to the program. Along with his record company, he said they could produce a CD with all funds going straight to ROMAC. He suggested that the album could contain his songs about children. In deference to the surgeons' work, it was named *Miracles*. Of course, we were delighted to accept the offer, and with the CD and the concerts, we raised over $30,000, all of which changed some young lives forever. I accompanied Kamahl on the road trip, and I have to say my one and only experience as a roadie was one I will never forget. His ability to relate to audiences and just people he would meet in restaurants or on the street was quite incredible. I remember our stopping for coffee in Coonabarabran, and the staff were very excited to see him. They asked if they could all take a picture with him. Of course, he did, and we went on our way. I went to that same café only a short while back, and that picture is now framed and hung prominently behind the counter almost twenty years later."

Kamahl's support for worthy charities outside of Australia has taken him far and wide. Often, these efforts have been initiated by circumstance and chance. When Sahodra decided to resume her own career in health care

at the Seventh Day Adventist Hospital in 2008, she and Kamahl became
aware of an outreach program it ran. Open Heart International had
started in 1986. The hospital encouraged staff to volunteer their personal
time to form teams that would travel to developing nations to provide
specialist healthcare in those countries. It was through this organisation,
Kamahl renewed his acquaintance with Papua New Guinea.

Operation Open Heart PNG was a team of Australian heart special-
ists who travelled there once a year. They would join with their local
counterparts to perform open and closed heart surgery, mainly on
children.

Whilst he had toured the country many years, mainly for benefit
programs, the opportunity had not arisen for a return over the past
decade or so. Through Sahodra, he was made aware of the hospital's good
work in the country. He was keen to see what he could do. This resulted
in the release of another album, with funds being pledged to the group.
To support the release, he also decided to do a promotional tour. He
recalls, "I hadn't been to PNG for some time. I had enjoyed the previous
occasions, but in 2008 I really didn't know what to expect, but Open
Heart was such a worthy cause, so I was happy to do whatever I could to
help. On the flight up there, I was seated next to an Australian guy who
was very friendly. He was a bit of a rough diamond, the type of regular
Aussie bloke you would meet in most country towns. I had no idea who
he was as he had introduced himself as Mick. He was also known as Sir
Michael Curtain, a business giant in the region whose civil engineering
business had been responsible for most of PNG's infrastructure. I caught
up with him again at a fund-raising dinner put on to support the charity.
In the program that night was an auction of donated items, one of which
was a platinum album of mine that I had given to them. Sir Michael was
the highest bidder with a bid of $16,500. He had been bidding against
fellow business giant and best friend Sir Brian Bell. He then surprised
everyone at the event by announcing that he was gifting the platinum

record to his best mate Brian. It was an incredible moment and was a real testament to the generosity of these two guys. Both had done so well through their association with PNG and were happy to do whatever they could to give something back."

Glenn Armstrong, who is a highly experienced media advisor and author with over twenty-years working in PNG was engaged to manage Kamahl's 2008 PNG tour. Glenn characterises working with Kamahl, "I have great memories of Kamahl's trip to PNG. He always had great popularity in the country but hadn't been here for quite some time. He was therefore in high demand with requests for interviews and appearances throughout the tour which made the schedule quite hectic. Despite the pace of the program he took on everything professionally with great humour. It made it a real pleasure to work with him."

In recent times, Kamahl has been actively supporting a relatively new charity named Destiny Rescue. The mission of this group is to rescue children from sexual exploitation and human trafficking and help them stay free. This requires their working closely with various authorities in third-world countries, gathering and sharing intelligence and, once children are rescued, providing rehabilitation support for victims. Kamahl's genuine concern for those most vulnerable in society, specifically children, has always informed his decisions about which organisations he chooses to support.

Of all the charitable organisations that Kamahl has been involved with, one has without a doubt, been the most enduring, is the Variety Club. The worldwide show business children's charity. When Kamahl became an International Ambassador, he joined notable names such as Sean Connery, Roger Moore, Shirley Bassey, to name a few. While Kamahl had performed at many Variety events in Australia and the US during the seventies, he would assume a formal role when he met Grahame

Mapp in the early eighties. One day Grahame called him and said, "Our wives play tennis together, so why don't we meet?" Kamahl was already familiar with Grahame by reputation. After all, he was one of Australia's most successful businessmen, having built an impressive empire over the previous few decades.

Kamahl was not as aware of Mapp's philanthropic life. He agreed to the meetup and the two men hit it off almost immediately. A Variety Club lunch invitation was forthcoming, featuring guest speaker Michael Parkinson. "My friendship with Grahame is one I value very greatly. He was definitely the prime mover in getting me so involved with Variety. The work they do in supporting kids is first class and so valuable. It is an organisation where I have been able to fully use the networking that I have access to from my many years in the business. Besides, where else could I say that I got to share an ambassadorship with not one but two James Bonds? Now that both are no longer around, maybe I could make a really late run for the role too … The name is Bond … Brown Bond. It has a ring to it, don't you think?" he laughs.

Grahame Mapp was so successful in his own role in Variety that he was Chief Barker in Australia before being elevated to the Head of Variety Club Worldwide. He is the only Australian ever to receive this honour. Grahame recounts Kamahl's Variety Club involvement with a great deal of fondness. "The thing about Kamahl is that he always brings such great energy to everything he does, and that was a great asset for Variety. Whilst many people can be stalled by setbacks, he just seems to refuse to accept them and just keeps pushing forward. As Chief Barker in Australia, I was delighted to recognise his involvement with Variety by making him a National Ambassador. I subsequently recognised him as an International Ambassador when the opportunity arose some years later."

Whilst Variety is a cause that both men hold very dear, Kamahl and Grahame's friendship extends well beyond charity. Grahame recounts, "Among quite a few other things I do, I have bred and owned racehorses for many years. Strangely I have never been much of a punter, something that I shared in common with Kamahl. In fact, this made him the best possible companion at the races, as we weren't fixated on the odds or distracted by the form guide. He was just happy to enjoy the atmosphere and the glamorous social aspects surrounding the sport. Like me, he also has a genuine love for horses. We had many terrific times at the track, but one really stands out. It was at Rosehill on the opening day of the Spring Carnival 2012 when my horses won the first three races of the day. As an owner, there are few things more exciting than your horses winning, but to have three in a row is really outstanding. I remember Kamahl telling me that it was all down to him, claiming that he had brought his black magic to the results."

21

What is Australia to me?

The house I live in, my neighbours down the street,
The proud and smiling faces of the people that I meet,
The children in the playground and Christmas in the Sun,
The G'Day and the handshake
That's Australia to me.
The town that I live in, the friends that I have found,
The people who just came here from nations all around,
Those who built this country, the air of feeling free,
The right to speak your own mind,
That's Australia to me
Words of Banjo Patterson, Henry Lawson and Mackellar,
The style of Donald Bradman, de Castella, Dame Joan,
There's Smithy and Ben Lexcen, achievers without peer,
And the dreaming of a people who've been here a million years.
This land I live in, the goodness everywhere,
A place of wealth and beauty with enough for all to share,
I love this sunburnt country, so vital, young and free
With a promise of tomorrow,
That's Australia to me,
But especially the people,
Yes, especially the people

Kamahl's Australian story, despite the odd setback or two, has been an overwhelmingly positive tale. Like many other migrants before and after him, Kamahl experienced challenges that at times may have seemed insurmountable. He believes that his great love for his adopted home developed through his many personal relationships and the connection with audiences he describes as the best in the world. He acknowledges that Australia still has a long way to go regarding social equity, tolerance, and fairness. Still, he feels that relative to many nations, Australia, on the whole, offers much more than any other he has known. He says, "The changes I have witnessed in my lifetime here are remarkable. The first minute I set foot on Australian soil, I felt like I was from another planet, not another country. I was filled with dread over what lay ahead. As I grew more assimilated, I started to see what I consider the real Australia, a place with people prepared to see beyond their preconceptions and prejudices. If we fast forward to now, we are a truly multicultural society, a country in which everyone, irrespective of creed, colour, gender, sexuality, receives fair treatment from most. When I got here, they called it the 'Lucky Country' and back then, it was pretty bloody obvious who had gotten all that luck. In navigating my life here, I found with Australians, if you just scratch a little below the surface, you find a unique characteristic that is not immediately obvious. Eventually, it becomes apparent that most Aussies accept anyone from anywhere as long as it is believed that they are prepared to 'have a go'." He acknowledges that there were, and still are, plenty who are deeply bigoted. They will always struggle with people who are not like themselves. "No country is perfect, but I genuinely feel that considering it is such a young nation, Australia has quickly embraced many positive things. We may be a country of extremes when it comes to weather but not our politics or beliefs, and we should consider ourselves a lucky country for that alone."

Reflecting upon his life in Australia, Kamahl recognises that he has been exposed to many iconic people enshrined in its cultural history due to his fame. He feels many of these people have played an enormous part in defining and influencing the Australian attitude. He also rejoices in having had the opportunity to meet and spend time with so many prominent Australians. People he feels have rightly earned the support they receive from the community. He thinks that Australian society is still where the powerful rub shoulders regularly with the masses.

As a prime example of his philosophy, Kamahl remembered being thrown the new ball in a lower grade game at a suburban oval in Adelaide back in 1955. His heart sank a little. After all, he considered himself a batsman and his opinion of his own bowling ability was reasonably modest. To add to his trepidation, his team's attack could quickly have been punished by what was a reasonably handy batting line up. His skipper's confidence in him, whilst comforting, was possibly misplaced. After all, this was indeed the first game he had played for this side, and it was the first over of the first game of the season.

Kamahl's first conversation with the skipper was short and to the point. He said, "What do you bowl?" The far from confident response "Off-Spin" was hardly the interview for a decision to be made to introduce him into the attack and turn the game around. Three balls into his first over, three wickets had fallen to his off-spin. His hat trick feat, it turned out, was just the beginning. He would take four more wickets that day, giving him the impressive tally of seven for fifty-five. Whilst very impressive, little did he know that this was the least exciting cricket experience to emerge from that day.

In the Kensington Cricket Club sheds following the game celebrating his heroics, the team was being congratulated by former players and officials. One of these men stood out, not because of his appearance but how others reacted to his presence. Observing that Kamahl did not recognise this evidently well-known individual, one of his teammates asked him if he knew who he had just met. Kamahl said no, "That is Sir Don Bradman", he was informed. Kamahl was shocked. "The legendary

Don Bradman? Surely not, I thought, a man with his reputation must be a giant towering above all like a colossus. This was possibly the world's greatest cricketer of all time. How could he dare to be so normal, so human?" he said.

Kamahl's introduction to the greatest cricketer who ever lived was not his last, however. Several years later, he performed at a Prospect Cricket Club function, where Sir Don was the VIP guest. Bradman, himself a keen music lover, would later recall to friends with fondness that on this evening, he had witnessed someone "destined to be a great artist." Interestingly Kamahl had no recollection of this happening until the great man himself pointed it out to him years later.

Fast forward twenty-seven years to 1988 when Kamahl, by now a passionate Australian, would write and record a song for the Bicentennial entitled 'What Does Australia Mean to Me?' The song's genesis was in Kamahl's absolute conviction that the New Year's Bicentennial Concert 1988 would be historical. It would feature a line-up of artists that befitted such a spectacular occasion. Promoters Kevin Jacobsen and Pat Condon promised to assemble the who's who of Australian performers. Kamahl felt that as one of the country's most successful recording artists in the past couple of decades, he was bound to have some small part to play. In preparation, he was determined to have a song that would befit such an event that spoke of his great love and passion for his adopted home. He took his inspiration from a Paul Robeson song that he had heard many years earlier. It was called 'The House I Live In'. The song was almost a love song to America. Kamahl believed that with a rewrite of the song's lyrics, he could capture the spirit of what made Australians love their country. He could think of no better time to convey that message than on its two hundredth birthday. He worked tirelessly to write the appropriate words whilst on a national tour. He would spend hours locked in his room, pen in hand scribbling down one idea after another until he felt he had cracked it. As he was never one to pass up an opportunity for an opinion, he even tried it out as a spoken piece to an audience in Alice Springs. The reception that the spoken performance received assured him that he was on the right track. All he had to do now was get the permission from those who owned the song to modify and record it. He managed to track down one of the two originators of the song in New York. Although based in Los Angeles, Earl Robinson was luckily on vacation in the Big Apple and had agreed to meet with him. Kamahl recounts, "I told him how much I loved the song but said that I felt the title was not what I felt the song was about. I also said I wanted to change the lyrics to include Australia. I think he was a little put out by the requests. He did offer a compromise. He wanted me to call it *Australia the Land I Live In,* which I thought was bloody awful, so we talked about it for quite a while later until he finally gave in. I'm pretty sure that by the time I was finished, he would've been prepared to let me call it anything as long as I let him go." He contacted song writing power couple Tony Hatch and Jackie Trent upon returning to Sydney. They were also migrants. Their journey to Sydney was from the UK where they had a celebrated career writing and performing. The couple lived not too far from Kamahl and, like him, were involved heavily with the Variety Club, so he arranged a meeting, and from that meeting came the song 'My Home'.

My Home
This is my home, this is my country
This is the land I've grown to love
My life began across the ocean
But I belong here, and though I roam
I say Australia, you are my home
I'll always love and honour
The place I was born It's part of me whatever else I do
Though once I felt alone here
I knew with each dawn

The people of this land will see me through
Those people from all nations Who live here and are free
Will share with me these feelings
With love and understanding
Let's pray we all may see
Our friendships growing stronger every day.

Whilst happy with the outcome of the collaboration he did feel disappointed by the couple not providing him a writing credit on the song. After initially agreeing to the credit, they reneged. Jacqui insisted that she and Tony were the only names ever listed on any song they wrote. Slight aside, the two pieces completed the single release, just in time for the Bicentennial and hopefully a set at the Bicentennial Concert. Sadly, the songs were to have little sway over the show's organisers, producers, and broadcaster as Kamahl's expected invitation never arrived. Whilst Kamahl pushed his then manager John Hansen to seek answers, the answers fell well short of what he expected. He took matters into his own hands by speaking to just about everyone who held some influence on the decision. This ran from the Premier of NSW to a whole host of bureaucrats, Channel 9 boss Sam Chisolm and all and sundry at Jacobsen's team. No one was missed. On a flight to London, he even cornered Kerry Packer on the subject. None of these efforts resulted in anything other than a flat 'no'. The one single word Kamahl has always had difficulty translating or comprehending is the dreaded N word. To add insult to what he saw as considerable injury at this time was the response that he got from David Mitchell. He had been referred to speak to Mitchell by promoter Kevin Jacobsen as the person responsible for the overall production for Channel 9.

Kamahl had sent Mitchell a tape featuring both songs and received the following reply in November 1987:

"Thank you for sending the tape of your parody of 'The House I Live In' on *That's What Australia Means To Me* and *My Home.* Unfortunately, we cannot fit either into our programme because we feel that Sinatra's version of the former is too familiar for the song to ring true. The sentiments expressed in H*ome* are already being dealt with in our opening ballet and the multi-ethnic finale. Best wishes with the records, and again, thank you for thinking of us." The letter felt like a dagger in the heart. When details of the talent line up were disclosed finally, he was gobsmacked to learn that the Australian talent included Cliff Richard and John Denver, neither being Australian. The ballet piece to open the show, supposedly covering the sentiment of his song, was to be performed to 'Waltzing Matilda'. Despite its broad adoption as an Australian anthem, it is actually an adapted German song. The producers even provided an apology for Irish comedian Dave Allen not performing. Whilst Allen was undoubtedly a great comic talent, he had only lived in Australia for a few years before returning to the UK. Kamahl was angry with many people and quite depressed over what he saw as an injustice. He recalls. "I was really down over the whole affair. I thought I was being rejected by the industry I loved and had worked for decades to establish myself in. When you run into that type of rejection, you naturally question yourself. It dents your confidence somewhat." Whilst never allowing it to affect his work schedule, he privately felt that he may have started to run out of the luck that had blessed him in the first thirty years of his career. The worst part of the rejection was that it reintroduced insecurity as a familiar but totally unwelcome old presence in his life. Later in the year, this was to change when at a chance meeting at a function, he encountered Sir Eric Neal.

Sir Eric invited Kamahl to perform his two songs at a Duke of Edinburgh Awards function in Brisbane attended by Prince Edward. The Prince was very impressed with the performance. In his performance, Kamahl explained his concept of FBAs and FDAs, foreign-born Aussies and fair dinkum Aussies, which Prince Edward was particularly taken with. When Kamahl was introduced to the Prince's father at a function the day after the show, Prince Philip mentioned that he had heard all about his FBA and FDA theory. To Kamahl's delight, the Royal seal of approval translated into his being engaged for the Royal Command Performance at the Brisbane 88 Expo. Jacobsen and Mitchell again had been appointed to run things, unfortunately. They put up quite a bit of resistance to the performance of the song. However, they met a force of objection that no one could resist… Premier Joh Bjelke Peterson. It turned out that the Premier was a bit of a closet Kamahlcoholic. The show was in Queensland, which Joh ran like it was his own fiefdom. There was little argument. Even if they were to discount the weight of a Royal imprimatur, this was Joh territory. Any such performance held in Queensland was unofficially the Joh Show! After all of the slings and arrows of outrageous fortune thrown his way in 1988, Kamahl got to sing his songs on a national platform at last. Through one of those songs, he was introduced to a great, long-lasting relationship with one of Australia's most legendary sons.

Within the 'What is Australia to Me' lyrics, Kamahl had referenced "the style of Donald Bradman" as a homage to a great Australian. Kamahl decided, as a courtesy, to personally send Sir Don a copy of the song. He reasoned that it was only polite to let him know that he had used his name in the piece. Bradman was impressed with the song and the courteous gesture reflected in the accompanying correspondence. He responded with a letter thanking Kamahl for his gift, returning the favour with a signed copy of his autobiography. After this warm exchange, the men developed a strong friendship with many meetings and a regular dialogue through correspondence discussing life, cricket and most of all, their shared passion for music.

In itself, their relationship Kamahl claims is almost an allegory of Australia at its best. It was two passionate Australians from two totally different cultural backgrounds, ethnicity, upbringing and life experiences to share a genuine friendship helped and not hindered by their differences. Interestingly, the relationship did have an early communications misunderstanding to overcome. When visiting Adelaide in 1989, Kamahl rang Sir Don to ask if he and his wife, Lady Jesse, would like to have lunch with him. Sir Don was more than happy to accept the invitation and Kamahl told him that he would pick out somewhere suitable and come back with details. Kamahl was staying at the Hilton and thought to approach their Marketing Manager to get her advice on where one would take a person of Sir Donald's stature. Without much hesitation, she recommended somewhere she felt would be highly appropriate. Later that afternoon, Kamahl rang Sir Don and informed him that he had made a booking for the next day for the three of them at an establishment called Cleo's. He sensed that the great man was a little less than enthused at the prospect, and so he pushed him to explain his apprehension about the reservation. Sir Don informed him that Cleo's was a topless bar as far as he knew, and he couldn't possibly be seen there, let alone be there with his wife. Totally embarrassed, Kamahl said that there must've been a mistake and that he would call him straight back. He instantly called the Hilton Marketing Manager and was about to read the riot act to her about her flawed X-rated dining recommendation. The lady calmly advised that she had told him to book Chloe's, not Cleo's. The former was Adelaide's finest dining establishment, and the latter a gentlemen's club of some notoriety. Sheepishly he informed the Bradman's of his gaffe and confirmed the booking.

One of the more surprising meetings involving another famous family came about a relatively short while back, even though it was initiated some sixteen years prior. Over the years, Kamahl has accumulated mountains of memorabilia, correspondence and keepsakes, and that mountain has sometimes proved hard to manage. He says, "Every few years, I commit to decluttering my archive of accumulated bits and pieces. Sometimes that turns up the most unexpected things. There's stuff that I either forgot

I had, I didn't remember where I had put or had become lost in the massive pile." During one of these decluttering exercises, he ran across an envelope that had remained unopened since it had been received. He opened it and saw that it contained a beautifully written thank you card from a lady named Heather Henderson. The note related to a fund-raising performance that she had attended at the Commonwealth Club. The big surprise was that the date of that performance was sixteen years prior. Kamahl remembered the concert and how he had been invited to perform, but the purpose of it eluded him. All he could remember about the event was that he had been asked to do it by his friend Tanya Shand who was with the Department of Foreign Affairs. When he opened the envelope, he found that it also contained a second note. In part, the second note apologised for what she described as the inadequacies of her first note. She then lavished even more praise on the performance she had witnessed on the evening. Kamahl, whilst delighted to receive the card, was embarrassed that he had taken sixteen years to find it and worse yet, had not responded. Immediately he decided to phone Mrs Henderson to apologise for the tardiness of his response and to thank her for her kind words of support. Her contact details were included in the correspondence, so he reasoned that there may be a slim chance that she may still be contactable at that number.

When he rang, the call was answered by Heather herself, who was completely surprised to receive it, so much so that she shrieked when he told her who it was. As it happened, Mrs Henderson was celebrating her ninetieth birthday that day. She was with her four granddaughters at home in Canberra, which she claims made the special day even more special than it already was. Heather Henderson is the daughter of Australia's longest-serving Prime Minister, Sir Robert Menzies. Over the past few years, they have kept in touch by calls, correspondence, and the odd get together. Kamahl reflects, "She is a wonderful lady with so many fascinating stories about her father and his life. She also holds fascinating opinions on civic responsibility. I value our friendship greatly."

His friendship with Tanya Shand and her husband Rick had begun when he was touring Malaysia in the early eighties. At that time, Tanya was the Australian Deputy High Commissioner in Kuala Lumpur. Kamahl had been invited to perform at the Royal Selangor Club Padang. Performing at that club was a bittersweet experience for Kamahl. "The place was very much a remnant from the worst aspects of racist colonialism. When I left Malaysia, a person like me would not be allowed across the front doorstep. In fact, the only people of colour allowed in came through the back entrance and were there strictly to serve. For me to even enter the building was incredible, let alone be the star attraction when I eventually did."

As a proud recipient of Australian Honours, Kamahl has many views on how recognising high-achieving Australians could improve. He received his Order of Australia in 1994 and the Centenary Medal in 2004. For him, the recognition was not only gratifying but a validation of faith in a society that had embraced him. "Whilst my early days in Australia were challenging, I persisted with my choice to stay despite the racism I sometimes felt. I was going against my parent's wishes to stay and, as a student I had to live with the ever-present threat of deportation. With all of this, I started to understand what the culture and spirit of my new home were." Through the lessons, he learned how to navigate a path toward career success and broad acceptance as a prominent person. In achieving this, he demonstrated his gratitude to the community that embraced him by giving back to causes that both he and the community strongly believed in. It has never occurred to him that this was anything other than the right thing to do. Still, he never actually thought that official recognition by honours was a possibility.

One afternoon in 1993, Kamahl was going through yet one of his periodic de-cluttering sessions at his Turramurra home. He and Sahodra received one of their regular visits from Nancy-Bird Walton. She came, as usual, bearing a beautiful floral gift, a massive box of camellias she had grown in her own nearby garden. The fabled Australian aviator, a close neighbour, had become good friends with Kamahl and Sahodra when they lived in the home that Rajan had dubbed the Taj Kamahl. "Nancy-Bird Walton was a lovely woman who had been a trailblazing feminist long before the term was even thought of. Her achievements should have taken several lives to live. She was one of the most humble and friendly people I ever met. She regularly brought us the most incredible flowers from her magnificent garden just as a neighbourly gesture. This particular day, I was up to my ears in the decluttering process. I had our 12-seat dining room table absolutely covered in correspondence I needed to respond to. It was not a pretty sight."

Noticing the mountain of mail, Nancy-Bird pointed at the pile, asking if Kamahl needed help handling it. Kamahl eagerly agreed that he did need help to get on top of responding, and she instantly said that she would send someone over. As Nancy-Bird Walton was such an estimable character, he didn't doubt for one second that help was well and truly on its way. Help indeed did arrive in the form of Margaret Hamilton. She had been the long-time Executive Assistant to Australian retail electronics giant Dick Smith. Margaret was a tremendously skilled organiser who was perfectly equipped to bring order and sanity to this correspondence conundrum. As she set about reading through the correspondence and suggesting responses to it for Kamahl, she enquired if he had a post-nominal included in the sign off to his replies. Kamahl said he had an OBE which surprised Margaret somewhat that she wasn't aware of it. "I told her I was an OBE, then explained that it stood for Overseas Born Entertainer, which amused her… these days I'm a different type of OBE, Over Bloody Eighty", he laughs. Even though amused by the joke, Margaret expressed her surprise that Kamahl had never been recognised by the Australian Honours system. Kamahl thought nothing more of the discussion. He was absolutely delighted that Margaret had done such a tremendous job getting his life and dining table back in order. The consequence of that discussion was to be realised some months later. Margaret Hamilton had shared her surprise at Kamahl's lack of letters after his name with Nancy-Bird Walton. In her own inimitable style, she decided something must be done to address the situation. Shortly afterwards, Kamahl received notification that he was to be made a Member of the Order of Australia. "To receive the award was a great honour in itself, but to get it by being supported by the nomination of one of Australia's finest is even more precious."

Kamahl is a great supporter of the Honours system. Even though he applauds the recognition they provide, he sometimes wonders why it was deemed necessary to depart from the existing honours that existed before Gough Whitlam's decision to Australianise them in 1975. "To all intents and purposes, they are exactly the same as they ever were. All that seems to have changed are the names. The nominations are put forward and approved by the same process that they always were. The titles may no longer extend to having prefixes to people's names like Sir or Lord but not the hierarchy of importance. Take Nancy-Bird Walton as a good example. She was a legitimate OBE and an AO. Which one was supposed to mean more? Both awards recognised an outstanding person for her great achievements? I think that we are sometimes too hell-bent on distancing Australia from British traditions just for the sake of it. On the surface of it, of course, it sounds like the right thing to do. After all, we are our own country and have long since cut the umbilical-chord to Mother Britain. I share this concern with the push to republicanism. It isn't that I am anti-republican; I am just unconvinced of the benefits it would provide. I think it foolish to take on something new if it doesn't improve things for the people. For all of is failings as a constitutional monarchy, we have had only one major constitutional crisis in our history. It seems that in the United States, they have one every other week. They seem to be in an eternal fight over who is really in charge and who has the correct interpretation of that document."

On Australian honours, Kamahl is often surprised by some of the inconsistencies he has perceived. At times he has questioned the merits of some awarded over the years but more those overlooked. A great example of this was his long-time friend Herb Elliot. Although Herb had been recognised under the old system in 1964 with an MBE, it wasn't until 2002 that he finally received recognition as a Companion of the Order of Australia. As far as high achieving Australians go, Elliot is a stand-out, widely regarded as one of Australia's greatest ever athletes. He represented Australia as a middle-distance runner at the Rome Olympics in 1960, winning a Gold medal in the 1500 metres in world record time. He also represented his country at the Cardiff Commonwealth Games in 1958, winning Gold in the 880 yard and one mile events.

Independently of his outstanding sporting achievements, Herb had led a very impressive life, having retired early from athletics at 22. Instead of continuing with his running career, he had decided to study at Cambridge. After graduation, Herb entered the world of commerce with Shell and then to a long career with sporting goods manufacturer Puma. He would also take several high-profile executive and non-executive directorships in long and successful business life and was a member of the Sydney Olympic Games Organising Committee. He was one of the torchbearers for the 2000 Games. Herb is a highly principled man, evidenced by his rejection of an offer in 1962 to 'go professional' in the United States. Publicist and promoter Leo Leavitt was at the time assembling a stellar line-up of track and field stars and was offering a staggering $250,000 sign-on fee to those he could recruit. Whilst generous by today's standard, this amount equated to a fortune in the early sixties. He was quoted when questioned why he had turned down the offer "If you were going to grow, your motivation had to be more than just winning or getting money". Herb was even compelled to return a gift to the French Embassy that he had received from their government. The gift was part of the recognition of him being their athlete of the year in 1960. He returned the very expensive clock to protest their testing nuclear weapons in the Australian desert. In 2000, Kamahl had the pleasure of meeting Herb for the first time. The two men hit it off almost immediately and found much in common. In Kamahl's estimation, Herb was such an outstanding nominee for the highest of Australian Honours. He was shocked to learn that he had not been recognised by Australian Honours until that time. "I will always be extremely proud and grateful to receive my award. Although I must question how a humble entertainer like me received recognition before one of our greatest sportsmen. In a sports-mad nation like ours, it just seemed strange. I was so motivated to rectify this oversight that I put forward my nomination and sought several others to second my submission. Thankfully, the Honours Committee saw fit to award Herb with Companion of the Order of Australia in 2002. Ever the gentleman, Herb not only wrote me a wonderful letter thanking me for initiating that process but he invited me to his investiture in Perth later that year."

Kamahl similarly was out on a crusade over yet another tremendous Australian sports star, Shane Gould. Representing Australia at the Munich Games in 1972, Shane won three gold medals, setting a world record in each race. She also won a bronze and a silver medal. The first female swimmer ever to win three Olympic gold medals in world record time and the first swimmer, male or female, to win Olympic medals in five individual events in a single Olympics. She is also the only Australian to win three individual gold medals at a single Olympics. Like Herb Elliot, Shane had been awarded an MBE in 1981 but was overlooked by the Australian Honours system. The thought of another of Australia's greatest ever athletes being ignored by Australian honours made no sense to him. A highly motivated Kamahl set about lobbying for Shane's rightful recognition. "The oversight just seemed a ridiculous flaw in our system. It is meant to be a more democratic and representative means of honouring our overachievers. When she did receive her honours, I was shocked and more than a little angry when they had only awarded her with an AM (Member of the Order of Australia). It was the same award that I had received. I thought that she was deserving of far greater recognition. Personally, I am mystified about how these things are arrived at. If the system we adopted all those years ago was not an improvement on what was there previously, why was it necessary to change it in the first place? How is someone with genuine outstanding historic achievement in their life and a stellar record of commitment to the country and the Community bracketed in with me a humble entertainer? It just seems so illogical."

Over the years, Kamahl has been directly lobbied by people or their representatives attempting to persuade him to support a nomination. In general, he has maintained that those who need to ask maybe don't deserve recognition in the first place. In his mind, honours are meant to be about being recognised for achievements from others and not demanded by yourself.

Kamahl's most recent experience with the honours system was inspired by watching the Australian of The Year award in 2018. The winner that year was a brilliant British born Physicist named Michelle Simmons who had migrated to Australia in 1999. When she was made Australian of the Year on Australia Day 2018, she gave a speech that inspired Kamahl greatly. Her theme connected with his own life experience in many ways. She spoke of the importance of not being defined by other people's expectations of you. She said, "Don't live your life according to what other people think. Go out there and do what you really want to do." The words yet again connected directly to Kamahl's own beliefs. He thought that she was precisely the type of person who should be nominated and receive recognition through the honours system. He immediately decided to lobby for Michelle's nomination for high honours. Subsequently, he found that she had already been nominated by a colleague. She had been nominated for Officer of the Order of Australia (AO). Whilst delighted that she would undoubtedly be recognised with an AO, he firmly believed her to be deserving higher honours and so was disappointed. Once nominated, it is not possible to suggest higher recognition in the current system.

Kamahl met Michelle shortly after her investiture. She was the guest speaker at a function convened at Wombat Hollow, a venue then owned by ex-NSW politician Michael Yabsley. "Michael is an old friend I have known for years, and he would convene these evenings at his place in the Southern Highlands. It was a nice set-up with a gallery and conference facility that he and his then-wife owned and operated. The functions were always designed to raise funds for some worthy cause. A suitable speaker would be engaged, and I sang the national anthem. They were always really well run, pleasant and interesting affairs with plenty of fascinating people there. It was a real credit to Michael for having such a great initiative. When I was invited on this occasion, I accepted as usual. I was delighted to learn that Michelle Simmons, who at that stage I had never actually met, was going to be the guest of honour and after dinner speaker. Hearing her speak, sharing her vision and her heartfelt commitment to advancing the cause of women in Science was brilliant. We spoke after her presentation, and I was even more impressed with her. She epitomises what we FBAs, Foreign-Born Aussies, should be all about. She is a new Australian making Australia a better place to be."

In early 2008 Kamahl briefly reunited with his alma mater, The Pembroke School or as it was known, when he attended, Kings College. The two-week tour of the United States by the forty-two-piece orchestra of year 9-12 children was quite an extensive undertaking. It included New York's Waldorf Astoria Hotel Ballroom for Australia Day celebrations and Washington's Kennedy Centre. The orchestra was also booked to appear at G'Day USA in Los Angeles at an exclusive black-tie dinner hosted by former South Australian Premier John Olsen. G'Day USA's stated aims are to bring together leaders from government, business, the creative industries and academia to deepen the Australia-US relationship. Whilst he was not scheduled to perform with the orchestra at the event, Kamahl decided to accompany the Orchestra on the assumption that this presence would be required. Organisers naturally would be aware of the tour schedule with the Orchestra and his participation. He recalls, "I thought that as a prominent Australian entertainer, I would actually be welcomed at the event. When I arrived, I mingled with the attendees, many of whom I knew really well, including fellow South Australian John Olsen who was chair for the event. When the hotel staff started to move people into the ballroom, however, it was discovered that my name was not on the invitation list. To be honest, I was embarrassed. I felt like a gate crasher at a function that I had not unreasonably felt that I had been invited to. Rather than create a fuss, I just beat a retreat to the bar. When I arrived at the bar, I noticed a large group of very glamorous model type ladies who seemed to know who I was. They explained that they were there as part of the G'Day USA program to promote Paspaley Pearls from WA. They invited me to join them, which I was happy to do and ended up having quite a pleasant night. I was just so annoyed with what I felt like was a real snub by Olsen. I sent him an email with a picture of myself in the centre of a line-up of the Paspaley beauties with just a line saying 'Dear John, thanks for a pearl of an evening'. He never responded, not that I would have expected him to."

Kamahl has now been an Australian for the better part of his life, well over sixty years. He refers to himself as an FBA, Foreign-Born Aussie, which he points out is not the same as an FDA, or Fair Dinkum Aussie. Like many who are grateful for the chances given him by this County, he tends to be fiercely patriotic and has endeavoured to become as knowledgeable about his adopted home as possible. For many years, he became a voracious consumer of information that would broaden his understanding of what made Australia tick. Such was his commitment, he managed to conquer the aversion of study he had in his youth to hit the books and absorb all that he could lay his hands on to better inform him about his adopted home. He says, "My background gives me an insight that not so many people have had through being a black migrant during the days of the White Australia policy. My introduction to Australian culture as a young man was incredibly mixed. Many combined their fear with ignorance which juxtaposed against so many others who showed me incredible, sometimes irrational kindness, people that I barely even knew. Over the years, so much has changed. The former group seems to have become a minority clinging to the fringes of our society. The latter is now most definitely the majority. They provide us with an environment of inclusivity and acceptance. It really makes me very optimistic about the future of Australia as a nation."

He says, "On ANZAC Day each year, I perform a wonderful piece of poetry called 'The Soul of Australia' by John Henry Macartney Abbott. Abbott was an interesting character, a veteran of the Boer war, a corporal in the Australian 1st Horse Regiment. He was invalided out of the conflict, badly wounded in battle. When he returned to Sydney, he used his own wartime experiences to write a best-selling book named *Tommy Cornstalk*. He would go on to a long career as a journalist, correspondent, author and poet. His words for 'The Soul of Australia' capture the mind of conflict, struggle and, in a way the emergence of a uniquely Australian spirit. It is written from a perspective that only someone who had endured bloody conflict themselves could accurately capture. I love performing the piece and, as long as I keep being asked to do it I will. I see it as a great privilege to perform such a wonderful poem for the veterans in particular for whom it was written and have sacrificed so much for our country and who deserve the utmost respect."

In the light of dawn, the break of day,
Through the waters chill they fought their way;
Like their sires of old, to the Motherland
They came o'er the sea, and they sprang to the strand;
And the blood of the Angles, the Scot, and the Celt
Grew hot in their veins as the war fire they felt.

In the light of noon, in the bright sunlight,
They fought up the cliffs from height to height;
And the sun shone down on that scene of strife
Where the 'Soul of Australia' came to life,
As the blood of Australians was shed on the sod,
For Australia, for Britain, Humanity, God.

Shall Australia mourn for the sons she has lost—
Should Australians weep? Nay! Great though the cost,
Joy mingles with grief, and pride mingles with pain,
For our boys died like heroes, and died not in vain.
And the 'Soul of Australia', new-born on that day
When her sons died at ANZAC, shall never decay

JHM Abbott

22

Listening with your eyes

People get to like a soul, but a satisfactory hat makes an impression at first sight.
Pearl Maria Teresa Mary Craigie

Kamahl has been acutely aware of the almighty power of perception throughout his long career. He states, "I am a great believer in appearance when I say that show business is all about perception. For that reason, I have made it a significant part of my persona. I have always worked hard to ensure that I was always seen in a certain way, and for me to deny that would be dishonest. I have always been dedicated to presenting myself in a way that my audience wanted or expected me to be. A manifestation of that is my appearance, and so I have always committed to never disappoint them in that regard. If you look carefully at my career, you will see that this is a pattern which has always been there … The Rolls Royce, the dinner suits, and the more flamboyant clothes like the kaftan. All of it was styled to create a big impression. It was all deliberately designed to make me more memorable, which made me more than just a singer. The truth of it is that I may very well have been a turkey. Still, I never wanted to settle for being a turkey, so I have always been deliberate to present myself as a peacock, and that is the difference. It is all there for show. To be honest, I will do anything and everything to distract from my voice. To be less reliant upon it, you have to remember that people listen with their eyes too, what they see influences what they hear." he laughs. Kamahl is humble about his singing talent primarily because whilst he acknowledges he has a good voice, he doesn't regard himself as a great singer. "You see, I know what a really great singer is, and I am not that. As I have said many times, I am that rarest of things, an operatic crooner if you like, not quite one thing nor the other. A hybrid of my own invention." It is his very own variation on that old adage 'if it looks like a duck, it must be a duck.' Kamahl's version is a case of 'if it looks like a peacock, it can't possibly be a turkey'.

While his very harsh self-assessment of his vocal capabilities is radically dismissive, it is hard to argue with the logic of the approach he has adopted. His strategy didn't rely entirely on the voice for success. It acknowledges that the world has always had more than a fair share of tremendous bass-baritone singers, but who could accurately name many?

Indeed there are very few performers in this genre that can be said to have achieved commercial success or recognition. By Kamahl embracing an approach that wrapped his personality, appearance, humour, singing talent into the glitter of success, he has achieved great things. He, most importantly, reached his most prized goal … acceptance. From the very beginning, it was always about acceptance. The fame and fortune just happily came along with it for the ride.

Kamahl recalls one rainy evening standing at a bus stop in Adelaide during the early sixties after just finishing a show. He was approached by an elderly man who had been an audience member at his performance. Looking genuinely puzzled at seeing him standing at the bus stop, the old guy asked Kamahl why he, the star of the show, was waiting for public transport. He honestly replied, "It is how I get around as I don't have a car". The old guy responded, "Don't worry son, with your talent, you'll be driving around in a Rolls Royce one day." The thought seemed wildly preposterous but hit a nerve with Kamahl, who vowed to himself that day not to disappoint the kindly old guy he met in the drizzle that night at the bus stop. So, it came to be that many years later, he received a phone call that would see this dream realised. "In 1978, whilst away on tour, I received a surprise phone call from my chiropractor, Manny Coroneos. He had called to let me know I would be in for a great surprise upon my return to Sydney. I had no idea what he was talking about. As he was being coy and refused to go into any detail, I had no choice but to wait until I got home to find out. He had certainly piqued my interest. When I arrived back in Sydney, I hurried home and there on my driveway was a metallic blue 1974 Rolls Royce Silver Shadow." Manny's companion, the car's owner Richard, would explain to Kamahl that he was reluctantly selling the car urgently out of necessity. He said Manny had told him he had a friend that he knew would fall in love with it at first sight. It appears that he was 100% correct. For a man who made his living working on people's aching bodies, Manny could be apparently quite adept at reading people's minds too. Kamahl thought the car was absolute perfection. Even though Kamahl had been happily swanning around town in a newly purchased green Mercedes, the Rolls was more than just a mere car in his eyes. To him, this was a masterpiece of engineering wrapped in sculpted excellence … it was more than that. It was a statement. "I still have a vivid memory of my feelings sitting behind the wheel for the first time. It was a combination of excited nervousness, and intimidation. Even though I had driven many prestigious cars prior, nothing had compared to this feeling. I have always believed in the influence of perception, how it is responsible for projecting an image of success. In show business particularly, it is the perception that rules supreme. It plays no second fiddle to reality… quite simply what the public perceive as reality is real. With this in mind, every instinct I had told me that this was to be. Thus began a more than four-decade relationship with The Queen as I had christened her. Sadly, after all of our time together, that relationship came to an end in early 2021. Unfortunately, by then, the Queen spent more time with the mechanic than with me. That was a love triangle that I couldn't sustain, emotionally or financially. We parted ways. Hopefully, she has found happiness with her new subject in Tasmania. On the day I farewelled her, I had a vivid memory of standing at that rainy bus stop in Adelaide many years before. I also saw the strange little old guy who planted that seed in my mind that I would own a Rolls Royce. Although I never did get his name, I am guessing it might have been Nostradamus."

Kamahl's early insecurities about belonging, gaining and maintaining social acceptance and his need to be valued and listened to were always the key driving force in his ambition. His self-consciousness paradoxically drove him to use a strategy of overt projection and high-visibility. He hurled himself against his own instincts with grand dramatic posturing. He not only sought attention, he eagerly and gladly embraced it and eventually became addicted to it. The spotlight not only gave him motivation; it gave him purpose. It unlocked his spirit and unblocked the path to success. He became Kamahl, not an 'other' to be at the mercy of preconceptions and prejudices, but someone of substance, someone of influence, someone to be reckoned with.

Kamahl, throughout his life, had plenty of remarkable things happen, which on occasion seemingly came looking for him. In most of those situations, he was proven to be more than capable of turning those opportunities into results. It is just as relevant that he was never found to be waiting for an opportunity to come knocking, far from it. In fact, whenever an opportunity was slow in arriving, he marched right out of the door and went looking for it. Moreover, when he could not find an opportunity, he would simply create one.

His unique journey had plenty of challenges to overcome, many of which were inherent, but he succeeded in turning them to his own advantage. The very differences that had made him the subject of taunts and mockery in his early days and often throughout some of his career, he had consciously fashioned into assets. Out of adversity, he developed what became the unique Kamahl brand. A brand defined by determination, hard work, humour, the strength of character and an indomitable will to lift himself ever upward no matter how big a fall that a failure may have threatened.

After a career spanning well over sixty years, Kamahl could be forgiven if he were to rest on his laurels. He could simply spend his time reflecting on his past glories. It is hard for many to fathom why he rarely refuses an offer for a performance or a speaking engagement.

Early in 2021, Kamahl, at 86 years young, agreed to be interviewed by Lyndon Terracini, Artistic Director of Opera Australia. The interview was to be screened at Opera Australia's online OA show. He not only agreed to a half-hour interview but would also gladly accept the invitation to perform an aria from the Magic Flute on camera. "To appear for a friendly chat with Lyndon, who is an old friend, was a joy in and of itself. Then to be allowed to perform Sarastro's aria accompanied by the incredibly talented Tahu Matheson, Opera Australia's Head of Music, was indeed a great and special honour. I was quite nervous as I hadn't sung a serious Operatic piece in decades. In fact, the last time, I believe, was at the Sun Aria Finals in 1966. Frankly, I was anxious about how it would turn out, so anxious in fact that I rehearsed the piece many times for at least a couple of weeks before the filming. I think it went fine … well, no one threw fruit at me anyway" he laughs.

Any appearance for Kamahl is something he always treats seriously. Of course, he would, he is Kamahl, and that is all there is to it. As he has always done, he prepared meticulously, rehearsing the aria multiple times, and on the day even coating his throat with honey to protect those vocal cords before singing. However, that wasn't all, ever the showman… He even went to the extra effort to don the kaftan to ensure that Opera Australia got that extra little bit of theatre that he is renowned for. At this point in his life, he simply refuses to do anything less than his best as he just isn't capable of doing anything other than his best. This is the performer persona that he created and has maintained all of his career. This is what the Kamahl brand is all about. To him, it is just as important today as it has ever been.

The fact is that Kamahl still has the drive and determination to entertain and to share the story of his journey, even if only to act as an inspiration to someone else who feels like they may need it. He feels that it may inspire someone by telling them that they too can overcome challenges, prejudices, setbacks, ridicule, rejection and most of all, self-doubt. To answer his evergreen question, "Why are so many people so unkind?" he proffers the following advice. "If you allow negativity and negative people to control your life, you'll always be destined to achieve very little. You should always be positive and try to seek out and surround yourself with positive people and positive things in your life. Do this, and you may well flourish, actually you may not be able to stop yourself from doing so. As for people being so unkind, I say to hell with them, let them be as unkind as they wish. People like that are seldom happy with their own lives. They merely validate themselves by tearing down others who are just trying to be the very best they can be. You know if you try to focus on seeking out the good in people, you might just find it. My life is littered with people who have shown me the almost irrational generosity at the most unexpected times. In Tennessee Williams' *Streetcar Named Desire*, his character Blanche Dubois famously said, '... I have always depended on the kindness of strangers.' Not to compare myself to old Blanche but I too have significantly benefited from the kindness of strangers. People who were prepared at times to show me almost irrational generosity. When I think of Harry Wesley Smith, who hardly knew me but would rescue me from being just another failing university student by arranging my enrolment at the Conservatorium. He set me on the path to a career in music. Then there was the incredible Bill Schneider from the Immigration Department who was prepared to stretch the rules to allow me to stay in this magnificent country despite having the power to deport me. Then there was Rupert Murdoch, who showed genuine faith in me by giving me those unbelievable early opportunities that set me on my path to success. He would even be kind enough to even put a roof over my head for over two years when I first arrived in Sydney. I cannot ever forget what these three individuals alone did to positively impact my life, nor do I feel that I could ever adequately express my gratitude to them. Of course I must also acknowledge another great source of kindness and generosity in my life. The support that I have been given from those who were gracious enough to allow me to be a part of their lives … My wonderful fans who have been with me through thick and thin. Without them there truly would have been nothing at all."

Quite often, you'll hear of people, rationalising that it was some unexpected inspiration that changed their life forever. They claim that somewhere in their travels, they experienced an event, a vision or an epiphany that triggered change and led them to fame or fortune. In Kamahl's case, it wasn't on the road to Damascus where he found his inspiration, it was the two minutes and fifty-one seconds of a simple song he heard in an Adelaide living room back in the early nineteen fifties. A song that just happened to refer to a strange enchanted boy, a little shy and sad of eye who'd wandered very far over land and sea. A boy who, wanted more than anything else, only to love and be loved in return.

Nature boy

There was a boy
A very strange enchanted boy
they say he wandered very far, very far
over land and sea
a little shy and sad of eye
but very wise was he

And then one day
a magic day he passed my way
and while we spoke of many things
fools and kings
this he said to me
The greatest thing you'll ever learn
is just to love and be loved in return

The greatest thing you'll ever learn
Is just to love and be loved in return

Eden Ahbez

About the Author

Keith Cameron lives on the Central Coast of NSW with his wife of over forty years, Amy. He was born in Sunderland in the North East of England before emigrating to Australia with his family as a 12 year old child. He began his working life as an advertising copywriter in the late seventies. In the years that followed, his role has broadened into developing advertising, PR and creative marketing strategies for some of Australia's best-known brands. As a self-described 'ten-pound pom', he has always been fascinated by the role that migrants have played, in developing and enriching the culture of modern Australia and the impact that they have played in its history.

A keen writer and eager correspondent, Keith had a chance meeting in late 2020 with show business icon and one of our most celebrated migrants Kamahl. That meeting led to a friendship which resulted in his being persuaded to capture his friends most remarkable life story.

Acknowledgements

For their contribution to this book we would like to recognise and thank the following people:
Denis Smith
Dermot Hoy
Dr Brendan Nelson AO
Grahame Mapp AM
Bill Davidson
Marianne Mellema
Phil Isaacs
Glenn Armstrong

US $24.99
UK $16.99